ESCAPE
FROM HERMIT ISLAND

Two Women Struggle to Save
Their Sunken Sailboat
in Remote Papua New Guinea

ESCAPE
FROM HERMIT ISLAND

**Two Women Struggle to Save
Their Sunken Sailboat
in Remote Papua New Guinea**

By Joy Smith
In Collaboration with Leslie Brown

Seaworthy
PUBLICATIONS

Port Washington, WI

Escape from Hermit Island
by Joy Smith in collaboration with Leslie Brown

Copyright © 2008 by Joy Smith
ISBN 978-1-892399-27-4

Published in the USA by:
Seaworthy Publications, Inc.
626 W. Pierre
Port Washington, WI 53074
PHONE: 262-268-9250
FAX: 262-268-9208
E-MAIL: orders@seaworthy.com
WEB: www.seaworthy.com

COVER DESIGN: Ken Quant, Broad Reach Marketing & Design, Mequon, WI, from a photo by Bernadette Willies

Library of Congress Cataloging-in-Publication Data

Smith, Joy, 1941-
  Escape from Hermit Island : two women struggle to save their sunken sailboat in remote Papua New Guinea / Joy Smith in collaboration with Leslie Brown.
    p. cm.
  ISBN-13: 978-1-892399-27-4 (pbk. : alk. paper)
  ISBN-10: 1-892399-27-X (pbk. : alk. paper) 1. Papua New Guinea—Description and travel. 2. Smith, Joy, 1941- 3. Brown, Leslie. 4. Women sailors—Biography. 5. Yachting—Papua New Guinea. 6. Shipwrecks—Papua New Guinea. 7. Coral reefs and islands—Papua New Guinea. 8. Papua New Guinea—Social life and customs. 9. Indigenous peoples—Papua New Guinea—Social life and customs. 10. Tok Pisin language. I. Title.
  DU740.2.S64 2008
  995.3—dc22
                                    2008001107

To the Memory of My Mother
Rena Phair
December 22, 1912 – September 29, 2006
Who told me to have adventures

To Leslie's Family
Sue Brown
Larry and Barbara Brown
Tammi and Scott Lauder
Who made it possible

Marianas Is.

Guam

PHILIPPINES

Palau

Caroline Islands   Truk   Pohnpei

Kosrae

Equator

Hermit   Manus

INDONESIA

PAPUA   Madang
NEW
GUINEA

Port
Moresby

AUSTRALIA

CHINA   JAPAN   North Pacific

Hawaiian
Islands

Ocean

PHILIPPINES

MARSHALL
ISLANDS

MALAYSIA   PALAU

INDONESIA   PAPUA
              GUINEA   South Pacific

                                  Ocean

VANUATU   FIJI   SAMOA

                      TONGA

AUSTRALIA

Tasman   NEW
Sea   ZEALAND

Indian
Ocean

CONTENTS

ILLUSTRATIONS

Drawings by Debra K. Thomas:

FOREWORD

Those who live on the fringes of the Third World understand well that, in the event of an emergency, they will probably be largely on their own. In many areas removed from population centers, access to telephone and radio communications is limited or simply non-existent, medical facilities are by Western standards primitive, and anything beyond the most basic supplies and equipment are unavailable. In addition, the people in some areas have a reputation for being less than helpful to strangers in need.

When Joy and Leslie struck a reef and sank on a remote atoll of Papua New Guinea, they faced all of the above difficulties and more. It is hard to imagine a more precarious situation. Joy was injured, their boat was on the reef, most of their belongings were scattered on the beach (or at least the part that had not already been carted off), and while some of the villagers were helpful, others were hostile. The only assets that Joy and Leslie had were their own resourcefulness, ingenuity, and a stubborn commitment that they would not leave their boat, and their home, on that reef.

By the time we met Joy and Leslie, they had refloated their boat, escaped from Hermit Island, and made their way to Madang Harbor for repairs. We were fascinated by their story: how they used their EPIRB to communicate to the "outside world" that they were okay; how they were befriended and helped by some of the nationals and targeted and harassed by others; and how they were finally able to repair and refloat the boat and leave the island on their own wind power alone. Over the past months we have watched them methodically repair or replace almost every system on the boat as they prepared to resume their cruising life.

Even though we already knew the story, we looked forward with anticipation to each chapter of the book as it was finished. This is a fascinating story, well told, of two women who overcame an impossible situation. They have truly been an inspiration to us.

Kyle and Kathy Harris
Pioneer Bible Translators
Madang, Papua New Guinea
November 2003

Hermit Islands

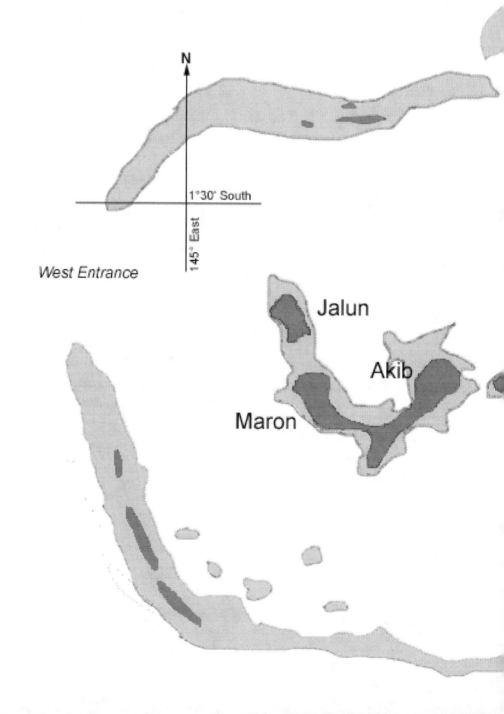

N

1°30' South

145° East

West Entrance

Jalun

Akib

Maron

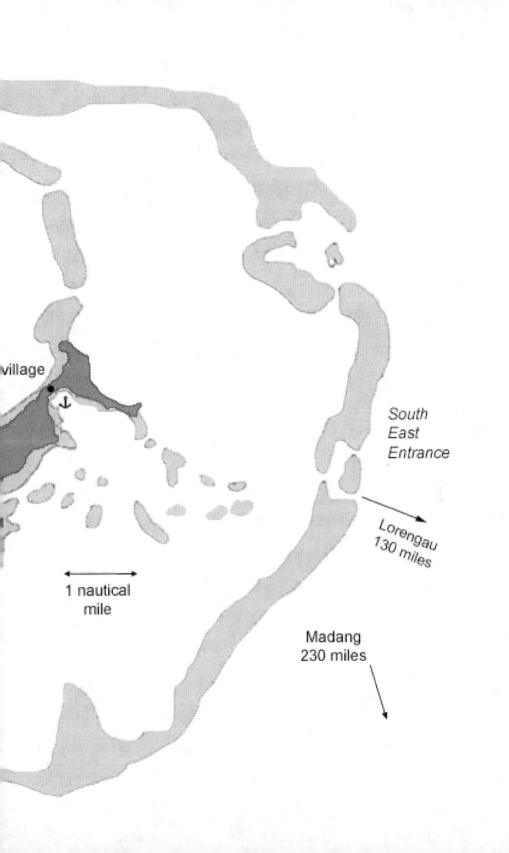

village

South
East
Entrance

Lorengau
130 miles

Madang
230 miles

1 nautical
mile

THE SINKING

Latitude 1° 31' South, Longitude 145° 06' East

After a few days of scuba diving in the isolation of Hermit Atoll, we are motoring *Banshee*, our 34-foot sailboat, back to the main village anchorage of Luf. We have made this easy lagoon jaunt several times already, and Leslie is conning the boat from the foredeck with the handheld remote for the autopilot. I step down below for a moment to put on a shirt. Suddenly, Leslie sees green water ahead. She frantically pushes the autopilot remote to turn the boat to starboard and out into deeper water, but it is too late—*Banshee* strikes the coral and, unbelievably, her thick fiberglass hull immediately starts to flood. I'm trapped below, held down by inrushing seawater that slams a door shut and jams my finger in its hinge. *Banshee* turns on her right side and sinks in ten feet of water, about a half-mile from the beach.

Our carefree, cruising life has come to an end; our ordeal has just begun.

Leslie, a 44-year-old scuba instructor, and I, a 61-year-old retired teacher, had been planning our voyage to Hermit Atoll for three years, while I completed a teaching contract at Palau Community College. Our Guam "boonie-cat," Booby, completed the crew. We had heard great reports from other yachts about Hermit, an isolated atoll belonging to Papua New Guinea. It has an idyllic lagoon, friendly people, and great scuba diving. We planned our voyage so that we would be sailing on the southwest winds of summer in the northwest Pacific. After visiting Hermit, we planned to go farther southeast to Kimbe, Papua New Guinea, for more diving, and in February, when the wind changed to the northeast, we thought we would head westward to the Philippines for a boatyard haul-out.

We had a pleasant twelve-day passage from Palau, making landfall at Hermit Island on October 12, 2002. We quickly made friends with the villagers, shared stories, taught them scuba diving techniques, repaired their fiberglass open speedboats (called "speedies"), traded, and generally did the things that voyagers enjoy doing in remote islands. They loved us, we loved them. We enjoyed their hospitality and soon became part of the community of Luf Island, a volcanic island inside the lagoon of Hermit. They took us diving on the untouched outer reefs, and they even named one of them "Joy's Reef" after me. Things could hardly have been nicer for a pair of ocean wanderers like us.

On October 21, after anchoring away from the village for a few nights to have a bit of privacy, we decided to return to the village. Leslie takes up the story.

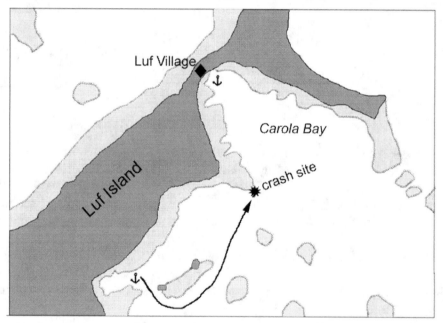

Leslie

It was about three o'clock in the afternoon. We were approaching the village—a route we had taken several times returning from various anchorages in the lagoon. It was a very hot, humid day and all the ports and hatches were open. The late afternoon sun's glare from aft was bright on the water in front of us. It reflected in my eyes, and along with the white sky of the thin cloud layer overhead, it made it difficult to see below the surface. I grabbed the remote and climbed up on top of the deck box for better visibility. I saw the color of the water go from dark blue to lighter green, meaning shallower water.

Horrified, I started punching the remote's control button to turn our course away from the approaching coral. I yelled back to the cockpit, "Joy, turn! Hard starboard, hard right! Now!" I looked back. Joy was not at the wheel. I dropped the remote and raced back to the cockpit, grabbed the wheel and slammed it hard over to the right.

Too late—I heard the sickening crunch of fiberglass against coral. The whole boat shuddered as we careened onto the reef. Joy, at the foot of the companionway, yelled up at me, "Leslie, my god! What have you done?"

Joy

In retrospect, I realize that we had become much too blasé about motoring around in tropical lagoons. I just assumed that we were in familiar waters and well aware of the short route we had to follow, and that Les would simply take the remote and guide us back to our mooring. Why should I think otherwise? We had been doing exactly the same thing every week for three years in Palau's lagoon with no mishaps. Complacency had set in. I was much too nonchalant in nipping below to grab a clean shirt while motoring through a coral-studded lagoon.

But I gave it no thought at all as I stepped down into the cabin, picked up my shirt, and turned to go up the ladder again to the cockpit. I felt the boat shudder as we hit, and I heard the awful, loud crunch of the grounding hull. I yelled to Leslie in a panicked voice. Then, to my utter amazement, I saw the floorboards under my feet start to pop up with the rising, intruding seawater.

"Reverse, Leslie! Go back! Reverse the engine. Get us out of here! Shit, we're sinking! Leslie, we're sinking!" I cried out in a terrified voice.

"Sinking? We can't sink! We're only in ten feet of water! We can't sink here. We're almost on land."

But then she said, "Joy, the water's coming up fast! I've got to cut the engine, got to turn off the engine—now! Water's coming in fast."

All I could think of was that *Banshee* was all that I had owned in the world for over thirty years, and she was going down fast.

I lurched forward and started closing ports and hatches, thinking only to stop the water from coming in. My brain was going in slow motion. All I knew was that water was coming inside my beloved boat and somehow I had to stop it. I felt *Banshee* heel over onto her starboard side, and then I saw water cascading through the open ports and hatches. I secured a few of them, and then my dilated time sense cleared and my brain kicked back in.

I was in the forepeak at that point, and looked back into the main cabin and saw the water rising quickly. *Got to get out of here!* I pushed myself through the inside door to the main cabin, grabbing the doorjambs to steady myself. I felt the rising, flooding water pushing at me. I moved my right hand and the door slammed shut on my finger. *Good grief, what pain!* My finger was caught in a closing hinge on the door. I violently shoved back that damned door and pulled my hand away, not even looking at it.

The cabin was almost totally filled with water now, but there was still a small pocket of air by the companionway, on the high side of the boat. I grabbed a lungful of air, dove, and swam for that air pocket. I gulped a breath, and then I saw that the wooden companionway ladder was floating upwards and blocking my way out.

Time and events were a blur—I knew I had to get out. I still didn't even have a shirt on. *Doesn't matter much now, I guess.*

Leslie

Joy was down below in the cabin and the water was coming in fast. Panic-stricken, I kept yelling, "Joy, where are you? Get out now, hurry, you'll get trapped—stuff's floating up—it'll block the hatch!" I had visions of the boat filling up with water and Joy drowning, unable to get out. I saw the ladder float up in front of the hatch, but still no sign of Joy—*where was she? What the hell was she doing?* Then I saw her swimming underwater for the hatch. I had no time to lose—I had to get her out now. I pushed hard on the floating ladder—the damned thing was stuck—it wouldn't go down. I started screaming as loud as I could and looked around the boat—and there in a canoe was our friend Ben. "Help, Joy's trapped! You've got to get her out. She'll drown—stuff is blocking the hatch." Ben leaped out of his dugout canoe and into the cockpit, shoved the ladder down, and grabbed for Joy.

Joy

I saw Ben in front of me, our kind village friend. His strong, dark body was crouched at the blocked hatchway opening, his arms outstretched to me, calling my name. I lunged for him and felt him grab me. As he was pulling me up out of the flooded cabin, I looked down at my hand. Blood was pouring out of my right ring finger. In horror, I saw that part of it was missing. But right then I felt no pain, just fright and terrible, awful, shaking fear. I heard Leslie say, "Get her out of here. Get her to the beach. Her hand—what's happened to her hand?"

I grabbed a cockpit cushion, jammed my bleeding finger in it, and clutched it to my still bare chest. I felt Ben pick me up and put me down on the cabin's coach roof, now the only part of *Banshee* that was still above water. I looked up and saw the mast leaning way over to the right at a strange angle. I noticed that Booby had climbed as high as he could go, up the boom and away from the threatening seawater. *Smart cat.*

Our small fiberglass dinghy with its tiny outboard motor was still floating alongside, as if nothing had happened. I heard Leslie say to Ben, "Get Joy and Booby in the dinghy and take them to the beach." Ben held the dinghy and I shakily got in. My brain was numb—surely this wasn't really happening. My cat friend appeared next to me, howling as only a scared, wet cat can do. I grabbed him along with my cushion and huddled down in the dinghy.

I saw canoes and speedies converging on our wreck site. Slippery and searing diesel oil fouled the seawater surrounding our sunken boat. Deck cargo, cushions, the generator, fuel jugs, and other floatable items were being swept away by the small wind chop now lapping at *Banshee's* sunken sides.

I called back to Leslie, "Tell them to grab our stuff, it's all floating away. Grab the stuff, quick." What more could I do? The pain in my hand was now excruciating, made even worse by the stinging diesel-laced saltwater. Blood was everywhere. *Endure, just endure, you'll make it.*

Ben motored our little fiberglass dinghy straight to the village beach. I couldn't look back at *Banshee* and Leslie. I simply could not look back at what I felt was the end of my life. I couldn't stop the tears, they just kept flowing. I cried out loud in pain and frustration. *My sailing life, my boat, my home and Leslie's home are gone—all gone in the space of a few minutes. Everything's gone.*

I looked ahead and saw the beach full of people rushing out at me. Newly-made friends that we had been joking and playing with just a few mornings ago were running up to the dinghy. Several women rushed out to me and covered me with a wrap-around *laplap*, grabbing the blood-soaked cushion away from me. I handed Booby—a howling, frightened mass of fur, claws and fury—to someone.

"Take him!" I yelled. "Lock him up in the health office or he'll run away." Booby disappeared with someone into the crowd.

The *meries* (women) helped me out of the dinghy, and someone gave me a rag to wrap up my bleeding finger. They half-walked, half-carried me to a well between the houses of the village. Several of them drew buckets of water and started washing away the diesel and blood that covered me from head to toe. Towels appeared and soon I was clean, dry, and dressed in a proper *laplap. Oh well, I'm just one of the meries now.*

I was led to the village dispensary, with a trail of *meries* and a few wary men peering from around corners the houses. Pauleo, the village Community Health Worker, came out to meet me on the path to the dispensary. His wry humor, calmness, and low-key nature, along with the fact that he spoke English fluently, calmed me down immensely. I knew there was nothing I could do to help *Banshee* at that moment. If anything could be done at all, Leslie could handle it. *This damned, stupid finger, what a rotten time for this to happen.*

The dispensary was the only structure in the village that could be called a "permanent house," i.e., one built of wood with a metal roof. When I asked to have Booby put in the dispensary, I knew that this would be the only safe place for him at the time. The building had conventional doors that shut so that he could be safely locked inside. I went inside and sat down, exhausted. Pauleo calmly chatted with me as he quickly cleaned up the mess that was the end of my finger. Booby was hiding under one of the beds, an appropriate place for a scared cat.

The *dokta,* as he is called, apologized for the lack of medical supplies but for bandages and soap. "Sorry," he explained, as he washed out the wound, "No stitches, no pain medications, no antibiotics here. We use herbal leaves on wounds instead, but they are very good. You'll heal. You are healthy." He instructed one of the meries to go pick some of the appropriate leaves in the bush. *Great, I know how fast staph infections grow in the tropics.*

My friend Lynnah, Ben's wife, appeared at the doorway and everyone indicated that I was to go with her. I picked up Booby and passively followed along with her to her pandanus-sago palm house at the other end of the village. People trailed after me; little *pikinini* (Pidgin for children) stared open-mouthed at me. They had always stared at me—the strange, tall, thin, older *waitskin meri* (white woman) who walked among them in their village. Seeing me this way was probably just too much for their little children's brains to comprehend.

"*Misis katim han. Em i havim pen* (White woman cut her hand. She has pain)," I heard as I went along.

Lynnah walked with me, proud that she and Ben had been the ones chosen to be our "family," and the ones who were to care for us from now on. I was pleased that the arrangement had been made, particularly as both Ben and Lynnah's English was quite understandable to us. My Pidgin was not exactly up to conversational levels.

We arrived at her house, climbed up the steps to her cool veranda, and sat down. "This where you and Leslie stay now," she explained. "This your place *long* (in) Luf. Booby like it *hia* (here) too. Ben and I like cats and we always want one." Booby jumped down and in cat-like fashion started exploring his new surroundings.

Finally, I had the courage to look out to where *Banshee* lay sunk on the reef about a half-mile away. I saw lots of men, women, *pikinini,* and boats of all types congregating around our pitiful stricken sailboat. I noticed piles of our gear being brought to shore and taken up on the beach. Speedies were roaring up to the village shore, dumping our *kago* (Pidgin for anything carried on a boat) and returning for more. Our lives, both personal and public, were being strewn in pieces along the shore. Our private lives were over—we were now living in a communal Papua New Guinea village.

SAVING OUR *KAGOS*

Leslie

The boats from the village were coming out fast now—canoes, speedies, even old logs and pieces of Styrofoam paddled by the village *pikinini*. I watched Joy in our little dinghy fade into the distance. *Joy, come back and help me! Oh god, I've let everyone down. We've lost everything—we've got nothing now. Oh, shit, what have I done? What have I done?*

The boats and people got closer. *Just leave me alone! Oh, Joy, help me. What am I going to do without you?* Then I felt a surge of adrenaline—*I've got to save this boat. It's all we've got. I'll do it, I can save her! I don't need anyone's help!*

Ideas raced through my head. *I've got to get the anchor chains out of the lockers. We'll need to set anchors to pull her off the reef. Then we can stand her upright with the boat's winches.*

What I couldn't understand was why *Banshee* had filled and sank so quickly! I knew her fiberglass hull was very strong—most older yachts had solidly laid-up hulls, and I had seen, firsthand, its thickness. Groundings on coral happen all the time, but they don't usually rip hulls apart and sink boats. *What had happened?*

Standing waist-deep in water on the bow, I looked down into the nearby dark blue of the lagoon—100 feet straight down. I shuddered and closed my eyes. *Just don't let us slip down there, we'll never get her back up.*

Crazy thoughts flew through my frenzied brain. *To hell with these people! They don't know anything. I can kedge Banshee off! I can do it all by myself.*

I sloshed back to the cockpit, reached down into the flooded cabin, and switched on the anchor windlass circuit breaker. I raced forward, kicked the anchor out of its roller, stepped on the footswitch, and heavy anchor chain started spewing out over the sunken bow. *Hey, you know, electrics usually don't work underwater like this.*

I called to one of the guys climbing aboard to dive down and kick over the growing pile of chain on the reef below. *I've got the chain out, now I can kedge off.* I looked behind me at the large, manual winch that we had recently mounted on the foredeck: Joy called it "the just-in-case winch." It was an old Barient sheet winch she'd had for over thirty years. When we'd installed new self-tailing winches in the cockpit, she couldn't part with it. She felt we needed a strong, manual winch on the bow should we ever completely lose power. I was very glad now that she had thought ahead.

By now, people were everywhere, climbing aboard, grabbing things, yelling at me and at each other. I heard Bob, a particularly aggressive guy, yell, *"Lusim* (stop) Leslie! What you do? You no be stupid. Why you *putim ol (*put all*) chain *long rip* (reef)? No *gud* (good).*"

"Get outta here!" I yelled back. I was at a fever pitch; nothing could stop me now. I was going to save *Banshee* or die trying.

I yelled at the men to go pull out more chain, telling them where to find it. "The winches, we'll use them to get us off the reef. With the winches, anchors, and chain, we can do it!" I shouted at their blank faces. I didn't grasp that they had no under-standing of English. They balked, saying we've got to save your *kagos.* I didn't know whether they were saving things or stealing them, and I instinctively believed the latter.

Assertively, Bob came aboard *Banshee*—there was no stopping him. He started shouting orders at everyone, including me. "We collect your *kagos. Givim* me (give me) important things. *Kisim* (get them) now. *Hariap (*hurry up)," he demanded in a mix of broken English and Pidgin. His children in dugout canoes were grabbing things that he threw to them. "Me *kisim kagos long ples* (place) *bilong* me—*em i olrait* there (they be all right there)."

No way, I've heard all about you—the meries say not to trust you, you steal things. Always the first one to visit a cruising yacht, always pushy, always demanding. I hadn't liked this guy when I first met him, when he pushed his way into my group of interested villagers who were learning diving skills with me.

People were now diving and swimming into *Banshee's* cabin. They were everywhere, it was sheer madness. Rape, that's what it was, pure rape. I had no control. People were grabbing things right and left. Bob yelled at me, "You *tokim* (tell) people, *kisim* me CDs, *givim* me CDs, diving CDs, now!" He didn't listen to me, just kept ordering everyone around.

Then Paul arrived, the village leader we had come to trust, a calm man whose inner strength more than made up for his small size. He raced into the scene in his speedie and jumped aboard poor *Banshee.* He took charge, and the villagers began to settle down. The circus-like crowd listened to him. Bob backed away. *The* bikman *(*leader*) has finally arrived, thank goodness.* It had been a scene of sheer anarchy.

Paul told me not to listen to Bob. "Don't give him anything," he said. I heard him say to Bob, "*Maski* (forget it)." Paul told me to put everything only in his speedie or those of his men and he would see that it got safely to the beach. He also designated several of his trusted guys to organize the safe removal of our *kagos*.

"Leslie, what is '*winis*' thing you yell about?" Paul asked.

"Winches, Paul, we'll use the boat's winches and anchors to pull *Banshee* off the reef and get her standing up." I didn't realize that neither he nor anyone else on this primitive island had any idea what a winch was or what it did. Paul gave me a bewildered look, shook his head, and said, "We do it our way."

Great. Where am I? I'm nowhere. The world and its machines don't exist anymore. I turned and looked at Luf village in the distance. *I'm on the ends of the earth, that's where. Where everything that gets here floats in over the reef, including Joy and me in* Banshee.

Then Stanley, Paul's most trusted advisor and a leader of their SDA church, arrived. I was glad to see him. With him was one-eyed Bento, a kind man from the nearby island of Wuvulu. He was more Micronesian and fair-skinned in appearance than the darker Melanesians of Hermit and PNG. These three guys, particularly Paul, spoke pretty good English.

Then Okip pulled alongside in his speedie. He was a loud, obtuse, heavy-set man whose purpose in life seemed to be the spreading of gossip, creating dissent, and hoarding things for himself. I certainly did not welcome his arrival. He, like pushy Bob, began shouting orders immediately. I tried to ignore him.

Paul and Stanley wanted to know where the scuba diving compressor was kept. "We *putim long nambis* (beach) and get running. We need it," they said. Again, Bob jumped into the exchange, yelling, "*Laikim* (want or like) compressor. *Putim we*? (where is it?)"

"It's in the big box in the cockpit, in back of the wheel" I yelled. Bob dived down, unlocked the latches holding the lid of the box, and wrenched it free from the suction that held it. Single-handedly, he lifted the heavy, bulky compressor on his shoulder and swam with it to an awaiting speedie. *Well, he's good for something, at least—brute strength.*

They asked me about our portable generator. "Yes, someone grabbed it. I think it's gone to shore," I replied.

Things were getting better organized. I was still worried about Joy, though. "Does anyone know about Joy? Is she okay? Is Pauleo taking care of her finger? Is Booby okay?" I asked each boatload of villagers as they came out from the beach. Not many answered. All were focused on the job at hand—saving the *kago*.

There was a regular back-and-forth run of boats loading our things and then taking them in to the beach. Adults and *pikinini* were all over the boat. Up the mast steps they climbed, and then dived off crazily into the water below. They hung on the nets of the lifelines, bouncing up and down on them. "Get off!" I yelled. No one listened. It was party time.

Then I heard men laughing. I had vaguely noticed that in the sweltering heat, I was feeling some cool breezes from behind, but I gave it no thought. The laughter increased. A *meri* yelled at me, "*Hia*, Leslie. You *putim long* pants. You no *ken* (can) go *long* no pants." In the melee, unknown to me, the rear of my thin cotton shorts had snagged on something, tearing the whole back of my shorts off. I was not wearing underpants, so the crowd had quite a view! To everyone's relief, I pulled on an offered pair of black knee-length tights to cover my immodesty. *Oh well, a bit of comic relief—now let's all get back to work.*

The distracted crowd returned to their circus. I was asked, "Diving gear, *we?*" They needed masks, regulators and BCs (buoyancy compensating jackets). As they all knew, I was a scuba diving instructor and had many sets of equipment. The guys that I had trained wanted to use the gear right now. The six scuba tanks lashed to the lifelines were easy to get at. I indicated where to find the rest of the gear. They pulled it out of the deck box, and Stanley, Bento, and of course Bob, suited up. The others just wanted diving masks. We had many old ones, so I passed all of them around to awaiting hands. They disappeared with them, diving into the water.

Finally, I suited up too, after failing to find my own or Joy's personal regulator. It appeared that those valuable items had gone to the beach in the rush to unload. I grabbed one of our "rental" regulators and got ready to jump in.

Someone brought a message from shore that Joy was in desperate need of her glasses—she's basically blind without them. I had to find them. Diving into the flooded cabin, I rummaged around in the chaos below. Then, *ah ha, found them!* Hanging by their safety cord, dangling over the open bilge and caught on the fixed crossbeams of the now floating cabin floor, there they were. *Good thing we're all swimming instead of walking in here. Otherwise, they'd have been crushed to bits.* Feeling very proud of myself, I stuffed the glasses in a pocket of my BC. I also spotted some little foil packets of Lariam, our important anti-malaria preventative drug, floating around in the cabin. *We'll certainly need this.* I grabbed them and stuffed them into my recently acquired black tights. *Really useful, these new shorts.*

Okay, enough of this. I've got to get Joy her glasses. Out I went, swimming back into the cockpit with my prize. There were approving smiles all around when I pulled them out. As I leaned over to hand them to someone in a speedie, I said, "Be careful, they're very fragile and she really needs them." They were snatched out of my hand, and then someone said, *"Lukluk, nogat* glass!"

"Shit!" I yelled. *Now how am I going to find a clear plastic lens in all this? Let's see—I remember that one of her lenses keeps falling out, so it must have gone into the water right off the side of the boat.* I dived down and started searching in the sand and rubble trying to find it. *Impossible, but I'll try—she's got to be able to see.* As I swam around underwater looking at every rock and grain of sand, I saw the lens reflecting a ray of sunlight—amazing. I surfaced quickly. "Here! Now get these to Joy quick!"

Isaiah, a kind and very huge young man, was free-diving under the hull on the other side of the boat, and he called me to come over and look at the damage. *I can't, I just can't look.* I kept putting it off, but I knew I would have to look soon.

Divers with tanks were swimming through the cabin. Bob, in his usual destructive way, had ripped off the hatches and the wooden companionway ladder leading below. "So man go *insait, autsait—mipela bikpela* (man go inside, outside—we big)", he told me defensively.

Okay, got to look at the damage. I submerged again and swam around to the port side. There was a long, gaping crack and a foot-wide hole in the hull. *My god, it's huge! Shit, how will I ever patch this?*

It was obvious that our massive external depth sounder transducer with its heavy bronze post had caught in the coral and rammed into the hull. The force of the impact had punched a huge hole, and there were cracks extending about three feet on either side of it. These long cracks had penetrated the heavy fiberglass to such a degree that the hull had actually sprung apart, with the upper side of the crack overlapping the lower. If it hadn't been for the transducer, we would have probably just scraped the coral with minimal damage. *This stupid thing finally sank the boat—the piece of shit never worked anyway. I wanted it gone a long time ago. Now look what it's done.*

It wasn't a clean-cut hole. The transducer was still firmly attached to a flap of the fiberglass hull and hung there, jammed in the hole. It was held by the tenacious 3M 5200 Adhesive—stuff that never lets go—and its clamping ring. I tried to pull the transducer back outside into its former position, thinking that it would bring the fiberglass flap with it and fill the hole. *If I can just do that, I'll be able to patch around it.* However, the thick flap of fiberglass hull was quite stiff, and when I let go of it, it would spring right back into the same position. Using only my hands, there was no way I could pull it out from the hole.

Sharp, rough shards of broken fiberglass tore at my bare arms and hands, leaving painful, bleeding scratches and cuts. My feet were also getting cut and bruised from the sharp coral. I just ignored it. I had no choice—my diving booties had been taken ashore with everything else in the afternoon's rush to unload.

After seeing and touching the terrible damage below, I realized that we had one huge piece of luck in our favor—when *Banshee* had struck the reef and torn the hull on her port side, the weight of our six heavy scuba tanks, lashed to the starboard rail, had caused her to heel over and then fall to starboard. This left her port side exposed, giving us access to the damage. We had only one chance to save *Banshee* now: by using the old two-part underwater epoxy that Joy had been carrying around for at least ten years. I knew exactly where it was kept.

The guys tried to calm me but I kept yelling "The underwater epoxy! I've got to get it. Get out of my way, I know where it is." I swam through the cockpit and dived into the main cabin. *Found it—both cans—parts A and B.*

Swimming outside again, I handed the valuable cans to someone saying, "This is very important, don't lose them. We're going to need this soon." Whomever it was, he nodded and took the cans from me.

Now for the crowbar. Diving back inside, I felt water-borne electric current nip at my skin. *Got to cut it off.* Reaching over to the main power box, I threw off the power switches to the solar panels, batteries, and windlass. *That should make it more comfortable down here.* The current was so bad I felt like a human firefly. Grabbing the crowbar, I swam outside and tried to use it to pry out the shoved-in transducer. Free-diving alongside me, Isaiah watched my futile efforts and then tried a turn at it himself. Nothing—it wouldn't budge much further than before and kept springing back every time it was let go.

Frustrated, I swam away and noticed that *Banshee's* keel had dug a grave for herself in the coral rubble, and the twelve tons of boat had become wedged in the coral heads. The thought of more damage from wave action grinding the starboard side of the hull into the sharp coral worried me. Surfacing for a rest, I talked to the others; I found that they had the same concerns. I suggested using old tires for protection. They looked at me in amazement, saying, "Tires? *Nogat* tires. *Dispela* place, *ailan* place (this place, island place). *Nogat* cars." *Of course, how stupid of me. Let's see, where am I again? Oh yes, nowhere island.*

While I was underwater, they had brought large fishing floats from shore to use as cushioning along the hull. I looked over at Okip in his speedie and saw him stringing some of these floats on a line. *Well, at least he's trying to be useful and has stopped yelling at me.* The divers took the floats underwater and wedged them, as best they could, into any open spaces they could find between the hull and the offending coral.

Now I had to get back to work and deal with that horrible hull damage. Diving down again into the diesel- and battery acid-laced water, I found Isaiah using our emergency tiller arm, made of heavy steel tubing, as a breaker bar. He had stuck it over our crowbar and was trying to lever the depth sounder transducer out from the hull.

No, no, stop it! I gestured, as I frantically grabbed at him to make him quit. He was a very tall, strong guy, and with the leverage he was using, I could see the crack in the hull expanding as it flexed in and out with each of his hard yanks on the bar. He wasn't going to stop on my authority, so I raced to the surface and yelled, "Paul, Stanley, stop him! He's tearing the hull apart!" Paul dived down and motioned for Isaiah to quit, and fortunately, before more damage was done, he obeyed his leader.

I was boiling mad at what Isaiah had been doing and at my total lack of control over the situation. It didn't seem to matter to them that this was my boat—that I legally owned it with Joy. They wouldn't listen to me at all. *Shit, it's their island, a boat has washed up on their reef, and they're going to salvage it their way, period.*

I knew I couldn't fixate on my anger. I had to get my momentum going again. I forced myself to focus. *If we can't pull that transducer and fiberglass back out, we've got to fill the hole with something else. I can make a patch out of wood and use the transducer to hold it in place while the epoxy sets up.*

"Okay, who's got the two cans of underwater epoxy?" I asked those around me.

Okip threw a can at me. "*Hia*, Leslie. Me *gat* (I have) *long* you."

"Where's the other can? Part A's no good without part B. It's two-part epoxy, like the stuff I used to patch your speedies."

No one, including Okip, seemed to understand me. They kept saying, "You *gat wanpela* (got one) tin. You no *laikim dupela* (two) tin. You *usim* (use) tin you *gat*."

"Listen, you idiots! I need both cans—part A and part B. It doesn't work without both cans."

Frustration at their ignorance was getting the better of me. *I have to calm down. Yelling and calling them names won't help.* I had to remember where I was and the lack of sophistication of the people I was dealing with.

Good grief, I have to find the other can; it must have been taken ashore. And I better get the first aid kit to Joy; she probably needs it.

Stripping off my diving gear into a speedie, I grabbed the first aid supplies and the sole can of epoxy—I wasn't letting it out of my sight—and directed the driver to take me ashore. I had to find that other damned can. I just had to!

OUR NEW HOME

Joy

Our new shared home was a pandanus and sago palm thatched house built on axe-hewn posts. The floors and walls were made of woven split bamboo. A shady veranda extended across the front and steps lead down to the ground. A separate kitchen, or *haus kuk* (cookhouse, from German "haus"), was nearby. We would share this small, three-room village house with our newly acquired four-member family who lived there. These wonderful people graciously opened their home and their lives to us and took us in as homeless refugees. Even Booby had found a space—safely hidden under a bed—a dark place of his own.

The house overlooked the lagoon where stricken *Banshee* lay, about a half-mile away on the reef near a mangrove-covered shoreline. Facing the other way, I looked across the flat isthmus area of the village and saw that the sun was getting low on the horizon. I stepped down from the veranda, crossed the tree-lined foreshore in front of our house to the beach, and walked into a chaotic scene. Men, women and *pikinini* were everywhere, swarming over our soggy belongings that were strewn along the beach. Sand and oily diesel-laced saltwater covered everything: parts and hardware, cans and Ziplocs of food, clothes and bedding. Paper items, charts, and books were rapidly turning into globs of *papier-mâché*. It was a nightmare scene in broad daylight.

Speedies roared up to the beach. *Kago* was rudely offloaded—just thrown onto the sand with a great deal of boisterous yelling. *Pikinini* grabbed at "treasures" and went running down the beach with them. They particularly liked our videotapes and CDs that became streamers and Frisbees for their play. *The promised Kago Kult has landed.*

Along the water's edge, fires had been lit. Dark smoke from smoldering, wet paper and whatever else they had decided to burn filled the air. Knowing the Papua New Guinean villager's love for bonfires of any kind, I wondered which of our things were now burning.

I wanted desperately to help—*damn this stupid finger.* Les was out there on *Banshee* without me, trying to save what remained of our life's possessions. But every time I reached to pick up something, throbbing pain tore through my finger. I knew I had to keep my bandaged finger dry and out of the surrounding filth. Even so, the thin gauze bandage soon became wet and dirty. I tried to ignore it.

Eventually, I realized that my best role here would be simply to move around through the crowds and direct what had to be done. A frustrating choice—I really wanted to dive in and work with two good hands. At least my much-needed glasses had arrived, hand delivered by a small messenger in a dugout.

People kept coming up to me with pieces of our bedraggled belongings, asking, "*Em i pipia?* (Is this trash?) *Putim paia? O holim?* (Put in fire? Or keep?)." I reluctantly accepted my new role as "Director of Clean-up" and stopped trying to pick up and move our things around—my painful finger simply made it impossible.

Lynnah, my new village sister, joined me, and her translations of my English to Pidgin certainly helped. I tried to mimic her spoken words, and this seemed to please the villagers—at least this *waitskin meri* is willing to try to speak our language. *The beginnings of my new survival-skills language lessons,* I thought. With some amusement, Lynnah noticed my westerner's inability to keep a *meri's* wrap-around *laplap* covering what it should, and she found a conventional tee shirt and shorts for me to wear.

Young Collen and older Namo, whose leg was badly crippled from childhood polio, were bent over our diving compressor and little Honda generator, cleaning out the saltwater with rinses of gasoline. They were the island's mechanics. I heard the generator cough into life and then the compressor reluctantly fired up. A few of our empty scuba tanks stood by ready for filling.

Twilight was approaching. I heard loud calls from an approaching speedie. It was Les, thank goodness. I was worried about her and had missed her intensely. We were so used to being together and sharing everything on our small 34- by 10-foot living space on *Banshee.* She bounded out of the speedie and rushed up to me, both of us asking each other at once, "Are you okay?" I just let her talk, allowing her to let loose of her pent-up feelings.

"Joy, it's bad, really bad. Half the hull's cracked open—wide open. The god damn transducer. It stuck out so far it caught in the coral and the bronze post punched a hole and the hull split. I told you that thing was going to kill us."

The realization of what she was saying hit me hard in the gut. In a flash, I knew what had happened. I felt so responsible; I had installed it myself. A wave of nausea washed over me.

"Oh god, Les. Can you patch it?

"I don't know, Joy. I just don't know. Okip took the other can of Splash Zone (Z-Spar's trade name for their two-part underwater epoxy). I've got to find it. I've only got part A. How's your finger? I found the first aid kit and the bottle of iodine. Where's Boo-Boo? Is he okay? Is the generator okay? What about the compressor?" Her words tumbled out. She was going on feverishly, talking to me and everyone else all at once.

I looked at her cut and scratched arms and legs with alarm. "My god, you're hurt. Let's get those cleaned up right now, or they'll get infected."

"Not now. No time—got to get the hull patched and there's no underwater epoxy to patch it with. Where's the other can of epoxy?" she yelled as she limped over to the guys minding the compressor.

Her words about what had happened kept ringing in my head, haunting me. I had bought that damned forward-looking depth sounder and had installed it on Guam, long before Les had teamed up with me. It was an Apelco 510, a unit of a discontinued product line now part of the Ray Marine Company. A nice graphic fish finder, but the forward-looking feature never worked well. Its bronze through-hull post was massive, and the fairing block shaped to fit the hull's shape made it stick out even further. I had mounted it forward, just outside the hull mast step so it could "see" in front of the keel. *I should have known better. Les warned me. Now I know why there are so many warnings in more recent transducer installation instructions.*

My private thoughts were interrupted as Okip came lumbering down the beach. "Why you yell, Leslie? *Wanem* now? (What now?)" Les started to explain, holding back her frustrations. Realization of what she wanted spread across his face. *"Em nau, em nau* (It is so)." He lumbered off towards his house on the other side of the isthmus. She turned to me, showing abject frustration. "See what I'm dealing with? It's impossible. Why would he take the stuff home, except to keep it? I told him I needed it here."

Leslie

I saw the generator and compressor sitting under the trees in front of the house. The men said that both pieces of equipment had been running, but the compressor kept stopping. My biggest concern was the scuba tank compressor—without it, we were finished. We had to fill tanks to salvage the boat.

I asked Namo, "Did you change the oil several times to flush the water out?"

"Em nau, me *save* (I know) *motos* go down *insait solwara* (engines go down inside saltwater)."

I grasped what he was saying, but my concern mounted. "Okay, but what about the compressor? It takes oil too. Did you change the oil and flush it also?" I asked. A look of realization flashed across his face. I didn't wait for his answer—I could see it in his face.

"Oh shit!" I screamed. "Saltwater inside will destroy the compressor for sure! It will get into the scuba tanks. We won't be able to breathe the air. Where are the damned fuel jugs from the tank locker? The compressor oil is in one of them. No wonder the compressor is stopping."

Panic-stricken, I followed their directions to an area under the house where all the jerry jugs had been neatly lined up. Grabbing a familiar-looking one, I opened it, looked inside, and saw clean, clear compressor oil. A feeling of relief flooded through me.

I hurriedly returned to Namo and the compressor. He watched intently as I explained the procedure. "We've got to open the oil fill housing, the condensate valves, and the filter housing to release the pressure so the oil can flush through and get the water out."

We poured oil through the indispensable machine. Namo exclaimed, *"Lukluk, bikpela wara come autsait* (Look, big water come outside)." Dirty, oily, dark-colored water poured out from the oil drain valve.

"You ran it like this?" I yelled. The crowd of onlookers watched with growing concern, knowing the importance of our procedures. *If we can't get this compressor working, we are truly finished.*

My heart was pounding—tension mounted inside me. Finally, the oil started to run clear, and I felt marginally better.

Now for the filters. I pulled out the existing filter from its housing, and it was dripping with dirty saltwater—not exactly the standard for a diving compressor air filter. We were going to have to breathe this compressed air underwater, so it had to be clean and free of water contamination. I yelled at the crowd, "My compressor filters. They're in sealed aluminum packages. We had lots of them—where are they?" I had found them when I was swimming through *Banshee's* cabin, pulled them out, and handed them to someone as important items to go ashore.

All anyone could find was a used filter in a Ziploc bag. My valuable filters had vanished.

I took the damp, used filter over to a container of fresh rainwater and rinsed it out, shaking it vigorously to rid it of water. *Okay, I know this isn't the preferred method, but what are the options?* Drying it off as best I could, I put it in the filter housing and screwed its top closed. What can we use for an air filter in the intake hose? Someone offered a clean rag.

I attached the high-pressure fill hose to an empty tank. We all stepped back, and I motioned for someone to go ahead and pull the starting rope—my tired arms ached too much to do that heavy chore. After a few tries, the machine coughed to life, but stopped almost immediately. "Try removing the engine air filter. The air here is very clean," I told Namo.

With another pull of the rope, the magnificent machine sprang to life, chugging away with its air pressure gauge showing building pressure. "Thank god" came out under my breath. Although I'm Jewish, I am definitely not a religious person. I patiently explained to the guys how they had to unscrew the condensate drain every ten minutes to drain off the accumulated water coming from the humid air. A few tries at this and they seemed to get it. We gave the Max-Air compressor a long run at first to vent any water-laden air, and then slowly filled the much-needed scuba tanks.

My attention was diverted from the tank filling when Okip returned bearing the part B can of the epoxy. "Okay, okay," he grumbled as he reluctantly handed over his prize. Grabbing the treasured can, I felt my spirit soar. "Thank god," I said again, this time almost reverently. *Now we can try to patch* Banshee.

Joy

It was getting dark rapidly. We were almost right on the equator, and in the tropics, there is very little twilight. My attention turned to Leslie's numerous bleeding cuts, scrapes, and scratches. Her skin and her dripping, wet clothes were covered with the oily saltwater that she had been swimming in. *Banshee's* sunken batteries had leached acid into the flooded cabin, and she complained that her skin was burning.

"Leslie, please, you've got to wash and take care of those cuts. And you've got to eat something. Lynnah has cooked food for all of us."

"I don't have time to eat. I've got to save *Banshee*," was her reply. Fortunately, Lynnah arrived carrying a large bath towel. "You *painim* (find) bath soap?" she asked. I pushed bottles of liquid soap and shampoo into her large awaiting arms. "Please, Lynnah, she won't listen to me. Show her where to bathe—she's filthy and cut-up. Look at her."

Big Lynnah was not one to be disobeyed, especially when it was a subject in which her motherly nature was concerned. *"Bakets* (buckets), you fetch *bakets*. Me *soim* (show) you." Off they went to the *waswas* place (shower or washing area). Tough little Leslie, barely standing 4'11", trailed obediently behind the tall, heavy bulk of Lynnah.

Ben, Lynnah's calm and gentle husband and my recent rescuer, had lit their treasured kerosene pressure lamp, and the bright light spread through the darkness. One of the *meries* handed me a plate of food. Some of it looked and tasted very familiar. *I think I know where this came from. Oh well, we're all sharing now, aren't we?*

Leslie returned, stepping into the lamplight wrapped *meri*-fashion in a large bath towel. She looked tired but clean. Someone gave her clothes—*pikinini* size, they said, as they teased her affectionately. After finishing a plate of food, she sat down on the veranda steps to paint her wounds in iodine and antibiotic ointment. I sat down next to her. People were staring at us, watching our every move—nothing is private in a PNG village. Her arms and legs were a mass of cuts and scrapes, and now a new enemy had arisen. Red welts and bites covered both of our bare legs. I gave a questioning look to the crowd and someone said *"Ol san* fly—*em i badpela hia* (sand flies—they are bad here)."

Yes, they certainly are. And now here we are, living on this blasted beach.

"Em i laikim blut bilong long lek (they like blood on legs)."

Leslie said, "I don't know which is worse, the pain from my cuts or the damned awful itching from these biting flies."

"Bug repellent," I said to her. "Our big purple bottle of Rid, where did that go? We're sure going to have to find it quick or we won't survive here very long." She grimaced and nodded in agreement.

She looked at the dirty bandage around my finger. "Why aren't you soaking it in iodine? Do you want to have gangrene?"

Everybody watched with great interest. *Marasin* (medicine) *bilong waitman*, they all agreed, was definitely *gudpela* (good).

Lynnah, seeing the valuable supplies, said to me, "We use *long* your *soa* (sore). Me *gat plasta* (plaster or dressing). Me *save. Sistas lainim* me (nurses "learn us" or teach us). Come *insait* house," she said, motioning to me with the lighted lamp she was carrying. "Me dress your *soa.*"

We sat down, cross-legged fashion, in the back room which was dimly lit by the smoky kerosene lamp. She carefully unwrapped the damp and dirty gauze that covered the cut-off tip of my finger. Every movement hurt, but she was gentle, admonishing me to keep it dry and clean, if it was ever going to heal. We poured iodine in a shallow bowl, and she left me there soaking my finger while she ducked outside to check on the rest of her responsibilities, including Leslie. I looked at what remained of the end of my finger. It reminded me of rather under-cooked hamburger. Redness and swelling had set in, and there were no antibiotic pills to be had.

A bottle of pain pills had survived in the drowned first-aid kit. I had told Les that I would take them only when I was going to go to sleep for the night—I was afraid they would mess up my thinking. I knew I was suffering from shock, and I didn't want to succumb further. I looked around, alone in the tiny, dimly lit room. *How did I ever get here?*

A Very Long Night Begins

Leslie

I was feeling better now. The bath and food helped, along with the secure feeling that I had both cans of epoxy and that the compressor was working. Sitting at the top of the veranda steps, I listened to it chug away.

Ben came up to me and said, "You go check *long* men filling tanks. I no trust them to do it right. You do it yourself." *More alarm bells.* I jumped up from my perch and rushed down to the compressor. "Are you guys draining off the water like I told you?"

"Okay, *em i olrait*. You no *ken* worry (It's all right. You no can worry). *Mipela save.*" I didn't trust them, and after Ben's warning I was worried. I opened the valve. Water flooded out in a heavy, pressurized stream; much more water than should have been there. *They haven't been bleeding it off like I told them. Damn, I can't leave them for a moment.*

"Look, you guys," I said, trying to be calm. "If you don't open up this valve and bleed off the water every ten minutes, there will be water in the tanks. Got it?"

I looked around—*Did anyone have a watch? Could they even tell time?* I kept reminding myself where I was—definitely not New York City where I grew up! *All right, I'll follow Ben's advice and sit here and do it myself.*

Joy came over and sat with me, covertly drinking a half-hidden can of warm beer. This was a Seventh Day Adventist village, so alcohol was forbidden for church members. However, we knew that many of the men, the *bekslaiders* (backsliders as they called themselves), would be more than happy to drink it, since they frequently asked for beer when I was alone with them. Ben had seen our cases of beer unloaded on the beach and knew that they would disappear quickly. He told me that he put them all in his back storage room for safekeeping. Joy and I had no intention of becoming teeto-talers while we were marooned on Hermit.

We agreed that if there ever was a time we needed a strong drink, it was now. Joy had simply explained, "Yes, we do have a drink in the evening, but we won't get drunk and no, we won't offer it to anyone else." With that they seemed to accept our habit. I shared a few sips of hers and then was told by one of the guys that it wasn't the thing to do before diving. Under my breath, I said to myself, *yes, yes and I'm a dive instructor too—so bug off and leave me alone.* At that point in our lives, a beer, even a warm one, was much appreciated.

We sat there with our nice warm beer and took turns with the bleeder valve, super-vising it and our drink carefully. The loud un-muffled noise from the compressor and the stares and closeness of the crowd made conversation impossible. We were satis-fied just to be able to sit together again.

I took Joy aside and asked her if she had seen our jerry jugs labeled "diesel." I knew she understood what I meant. "Good lord," she said, "I completely forgot. Where are they? Have they figured out what's in them?"

"They're just sitting there with the rest of the jugs underneath the house. I didn't want to draw attention to them. They've already asked me if they could use "it" to soak sunken parts, but I headed them off and told them to use the diesel in the large blue containers."

She was trying unsuccessfully to keep a straight face. "Is the stuff okay?"

I nodded. "Oh yes, came through just fine—had a nice "whiff" a little while ago."

"Guess I'd better hide them quickly," she said, grinning. The "it" in those two jugs was almost five gallons of Philippine rum, bought cheaply in Palau. Joy does like her rum, no doubt about it. We carried them on deck with the other jugs, plainly labeled "diesel." No one had ever questioned their contents. I watched as Joy, poker-faced, headed off to the house on a mission to secure her valuable potion. "We may be here a very long time," she whispered.

It was slow going, but finally we had three full tanks. Paul and Stanley arrived to have a talk. "Men ready to go back out now," they told us. "We put our generator in speedie and use *bikpela* light from church out there. Done *bipo* (before). We need light."

"Great," I agreed. *What a good idea.* I had been concerned that our diving lights wouldn't be enough for the job ahead—patching that gaping crack in the hull.

With three of the tanks filled, they wanted to get going now. "We take compressor out *long* boat and fill tanks *long* speedie."

"Okay," I agreed dubiously. I had reservations about this, but they seemed to be-lieve it would work. They loaded my precious compressor into the awaiting speedie, along with the diving gear, their generator, and the church light.

Everyone was eager to get started with the night's work. Some had had food and rest, and now a crew of fresh guys joined the rest, ready to go at it. Joy, reluctant to see me go out again, wished me luck and sat down alone by the fire on the beach. I watched her sitting there as I left. I knew it was up to me at this point—Joy's injury kept her from doing anything physical at all.

Joy

The speedie carrying Leslie and all the gear left the beach. I watched her go out into the night—back to what used to be our world—our former private home and life. I was so frustrated and depressed over the fact that I was unable to do anything useful. *I should be out there with Leslie right now, helping her. I don't want her to be alone out there with all those guys, trying to do it all by herself.* For a while I just sat there, numb with my agonized thoughts.

One cannot just sit alone for very long in the communal village. I really didn't want to talk with anyone—most only spoke Pidgin anyway, and I was really at a loss with the language. I longed for the solitude and peace of our boat.

I got up from the warm, cheering fire as more and more people, mostly men, congregated, and I walked back to the house. If I had to, I could talk with Lynnah; her English was pretty good. She was making up a bed on the veranda with clean sheets, covering the few old cushions that she had scrounged. Up to this point, I had no idea where we were going to sleep.

As I sat down and started talking with Lynnah, Booby came wandering out onto the veranda. *Oh, he's heard me, and it's about time for his evening meal. Some things never change, even with cats.*

Fortunately, I had retrieved the large container of dry cat food from the crowd on the beach. As our things came in, they were opening and trying out anything that resembled food, including the cat's stuff. I had to explain, much to their amazement, that we carried special *kaikai bilong puskat* (food for the cat). This decadence was a stretch for their imaginations: *puskats*, of course, found their own food, and are very good to have around because of it. Everyone knew that. Booby greedily gulped down his usual Friskies, and slinked back to the safety of his hidey-hole.

Lynnah soon let me know that Leslie would be sleeping in her son Bently's room, and I would be out here on the veranda. "It okay for you, older woman, to be out sleeping on veranda," she said, "but Leslie, oh no, never. She *no ken* stay out *hia* alone. She *yangpela* (young), and, well, you *save* men. It just wrong."

I guess that we definitely will not be sleeping together while we're here in this house.

I'm sure Lynnah never thought that we might want our sleeping arrangements any other way. This was village mores speaking; what could I say? *Good heavens, to her it doesn't even matter that Leslie is out there right now working her tail off in the dark water of the reef, alone there with only men. But when she is here under her roof, she is a* meri *of the village and village rules apply.*

Good grief, where have we ended up? Leslie and I—two women, one from New York and the other from LA, sharing an ocean-going sailboat and a long-term couple relationship, are stranded in a remote, primitive culture totally cut off from the world.

The irony and insanity of our situation hit me in the face. I realized that these people were basically naïve, uneducated fundamentalist Christians, only "missionized" from their pagan, animist beliefs since 1950, when they were indoctrinated with the missionary's unilateral view on matters of human relationships. It definitely never occurred to Lynnah, or anyone else here, that we were a couple. We had stepped back into a time warp where western big city acceptance of all kinds of relationships had not permeated. As long as we had had the privacy of our own boat—our floating "spaceship," we called it—we could venture into their village life and then retreat from it when it got too close and personal.

We had been through a ghastly experience. What we needed was some privacy and some time to be together in our own room. We desperately needed to comfort and console each other over our tragic loss. I knew full well that I could not ever explain this concept to Lynnah or to anyone else in the village.

The Christian missionaries have done an incredible amount of good in so far as stopping the warring and killing between tribes and in bringing literacy to an illiterate people. However, as they do this, they also teach their own views of the rights and wrongs of human existence. These people with whom we now lived had been completely indoctrinated into a belief that viewed our very lifestyle with horror.

If they only knew what had floated into their midst. Our fragile existence was completely dependent on them. If they even suspected this of us, our boat and perhaps our lives hung in the balance. *How do I handle this? Please let me find the strength.*

Although my mind was racing, I kept my thoughts to myself and helped Lynnah with the bed-making. She was particularly insistent that my bed on the veranda be covered with a mosquito net treated with insecticide. "Malaria," she said, "is *bikpela* problem *long hia*. We all sleep *aninit* (underneath) nets, every night, *tasol* (that's all). Where Leslie sleep, in Bently's bed, there is net *bilong* bed. When she go to sleep, you *soim* how *putim* net *long* bed. Me and Ben go sleep *bipo* time she come *bek* (before time she comes back)." I took mental note of the procedure for arranging one's nets for the night. "Lynnah," I asked, "what about the toilet? Um, it's very dark out there." I already knew the island's sanitation set-up, which was basically the same in all villages. I had had a lot of fun explaining the concept to Leslie when she first encountered it with me on Nukuoro Island several years ago. Yachties jokingly refer to the little above-water outhouses as "beach post-boxes"—with the admonition, "the area near them is not exactly the greatest place to swim."

At Luf, several little huts stood on stilts in front of the village. Logs formed a narrow one-way bridge for walking (with a great deal of careful balance) and connected these toilets to land. I felt that there was no way that I could safely navigate that log bridge at night. For me, even in daylight, the rolling logs made it an act of daring. On the beach, where the log bridge met land, there was a sharpened stake pounded into the ground—pointed end up—with coconut husks lying around it. I knew what this was for when I showed it to Leslie before we sank, but let her guess. "Why husk coconuts here?" she had puzzled. Then she said, "Oh, yeah, I get it," and made a disgusted face. "Really?" "Yes, Les, be glad we have our own toilet paper and our own living place." How ironic that we now had to use the husks ourselves.

Lynnah, sensing my concern and immediate needs, said kindly, "Oh, you go *long nambis*—we all do." She laughed and said, "We no *laikim* come fish you out *long wara long* night. You walk down *autsait lamlait*, use *san* (outside lamplight, use sand). *Wara* come up *long moning* (morning), make clean, *tasol*."

"Okay, I'll give it a try," I replied as I left for a trial run. *Whatever works—it's their custom and their beach. I'll endure. Just go along with the program.*

With the swarming, biting sand flies and mosquitoes, the marauding coconut crabs and their open holes, and the unseen rocks, logs and brambles, my squatting on the sand was an experience to test the sanity of any western woman. *There has to be another way.*

After that trying experience, I trudged back through the dark and up the steps to my net-covered bed on the veranda. The bright kerosene pressure lamp was on, and a crowd of people, mostly men, sat around the *haus kuk*. A bed sheet had been hung over the open area on the front of the veranda. I appreciated that kind and polite attempt to give me some privacy, but with the continual talking and the bright light, all I could do was lie there and worry about Leslie, my friend, who was out there in the dark water without me to help her.

As the people drifted off to their homes, the light was finally turned off, and I lay there listening to the land sounds of the tropical night. I heard a familiar scratching and soft mewing. It was Booby, perched on the windowsill, sniffing the new smells of the leaf house. He hopped down on my bed, "talking" cat-fashion to me, nuzzling my face and then proceeded to explore the inside of my net-covered bed. Satisfied that it was really me in there, he jumped back up on the sill and down into the yard below. *Such exquisite smells, sights, and noises for a little pussycat who never got off the boat—freedom, and a whole new world to explore in the fascinating night ahead of him. Take care of yourself, little cat friend, you're on your own now.* Slowly, I fell into an exhausted, restless sleep, alone, under my mosquito net.

THE HULL IS PATCHED

Leslie

Off we went into the black tropical night. *My god, it was dark.* On the way out to *Banshee,* I set up three sets of diving gear using the full tanks that we had. The other three empty tanks remained lying down in the bottom of the speedie. I wanted to be ready to get in the water when we arrived, so I geared-up with tank, BC, reg, weights, and mask. We didn't use fins as the diving area was very constricted, and we could pull ourselves along with our hands.

I noticed that there was an older, gray-haired man sitting in the boat near me holding the two valuable cans of underwater epoxy. In quiet Pidgin, he said, "You come *long* me *long* epoxy, *tasol*. Me *holim dupela* tins. You *laikim,* you *askim* me, *tasol.* Paul *tok stret* (to speak truly) *long* me, true. (You come to me for epoxy, that's all. I keep the two cans. You want them. You ask me. Paul told me straight, truly)." He clutched the two cans close to him as he sat there. The others showed deference to him and smiled as he spoke. He was Paul's father, Kalu. As the respected head of his extended family, no one would have taken anything from him.

Paul and Stanley were still with us, but the former diving crew was replaced with fresh guys. I was quite tired but adrenalin kept me going. None of them moved to do anything on the way out, just sat there watching as I hurriedly set up all three rigs myself. I was becoming frustrated at their lack of activity. The speedie arrived on site and the guys tied it alongside *Banshee's* ghostly wet form in the darkness.

I was sitting on the side of the speedie and immediately back-rolled into the black water with my dive light turned on. I was near enough to the surface of the water to suddenly hear yelling and banging on the hull of the speedie above me. Surfacing, I heard them all scream at me, "No, not now, salties *hia*. You *stap. Mipela putim bikpela* light *antap (on top)*."

"What're you going on about? Salties? What're salties?" I yelled back, eager to get underwater again. They went on yelling, "You *long manggros* (mangroves). Salties *hia*—crocodiles. *Em i* come out. *Dispela rip bilong em. Sapos em i* come out *na lukim dispela bot long rip?* (They come out. This reef belongs to them. Suppose they come out and look at this boat on reef?)"

"Crocs! Shit! Should I get out now?" I asked, panic-stricken, as I tried to climb up on the shallow coral heads below me, cutting my bare feet. I felt as though I could have levitated and walked on the water.

"Okay, okay, Leslie, *mipela gat bikpela* light now. You *olrait* (all right) now."

Wonderful, those words don't do much to stop my heart from pounding. I stayed there hanging on the side of the speedie, catching my breath, while they asked, *"Wanem plen bilong you? Hausat you no mekim plen?* (What plan is yours? Why don't you make plan?).

"Plan? What plan?" I yelled. Then, trying to calm down and stop thinking about crocodiles, I gave them directions.

"Okay, look, there are two more diving rigs set up. Get them on and get in the water. I'll go inside and get the axe, chisels, scrapers, and wet-dry sandpaper. You guys go in the cockpit, open the engine room hatch by the wheel, and get the gear bags out. They have wood in them. We're gonna to use a piece of wood to patch the hole."

I disappeared underwater and into *Banshee's* submerged cabin. *Anything to get away from dealing with them and thinking about crocs. I want to get this job done now.*

As I descended into the darkness of the flooded cabin, our foam seat cushions floated up at me, blocking my way. The loose, floating cabin floorboards had been removed earlier to allow access, but not the heavy saturated cushions. I pushed them aside and sat down on the strong cross stringers built across the now open bilge. My big UK diving light was getting dim. *Who would have planned ahead for a sinking and re-charged its battery?*

No matter. It was my cabin and I knew it with my eyes closed. The heavy toolboxes were still held in place on the floor under the table by a restraining aluminum tube securely fastened across their sides. I wasn't focused on the consequences of removing the tube over an open bilge and just pulled it loose. Tools went everywhere as the boxes fell over, spilling their contents into the bilge and down under the water tank. *Well, maybe they'll be out of sight and safer down there.*

I found the needed tools exactly where I had left them, and the plastic bag of wet-dry sandpaper was still lying on the wooden bench of the settee in its usual place. Grabbing the things I needed, I swam through the heavy floating cushions towards the main companionway opening and out into the cockpit. The left side of the cockpit was slightly above water and provided a sitting place, and it was now crowded with men just sitting there, waiting and watching the show.

"Leslie, no *ken painim bek bilong diwai insait long hasis. Painim rop, tasol* (cannot find bag with wood inside hatch. Find rope, that's all)."

Shit, it doesn't even occur to them to look in the hatch on the other side. "No, no, the hatch on the other side of the wheel—down there," I said, as I motioned in frustration to the hatch cover on the submerged, opposite side.

Complaining voices said, "Oh, no, *em i insait long solwara.* No *ken* go down *insait long hasis. Dispela* tanks *bikpela tumas.* You *lusim stia?* (No, it's underwater. We can't go down inside hatch. These tanks too big. You take off wheel?)"

"No way—forget it guys," I said. *They'd just love to have our steering wheel decorating someone's house. My, I am definitely becoming paranoid.*

Then a drawn-out discussion ensued about how they preferred hookah rigs to tanks. "Come on guys, back to work." I had little patience for their dawdling around. I dove down and opened up the hatch lid and, presto, the bags filled with wood scraps floated up.

"See, there you are, just reach down to the hook, unclip the bags and pull them up," I said. *With my aching back, cuts, and tired arms, I am not going to lift those heavy bags out of the water by myself with these young guys just sitting around, staring at me.*

More whining. "No *ken* go down *insait na lusim* hook. *Em i pas* (We can't go down inside and loosen hook. It is stuck)."

Frustrated by their lack of action, I grabbed my expensive, ever sharp Myerchin knife from its sheath next to the door, dove down head first into the hatch, and with one swipe, cut the cloth handles of the bags, and they floated free. They gasped when they saw how easily it cut. That was the last time I ever saw the knife.

Totally frustrated by this waste of time, I told them, "Get those bags into the speedie and start looking for a piece of wood big enough to patch the hole. Grab those chisels, scrapers, and sandpaper, and go down and start scraping off the bottom paint and muck around the crack and the hole. I'm going down there and make a template of the hole with the sandpaper. Let's move and get on it. Come on, guys."

Without waiting for them to respond, I dove underwater, a place that I was comfortable with. *Much more peaceful down here—all I have to listen to are my bubbles.*

The only way I could work on the template for the hole was to be head down in the water with my bare feet splashing at the surface. The coral bank and nearby rubble bottom didn't give me space to work any other way. That's why I was so glad that I had found my newer Scubapro regulator. The others were not as comfortable to breathe from when working upside down.

The two divers scraped and sanded the hull as directed, but the rest of them, free-diving down to see the action, just got in the way. I kept kicking them with my feet. I boiled to the surface and yelled a blue streak of profanity at them, telling them to get their useless selves away from me. I work very well by myself and like it that way. However, in PNG, one does not do anything alone—there is always the inevitable crowd of onlookers, especially as we were women.

Underwater, in the dark, I kept seeing a bright flashing light inside the cabin. I thought it was the guys above shining my underwater dive lights into the water. But something didn't seem right about that. *It's more like a strobe light. Shit, it's the EPIRB! It's water activated, so now the whole world knows we're sunk. Oh, my god, our families…my poor mother.*

I surfaced, yelling, "The beacon. It's under the shelf on the nav station. Untie it and pull it out. Get it out of there." Someone dove down, did what I asked, and handed it to me. Everyone stared. Hermit was now on the world map.

It must have been transmitting for hours. I had completely forgotten about our ACR Emergency Position Indicating Radio Beacon (EPIRB). I couldn't remember how to turn the damned thing off. *I'll just unscrew the antenna. That ought to stop its signal from going out.*

"Get this to Joy on the beach, quick."

Joy

Loud cries came from the beach, and a little messenger came running up to the veranda carrying our EPIRB, still flashing its bright strobe light. *"Misis, misis, laikim dispela? Em i tokim me, long givim long Joy. Hia.* (White lady, you want this? They tell me to give it to Joy. Here)."

I grabbed it and disabled the switch. *How long has this been on? Has the signal been received? Please world, we're taking care of ourselves just fine. Let us do our work. Oh god, I don't want anyone to worry.*

All faces turned to stare at the strange, blinking plastic box. Lynnah was amazed and listened intently as I explained to her how this beacon "talks" to a satellite in the sky and will tell our government and then our families that *Banshee,* Joy and Leslie are now wrecked on Hermit Island. The thought crossed my mind that if these people get the idea that the outside world knows about us, they might be a little easier on us. I was becoming increasingly concerned about the security of our possessions that seemed to be littered everywhere.

Lynnah's Pidgin translation of my explanation and the villager's reaction was something to behold—the expressions on the faces of these primitive people as they kept looking skyward said it all.

I went inside the house and safely hid the beacon. *I need to keep this for later. We may need it, and I don't want it stolen.*

Leslie

"Now back to work," I told the guys. *I don't need any more interruptions, please.* Underwater again, I placed a sheet of sandpaper over the hole and folded its corners to fit the hole. I wanted to fit the wood into the hole, pressing it between the inside of the hull and the pushed-in, still attached flap of fiberglass holding the transducer bulb. The sheet of sandpaper was a little small, but it would have to do.

Satisfied with my template, I swam out to Paul, who was waiting in his speedie, and handed him my art work. "Here it is. Just make it a little bigger for the overlap so the transducer doesn't push it back out when the board is pressed between it and the hull."

I climbed aboard, and asked for my bag of wood. He pointed to a wet bag on the floor, and I began to rummage around in it. I was looking for my marine plywood, but had to settle for a wide piece of teak. The hole in the hull was almost a foot in diameter. "Okay, this'll do. Now shape it up with the axe." I watched while he chopped at it until we were both satisfied with the shape. *Cutting with axes, they're good at. I couldn't have done it that easily.*

The guys with the other two diving tanks had been continuing with the job of salvaging stuff from inside the boat. I doubt if it ever occurred to them to manage their air consumption—they just gulped it down. They both surfaced and I checked their air: only 500 p.s.i. "Almost empty," I told them.

The complaining started again. "You *filimap tanks*. You *tokim mipela* you *havim planti win*. *Filimap* now. *Laikim win long* dive (You fill tanks. You tell us you have plenty air. Fill them, now. Want air to dive.)" My rig was lying in the boat, so I gave it to one of them thinking he'd just go away while I tried to start the compressor.

After several pulls on the rope, it became obvious that this idea of running it in the speedie was not going to work. *I guess the rocking boat upsets it; perhaps another oil change is in order. Oh well, no spare oil out here now.*

Shit, now I've got to get my tank back or I can't finish this job. I yelled at one of the guys snorkeling without scuba gear and told him to go down and get his friend so I could to get my rig back. He wasn't happy with giving it up, but did let it go. *What a waste of valuable air.*

Now for the epoxy still held by Kalu. "Does someone have something to open these cans?" Paul opened them with the axe. I reached in and grabbed a handful of each part of the gooey stuff, mixing it together on one side of my newly made wood patch.

Diving down to my work below, I shoved it into the hole and, presto, perfect fit. The new wood patch was firmly secured by the pressure of the springy fiberglass flap and the transducer pushing it against the inside of the hull. Magic! My idea worked perfectly.

The gooey epoxy was all over me and my diving gear now—*no matter, no time to worry about that.* Back up to the boat for more of it I went. Surfacing, I found Okip had arrived, running his speedie almost up on top of me. "Get him outta here. He's in my way!" I yelled at Paul. *All I needed was another go-round with him.*

I heard him arguing with Paul. "You *givim* me epoxy. You no *tokim* me *rausim* (leave). *Ol* papa *bilong* me *na* you, *em i brata*. Me papa *em i bikpela* 'Chief.' Me *stap long hia, tasol*. Me *wok long* Leslie. You *rausim*. Me *kisim* epoxy. (You give me the epoxy. You don't tell me to leave. My father and yours are brothers. He is the bigger Chief. I stay here, that's all. I work with Leslie. You leave. I keep the epoxy.)"

Good grief, I'm trying to save my boat and they're arguing over who keeps my epoxy!

"Look, you guys, just give me the epoxy. Where is it?"

"You come *hia*, Leslie. Me *givim* you. Me *gat* epoxy."

It appeared that Okip had won the battle of the epoxy, and I was to go to him to get my handfuls of the stuff. *Dammit, it's my epoxy. Why's he got it? He's been trying to keep it all afternoon. What's with this guy?*

Trying to hold my temper, I swam over to his speedie and said, "Okay, give me a handful from each can."

"No, you *kalapim* (get aboard). *Em i hia* (here it is). Me no *holim* (touch) epoxy. *Em i* poison. You *rausim* tank, *kalapim long rip long bot* (boat). You *putim han* (hand) *long* tin, no me."

All right, they've got me. What else can I do? I'll do it your way. I've got to get this patched. Off went my tank and up on the coral I went, my bare feet getting even more cut up. I had been asking for my dive booties since we sank. No one knew where they were. Just gone. *Those are valuable items in a primitive fishing village.*

Now we had an exhausting routine. I would surface, remove and float my scuba unit, climb up on the coral, grab handfuls of the goo, mix them together in my hands and then go back in the water, put my rig back on and smear the stuff around the damage below. When I felt I had enough epoxy around the wood piece, I started working on the cracks. They extended about three feet out from each side of the hole. I shoved my epoxy goo into any spaces that I saw.

I was trying to be very sparing with my precious epoxy. The cans were only one liter each, and they had not been full. I figured I had covered enough on the outside of the hull, and now I wanted to smear some on the inside of the patch. However, I didn't trust any of the men, so I sat there, underwater, next to my lovely patch, and waited for the stuff to harden. *One of these guys can easily come down here with the axe and smash it in.*

Satisfied that my wood and epoxy patch was becoming permanent, I turned my attention to covering the inside. When I came up, everyone wanted to leave. *"Inap tunait, pinis long moning* (Enough tonight, finish in morning)."

"Give me more epoxy. I'm not done. Got to put some on the inside around the patch. Got to make it strong." *So one of you doesn't come and smash it in when I'm not here.* I had heard too many scare stories about stranded yachts in remote villages being stripped. *I'm going to make this strong now before I go ashore tonight, that's for sure.*

I grabbed two more handfuls from Okip and swam down into the dark cabin, holding my diving light under my arm. The hole couldn't have been more inconveniently located. It was under a low shelf and deep inside a bin covering the hull. Being short, so are my arms—too short to reach the hull through the bin. *Now I do need long-armed Joy. She could reach this.*

Plopping my gooey ball of epoxy on a cabinet, I removed my diving rig, set it on a seat and kept the reg in my mouth to breathe. I tried to position my light so that I could see into the bin. *This is not going to work. I'll have to do it by feel.* I wedged my head and upper body in under the shelf, arm extended as far as I could reach, holding the ball of epoxy in my outstretched hand. The fiberglass shards tore at my wrist and fingers.

Okay, I feel the edges of the patch, and, good, the transducer is there pressing down on the wood. I wanted to cover the outside edges that were touching the hull and not get any epoxy on the transducer, because I needed it to be free of the hull. My idea was that later, when we were floating, I would saw off the flap of leftover hull and transducer and get rid of it. Then I would be able to patch over the whole area from the inside with more epoxy. I knew I had to be very careful, especially doing it by feel.

Make a bead of the stuff around the outside of the patch, cover all the edges, and swim out for more precious goo. I did this three more times, until I was satisfied that the patch edges and the parts of the crack closest to the hole were all covered with hardening epoxy.

I think I've done it. I think it's patched. Tomorrow I can fill in what I've missed. I need to get out of here before I collapse. God, I'm tired.

"All right, guys. Let's go. We'll finish it in the morning." They looked relieved. We sped off to the light from the fires on the beach.

The house was dark and quiet when I climbed up the steps to the veranda where Joy lay sleeping under a mosquito net. She stirred as I came near. "It's patched, Joy. The hull is patched. *Banshee's* going to be okay—we'll make it."

Joy

In my sleep, I heard Les say, "It's patched." She was kneeling next to my bed and had pulled back my net. *God, she's a mess—wet, dirty, cut all over, and she has epoxy globs in her hair. Poor dear Leslie, she'd die trying to save* Banshee.

I got up to help her. This time her bath was just a few buckets of well water poured over her shaking body. "I'm cold, Joy, so cold. I can't stop shivering." I dried her off and led her into her bed in the other room. Her whole body was shaking so badly that I was afraid she would go into shock. *At least Lynnah has provided blankets.* She wouldn't stop talking—going on and on about what had happened out there. I bundled her up with blankets and pulled down the mosquito net over her bed, explaining that she needed to keep it around her.

"I'm freezing. It's so cold—I've got the chills. Oh, Joy, hold me, I need you so much. I didn't want to be alone out there without you—those guys—it was so awful. Stay here with me, please."

I tried to calm her. "Please don't talk now. They can hear everything, and you need to sleep. We'll talk later when we're alone." I sat there on the bamboo floor next to her bed, holding her hand, until she calmed down and some of her shaking stopped as she fell asleep.

She woke up and came out to my bed several more times during that awful night, shaking with chills and fright. It's the shock. She's got to stay warm and in bed. Each time I took her back to her bed and comforted her as best I could; the lack of privacy was awful. *If we could just be alone and hold each other, it would be so much better.*

Leslie

I was finally asleep—dead asleep. It must have been around two or three o'clock in the morning. A little girl was tugging at my bed. *"Misis. Misis, ol* man *laikim* you come out."

"Go away. I'm sleeping. Leave me alone. Get out of here." I turned away trying to ignore the voice.

A woman appeared. It was Joen, the schoolteacher, Okip's daughter. "Leslie, please come out and pump tanks. The men want to go out and save some more of your *kagos.* They say you give them more air. There are lights on *Banshee.* They afraid some people steal out there. Please get up and help them."

I got up from my warm bed, wrapped a blanket around me, and followed Joen to the beach where the men had gathered around the compressor. Somehow, in my dazed condition, I got it running and pumped two more tanks. I sat on the veranda steps while it ran, checking it every so often. Joy called to me, half awake, saying, "What now? Why are you pumping tanks at this hour? Let it wait till morning. Les, you've got to sleep. Please, don't go out there again." I assured her that I was just pumping tanks for the guys—they were going out without me—and as soon as two were full, I would quit and go back to bed.

I sat there, putting more antibiotic cream on my festering sores, as the machine chugged on. Booby scampered around in the darkness, checking in with me every so often. I looked up in a tree while tending to the compressor, and there he was looking down at me.

After the two promised tanks were done, I shut it down, ignoring their complaints for more. "Get out of here, guys. You got your tanks, now go." *Probably they'll do a little fishing too,* I thought, as I went back up to the house.

Sleep—please, all I want is sleep.

DAY ONE ON HERMIT

Joy

The chickens start in early—about four o'clock—in a small village. Their unwelcome crowing and clucking roused me from my exhausted sleep. My net-covered bed on the open veranda provided no protection from their incessant noise. *This is going to mean early morning wake-up calls from now on.* Still trying to catch some sleep, I contemplated the options for the morning's needs. *It's either a run to the beach while still under cover of darkness or walking the plank to the beach outhouse later.* I opted for the beach, even with its hazards.

The sand flies on the beach were awful, making me resolve to find my big bottle of Rid insect repellant as the morning's priority. *And the toilet situation: I've got to do something, even if it's only a jug under the bed.* Crawling back under my net and covers, I savored my last private hour before the communal village day began.

As the sky lightened, the village came to life. The sounds of children playing and yelling and mothers yelling back, families beginning the day's work, more chicken noise, dogs barking and then the gong—the damn omnipresent banging village gong—destined to become a part of our life's activities from here on. It tolled the time of day, the meetings, the school hours, the call to prayer, the church services, and many other things I didn't care to ask about. It was an old empty welding gas tank as tall as I was, hung from a tree limb and struck with a metal pole.

Ben and Lynnah were up now, stirring the smoldering fire in the *haus kuk*. I heard Ben chopping the day's firewood supply and smelled the rising smoke. *Coffee! Now where was that strainer? I've got to have a cup first, then I can handle anything. At least I hope I can.*

I passed by Les' curtained-off doorway (she was still sound asleep) on my way to the back room of the house. I knew she needed all the rest she could get. My whole hand ached now—I knew just by the feel of it that infection was setting in. *Got to ask Lynnah to help me clean and change the bandage this morning. Good, the coffee strainer still's here.* I had put it along the wall with several rescued cans of our unopened Chase & Sanborn ground coffee. *Not exactly gourmet stuff, but still wonderful.* Carrying my prize, I went outside and entered the smoke-filled *haus kuk.*

The extended family was gathering in the screened eating area in a room walled-off from the cooking fire, complete with a table and benches. Ben smiled when he realized what I was carrying. Coffee is a treat; the usual beverage, if they have it, is black PNG tea. Ben and his trusty bush knife had the big can open in a flash. The process of pouring boiling water from the fire-blackened kettle through my tiny strainer over the ground coffee was watched with great interest. A big can of our New Zealand An-chor-brand powdered milk had found a new home. It stood on the table, newly opened and by now almost half gone. *Milk is such a treat in these places. They could hardly resist.* Cups were laid out on the table and a jar of sugar was offered. Eyes gleamed with expectation as I poured out the treasure they rarely had. Standing there as a stranger among people from a primitive culture, all of us with cups of the wonderful, steaming liquid, I told them: "This is Day One. We'll make it, guys."

Someone said, "Leslie, *we?*" "Still sleeping," I replied. "She was so tired, let her rest." Heads nodded. *"Liklik meri wokim* (little woman works) *bikpela long* night." At her full-standing height of 4'11", it amazed the villagers that she could easily do *"wok bilong man"* (man's work).

After a while, a disheveled Leslie appeared at the *haus kuk* door. Her pained expres-sion told me her first order of business was the dreaded toilet ritual. I nodded, shrugged, and raised my eyebrows toward the nearby beach. Soon she returned, standing there in her soaking wet clothes. "A necessary early morning swim" she said. Lynnah didn't have to say anything; I got her look: not dripping wet in *my* house, please. I fetched a towel and some of Les' herbal tea that I'd found among our things in the back room.

Before we left Palau, we had stocked up on our favorite brand of granola cereal, carefully stowing it in Ziploc bags. Many bags had survived their time underwater. *How fortunate, because there's nothing here I want to eat for breakfast, and shops are nonexistent.* Lynnah's family was making a meal of left-over fish heads and bones that had sat all night in greasy coconut milk, and cooked *tapiok* (cassava) that the flies had been feeding on since the day before, even though it was carefully covered with banana leaves.

The villagers were already out at *Banshee,* and speedies were arriving on the *nambis* filled with our belongings. People swarmed over them as they arrived, grabbing and throwing our things onto the sand. Some ran off to their houses with their arms and hands full. Others threw our things into piles, opening and dumping carefully-stored Ziplocs filled with important parts into hand-woven pandanus baskets. *"Long waswas, ol waswas. Solwara* no *gud long kago."* A chaotic circus was going on around us. Our world had gone mad.

Leslie

As I walked out on the beach among the throng of villagers, my impulse was to jump in my dinghy and go out to *Banshee*. People were out there and I needed to be there too. But first I had to find something to protect my feet. I was having trouble walking, the pain was so bad. Neither of us had any shoes. On the boat we had had so many pairs of shoes—thong sandals (called "slippers" in the Pacific), expensive Tevas, sports running shoes, rubber sea-boots, and some dressier loafers. Now all of our shoes were gone. Very few people on Hermit had shoes; finding ours was a goldmine. *Booties, where are some diving booties?* I asked everyone to no avail. Finally my loud nagging had an effect, and someone appeared with a net bag with assorted pairs. Putting them on was painful, but I had to protect my damaged feet from the rocks, sand, and sharp coral.

The guys were quick to tell me that tanks needed to be filled. *Okay, let's get going, six tanks coming up. What would we have done without my Max-Air 35 compressor?*

Our dinghy was pulled high on the beach, filled to overflowing with high-priority salvaged items to keep them away from the melee of foragers and cleaners. My idea was to get these things into the protection of our storage room in Lynnah's house. Once the stuff in the dinghy was cleared out, I could come and go to *Banshee* on my own with our small outboard. I yelled for help but they refused, telling me to get in one of their speedies and go with them. I got the idea that they didn't want me to be coming and going on my own.

"You go *long mipela*—no go *long dinghy*. You *lukim, tasol*. *Mipela save wok long bot*, no you. You *meri,* no man. *Dispela wok bilong* man. (You go with us—not in dinghy. You watch, that's all. We understand work about the boat, not you. You woman, not man. This is man's work)." *Wow, they're certainly getting defensive about what I did yesterday.*

Paul arrived, and again I tried to explain how we could use winches and anchors to kedge *Banshee* off the damaging coral. As before, he and the others didn't understand and wouldn't listen. Paul kept telling me that we needed to "position" the boat under-water first and that they knew very well how to do that as they had done it many times before with other sunken boats. They were bull-headed in their conviction that they could do it by sinking empty fuel drums and then floating them.

"Em pinis, tasol!" (finish, that's all), and they turned their backs on me and walked away. In PNG, it's unheard of for women to tell men what to do.

To keep the peace and avoid a standoff, I went along with the guys in their speedies, *meri*-style, obeying my male "bosses."

The scene at *Banshee* was insane. *I'm glad Joy isn't here. If she saw* Banshee *like this, being taken over and scavenged by these wild, crazy people, she'd be devastated.* Men and women swarmed over the boat, swimming inside and out, laughing and shouting. They were grabbing anything that was loose and throwing it to others in canoes and speedies. *Pikinini* climbed up on the cockpit overheads and rigging pinrails and dove off into the water, only to climb up to do it again. They leaped back and forth between the forward hard dodger and aft hard bimini, jumping on the solar panels as they went. *Meries* swung in the nets on the lifelines, bending and moving stanchions. It was an island free-for-all party. The fabled *Kago Kult* (Cargo Cult) had finally arrived, and it was all theirs.

"Stop it, get off!" I yelled at them. I swore. No one listened.

Then I turned to see the amazing sight of thirty men in the water, laughing and shouting. In unison, they would sing out, *"Wan, tu, tri, siuvim* (One, two, three, shove)," and then dive down and shove on the hull. Then they would surface and do it again. If it wasn't so pathetic and ignorant, and if I hadn't tried so hard to explain kedging using the winches, it would be laughable. Grown men trying to push twelve tons of firmly-grounded boat while swimming! Even Paul was in the midst of the melee.

Paul's wife, Hedis, usually a responsible, serious type befitting the wife of the community leader, was gaily swinging in the nets, shouting and laughing. *She'll listen to me.* I tried to explain things to her and noticed that an attractive young woman sitting next to her was translating my words into Pidgin. I stopped, stared at her, and she introduced herself, in perfect, educated Australian-accented English, as Paul's sister, Natalee.

I was dumfounded—*what is she doing here?* Then I remembered that she had been one of the few women in my diving class, and had been identified as the "only *meri* tour guide" for visitors to the village. However, up till now, she had never spoken to me directly.

Why am I wasting all my energy trying to speak to people who don't understand me when here's a translator right in front of me? "Natalee, please help me to get all these people to calm down and be useful. They're gonna break things and lose valuable parts; we don't need any more destruction. Tell those stupid men to stop pushing—they'll never move this boat that way. Get the men to listen to me, please."

Natalee spoke quietly as though she didn't want anyone else to hear. "Yes, I have been watching and listening to you for some time, but I cannot help you talk to the men. As a woman, and as the sister of our leader, my loyalty must be to him. It is not my role to tell him or any other man what to do or how to do it. That simply is not allowed, even if I am only translating for you. The roles of men and women are very strict here, and I must obey the rules if I am to live here or have any connections to my family. That's the reason I've just hung back and not talked with you. I didn't want you to know how well I spoke English because then you would ask me to help you. I'm sorry, I wanted to, but I couldn't. I was really torn, but Paul is in charge, and I must not question his authority. I chose to be quiet. I thought it was best. You do not act like a woman in our culture."

That's for sure! I'm a liberal Jewish woman from New York City, where women do exactly as they please without being questioned about "roles" by the male establishment. I thought of my mother, who owns and operates her own exclusive travel agency and employs an all-female staff. And of my sister, an executive stockbroker. And my well-traveled father, a liberal New York maritime attorney, in today's modern world. And then of me and my relationship with another woman. *Did Joy and I ever subject ourselves to the expectations of men?*

"Okay, Natalee, I understand. You *are* allowed to talk to the women, aren't you?"

"Sure, as long as it doesn't reflect poorly on Paul, the church, our values, or any of our men."

All right, I'll try to go along with that. *Just give me strength.* "Please help me organize these women to remove our stuff and get it to shore. And the *pikinini*—can't you get them under control? They're breaking things and getting in the way. Why are they here at all?" Natalee grinned and started speaking in rapid Pidgin. With chagrined expressions, the wild *pikinini* retreated to their small children's canoes and a semblance of order returned. I still couldn't contain myself from raging at the men and their stupid water game. Some gave up and drifted off ashore. Even though many stayed at it, the game didn't seem as fun anymore.

I did notice that there was one man whom Natalee had no problem telling what to do—Bento, the gentle guy from Wuvulu who had helped us before. He followed her directions without a whimper. *Ah ha, I see. He's not from Hermit or Ninigo* (the neighboring island with close familial ties). *He's not a wantok* (literally, one-talk or same local language), *so she is allowed to give him orders.*

With people organized and working, I put on my diving gear, took the remainder of the underwater epoxy, and finished the patching work, inside and out, until every precious drop was gone. *Well, it's got to hold now because there is no more. Let's just hope it works.*

Paul and Stanley returned in a speedie piled high with empty 55-gal fuel drums. They placed them around the perimeter of the hull with their edges scraping into the paint, fiberglass, and teak rails. I objected to their lack of cushioning, but was quickly shouted down by Paul: "Look, Leslie, you *laikim* save boat or save paint?"

"At least put them where they're going to do some good! Tie them around the keel," I replied. No one paid a bit of attention to me.

The men sat on the drums to fill them with seawater. When the drums sank, they dove down and tied long lines on them, tying them off to every above-water structure they could grab: overheads, rails, stanchions, rigging, chain plates. Then they blew out the water with compressed air from the scuba tanks. Because the drums had not been correctly placed and tied securely around the keel, they simply popped right back up to the surface. It was useless, of course, and *Banshee* lay steadfast in her grave.

It was obvious that they had never dealt with refloating a heavy, deep-keeled boat, no matter what they claimed. *They have no idea of the huge weight of a lead keel.* Their oversize male egos were on the line. We were not dealing with logic here, just emotions. In agony, I listened as the empty drums banged and crashed into the hull. A day was passing in useless enterprise. *When will they listen?*

As the end of the day approached, speedies filled with men, women and gear started going back to the shore.

"*Misis* go home. *Em i no wok. Mipela* no *ken movim bot. Em i pinis.* You pray, *tasol.* (It won't work. We cannot move the boat. It is finished. You pray, that's all)." Hedis and Natalee came to me, held my hands, and told me to accept that the boat was gone and to pray with them. Now, Joy and I are definitely not religious. Neither of us believes in any higher power—we simply believe in ourselves and what we can do—so this continual praying stuff was getting on my nerves. It took an effort to hold my tongue. *Yes, they're trying to be kind, but I don't need this. I know* Banshee *can be saved. We have winches, damn it!*

Joy

All day I watched speedies come and go, dumping their *kagos* and returning to *Banshee*. Villagers came and went. I kept watching for Leslie to be in one of the boats, but she never appeared. *What is going on out there?*

There was little I could do physically except to act as "Director of Clean-Up." My finger hurt terribly. Lynnah changed the dressing. It was obvious that infection had set in, it was so ugly. *What the hell, I've got to do something useful.*

A crew of diligent *meries* and older men worked long and hard sorting and cleaning our things as they were brought to the beach. Trash fires continued to burn with items that were beyond saving. Everything was covered in salt and filth. Our more durable possessions were dutifully washed in water from the tidal wells. This well water was all that was available for washing, although it was brackish and a bit sandy. They needed soap to get things clean, so I gave them soap powder from our sealed plastic containers. Soap was a scarce commodity on Hermit.

The village was quite limited in potable water. Rainwater collected off corrugated iron roofs was the primary source. There were several freshwater springs, but they ran down steep slopes into the sea, and they were only accessible by canoe from the lagoon.

Shallow tidal wells were dug close to houses. To hold them open, empty fuel drums with cut-off ends are pounded into the well sides. The flat land of the village was a sand-topped coral shelf, which is very porous. Rainwater filters down and floats on the seawater coming up through the coral under the sand. As the tide rises, so does the level of the fresh water in the well; as the tide falls, the level of the fresh water drops. These tidal wells enable a village to exist where river or spring water is unavailable. This brackish well water could be drunk, but it had to be boiled first. Washing with well water got the salt out of our things but left a sticky, sandy film on everything. How I longed for running water from a hose.

Finally, I saw Paul's speedie head into the beach. Leslie was riding in the bow. Her thumbs down gesture and shaking head told the story . "Joy, they won't listen to me. They can't move her. What are we going to do?"

We had to talk with Paul and Stanley. Even though they were tired, the two men finally agreed to come after dinner and listen to us, but with a surprising proviso:

"You bring coffee, milk and sugar. We listen, but Joy tell us what we do next—no you, Leslie, you talk *kwiktaim tumas*."

Dusk was settling in and our flashlight batteries were about finished. *Another night of stumbling around in the darkness. Great.* At least my large bottle of Rid insect repellant had appeared in one of the speedies, for which I was grateful: the evening sand flies were biting fiercely.

Les was sweaty and salty, and I hadn't had a bath since the *meries* washed me down from the sinking yesterday. I had our bathing stuff, fresh clothes, and buckets ready to go, as instructed by Lynnah. I told Leslie that I would need help bathing. Teasing me, she replied, "Of course, I'm happy to play nurse."

In the dusk, led by Lynnah, we crossed through the central, grassy soccer field and over to the houses that faced the other shore of the isthmus village. "Shower *bilong* Daniel—*nambawan* (number one) *long* village," Lynnah announced. Leslie, who had had her shower instruction last night, was waved on ahead with an *"Em i olrait."* Patiently, Lynnah showed me, the novice, the fine art of a PNG bucket shower.

The *waswas* was a bamboo and palm enclosure, open to the sky. Water came from a nearby well. One had to lower a tin pot attached to a long bamboo pole into the well, fill it, pull the pole up, and empty the water into one's bucket. This procedure took many dips and required a certain knack to keep as much sand out of the water as possible. After filling our five-gallon bucket, we lugged it into the shower enclosure. A plastic bowl was used as a "dipper" to splash water over oneself. Then came a soap-up with the washrag , followed by another rinse. And that's it—a one-bucket traditional PNG *waswas*.

To keep my finger dry and out of the well water, I had to hold it up in the air while Les splashed water over me, but at least I still had a left hand left for washing. I appreciated Les' efforts, but hated to be so dependent for basic needs. She was eager to get back to Lynnah's, as she was looking forward to tonight's promised conversation with Paul and Stanley. In her haste, she grabbed our only flashlight and left before I was finished.

It was quite dark by then, and stars appeared as I looked up from my open air shower. *Damn, no flashlight. When it's dark on a remote tropical island, it is very dark.* Still not very familiar with the surroundings of the village, I went stumbling around houses and through the grass in the pitch dark, trying to set my course for the bright light of Ben's pressure lamp. Coconut crabs and their treacherous holes in the ground were everywhere, tripping me several times. In some villages these crabs are eaten as a delicacy, but not here with the strict SDA Old Testament dietary restrictions. I hated these ugly critters.

Arriving back at Lynnah's, I was sore at Les for taking off with our sole flashlight, but a hot plate of food (from our own supplies) was placed in my hands and I gratefully accepted.

Paul and Stanley arrived a bit later. We sat around the *haus kuk* table for our discussion. They couldn't understand why we, two women, continued to believe that our very heavy boat could be moved off the reef and refloated. They had run out of ideas; it hadn't worked as they had thought. *What to do now?* Using some pages from a school exercise book, I gave a lesson on the mechanical advantage of winches, the physics of kedging by setting out anchors, and the leverage of using the mast to pivot and slide the boat.

"How can small machine like winch have *bikpela* strong power like many men?"

The old science teacher in me had them listening for the first time—a bit dubiously, but they were listening and learning.

Finally, Paul slapped the table and nodded.

"Em i gudpela plen. Traim tumora."

KEDGING AND *KAGOS*

Joy

Grey dawn, crowing chickens announcing the sunrise, the clanging gong to awaken the village—another day on Hermit. It had been a better night. *I'm learning how to survive. The sand flies are voracious. Putting Rid cream on before climbing out of the net helps a lot.* I had found a covered plastic jug that worked for a nighttime toilet and hid it along with our bottle of Rid under my bed. *In this communal society, if you have something you value, don't talk about it; hide it away. "Out of sight, out of mind" works best.*

Booby had had a great night for a little *puskat.* A few times during the night he had perched on the window sill next to my bed and softly announced himself, but I hadn't seen very much of him. It was his bowl of Friskees that he wanted now. Lynnah came out as I was feeding him, smiled, and said, "My cat now—*gud puskat*—my *pren* (friend). *Em stap long* my window *olnait* (all night)." *I see he's made friends and has been adopted into the family already. Didn't take him long.* When Les got up she told me that she had watched him "streaking" across the grassy yard in the moonlight, chasing shadows and chickens all night. *What fun.*

Now for the coffee ritual. People had gathered in the *haus kuk* awaiting my arrival. *I see I've started something.* I could hear the compressor running on the beach. *So Les was already at work pumping the morning's tanks. More granola cereal and more milk—as long as it lasts.*

Les had been giving me training in "walking the plank," as we called a trip out to the toilet, balancing on the unstable logs. She had caught on to this maneuver quickly. When I expressed fear that I might fall in, the *meries* laughed, pointed to a long bamboo pole, and told me to use the "pole *bilong lapun meri*" (old lady's pole) for balance. It worked, and I used it from then on.

Soon, Paul and Stanley arrived ready to plan the day's activities. "We *movim bot* today your way. *Bikpela bot*, got to get heavy *kago* off."

"Okay," I agreed. "Take everything off, batteries, tools, clothes, mattresses, everything, and bring it here. We've got to clean the stuff anyway. And the solar panels—there's six of them over the cockpit. Please be careful; they're glass, you know."

"We *save* solar panels. *Ol* people *hia laikim tumas*. We *bringim*."

"Those batteries are leaking acid all over the place. Be careful, they're very heavy—don't tip them over."

"Yeah, we *save*, no *capsaitim* (capsize them)," they replied. I enjoyed this Pidgin term—the language was colorful with a lot of words from the old days of sailing ships and whalers.

"Now about the drums out there," Les said. "We've got to sink them again and this time they have to be tied tightly around the keel where they'll do some good."

She drew a picture in the wet sand showing how it should be done. This was a sore subject for the men. They had been so sure that their way would work—it always had before, even with large cargo boats. They were embarrassed that their way had failed and that a "simple" *meri* thought she knew more than they did.

They grumbled and said, "Look, it take *longtaim filamap long win* (long time to fill them up with air) underwater. Can we take tanks down—no regulators—and *putim long* opening and *tanim* on? *Em i filimap kwikpela* (Put over opening and turn on? They fill quick)."

"What? Are you crazy? That'll get water in my tanks! No way."

Trying to stay calm, Les told them that she had some spare first stages with cut-off hoses just for this purpose. All they had to do was stick the hose from the first stage into the barrel and blow it out.

More pictures were drawn in the sand, this time showing how the anchors should be laid out for kedging. *Banshee's* bow was wedged between coral heads on both sides and her stern was sticking up above water. She would have to be pulled backwards, away from these coral obstructions. Fortunately, she was leaning to starboard and could be slid into deeper water by kedging her along on her side until she was clear of the coral.

With the drawings done, explanations given, plans made, and gear loaded, off they all went to what was now known as "Banshee Point."

Leslie

As the speedie plowed along through the light chop in the lagoon, I realized that the wind had come up. *Shit, those damn drums from last night.* I could hear them crashing into each other and the boat before I even got near. They were pulling on the rigging, denting the teak toe rails, gouging the fiberglass and paint, and tearing off parts of the cockpit overheads. They were literally eating away at my boat. *And that strange green color, it's everywhere. What is it?*

"Get those drums off! Haven't we got enough damage already? Do something."

The men stared at me. Paul grimaced, spoke some fast Pidgin, and they pushed at the drums, moving them out of harm's way. I could tell by the look on Paul's face that I had better calm down; a repeat performance of yesterday was not what we needed.

Most of the villagers were set to the task of taking everything movable from *Banshee*. We had to lighten the boat as much as possible, if we were going to stand her up and refloat her.

As I looked around, I noticed that the green color in the water had a fluorescent tinge to it and was concentrated near the hatches. It seemed to be steadily flowing out of the cabin and into the surrounding water.

We had stocked up with marine paint in Palau in anticipation of a major repaint job in the Philippines. Now I was worried that the pollution might be from the cans of epoxy. Some of the epoxies had pumps in them, making the contents open to the air—and now the water. *That stuff's damned toxic, and so are all those thinners and half-used spray cans of lubricants and paint. God, what a mess if that stuff starts leaching out of the boat and into the lagoon. An ecological disaster, for sure. This green stain—what can it be?*

"Paul," I said, moving away from the others, "You see this green stuff everywhere?"

"Yeah, I see. *Wanem?*"

"I don't know, but there's still a lot of hazardous stuff in there—cans we didn't get out when we did the repair."

"I think we get *olgeta asade* (all of it yesterday)."

"There's more, Paul. I've got to get it. I know where it is."

"*Kisim* out now—all of it," he commanded. "*Em i bagarap* lagoon, *planti*."

As I swam down inside my former home, the water was like pea-green soup. I couldn't see anything, just green. A diving light would have been useless.

Panic struck.

What is this stuff? Some of the cans must have opened up; I don't want to touch them. I've got to get out of here. I've got to be careful about what I say, or they'll get really weird.

I swam into the forepeak. *Gosh, it's really bad up here. I can hardly see.* I climbed out the forward hatch and saw Natalee. *I can tell her, she'll handle it okay.* "Um, Natalee, this green stuff—you know where it's coming from?"

"It seems to be coming from some bags up in the bow. I'll go pull it out. But I can't see in there. I need a mask."

"Here, take mine," I said, not wanting to be down there one second more.

She dove down and grabbed a Ziploc bag that had started to open. Coming up for air, she waved it in front of me. Bright green dye poured out into the surrounding water. I could see her questioning look behind her mask.

Relief flooded through me. I could hardly control my laughing. It was the sea dye markers! Water-activated yellow pouches of fluorescent green dye, enough to mark several wrecks. They came from my boat in Hawaii, and I had brought them with me when I joined *Banshee*. They'd been around a long time, but obviously still worked.

Problem solved. She showed the little bags to the others on deck, with a fast Pidgin explanation as to why everything and everyone was slowly turning green. There was lots of laughter as they looked at each other. Paul looked especially relieved.

"*Em i wara pen* (water paint). *Mipela ol* green man, now."

Wow, if anyone was looking for us from the sky, they could certainly see us now.

Yesterday's carnival atmosphere was replaced by the serious, purposeful work of a job that had to be done. After that scare, Paul was insistent that I locate anything hazardous and personally remove it immediately. Bento and I worked in the green gloom, pulling things out of lockers and handing them topside for transfer to a speedie.

Stanley started removing our six large Trojan batteries. I shuddered as I watched him pull some out by their cables, breaking off some of the studs in the process. What could I say? We were all working underwater together in miserable conditions, and he was trying his best. I couldn't be picky.

While all this was going on, Paul and some others were ready to get to work on setting out the anchors according to our plan. *Okay, now we're getting somewhere.* I alternated between the two groups, helping where I could.

We had four anchors: two 35-pound CQR plows, a 22-pound Danforth, and a lighter 12-pound high tensile Danforth. One of the CQRs was our main bow anchor and was attached to a 300-foot chain rode. When *Banshee* sank, I had dropped it into the water along with much of its chain.

To start, we worked with the three other anchors—those with combination rope and chain rodes, as it is very difficult to move an anchor around with an all-chain rode. The plan was to set two of the anchors in deep water, one to starboard and a little aft of amidships and the other also to starboard but much further aft of the boat. This would give a diagonal pull to move *Banshee* to the right and astern, away from the coral heads and into softer sand. They left the third anchor, the large Danforth stern anchor, on the boat.

The men loaded up a speedie with the two anchors—the spare CQR and the small Danforth—along with their chains and rodes. I jumped in too, eager to go. Handing one bitter-end of a line to guys on *Banshee* to cleat on the deck, we took off to where I thought was a good place to drop it, stretching the line as far as it would go. Then we came back and handed them the second line. This one I had to piece together with bowline knots to make it long enough. One line was cleated to the bow and the other to the starboard stern near the winch.

I had been so particular with rope before: nylon three-strand for warping and anchoring, one kind of Dacron braid for sheets, and another for halyards. Now all I care about is, is it long enough?

Back aboard *Banshee*, I showed them how to wrap the line around a winch. Although the cockpit sheet winches were underwater, depending on the tides, they could still be worked from above the surface. We led one of the anchor lines to a sheet winch and the other to the large winch on the foredeck, Joy's "just in case winch," which was several feet underwater.

Paul and I floated on the surface above the foredeck. I handed our large winch handle to him and motioned in which direction to turn it.

All eyes fell on Paul. No one else moved. He took a gulp of air, dove down, shoved the handle in the winch, and turned. The line tightened. I stood on the exposed port side cabin and tailed the line. Soon the line was bar-taut.

Shouts and screams rang out.

"Em i movim! Bot movim!"

People were cheering wildly. Paul shot up for air, holding the winch handle high. Grinning, he slapped me on the back.

"Now we see what *winis long rop* do. We *save.*"

Oh, Joy, now we'll get out of here. It's working!

Paul continued to crank the winch like a man possessed. Up for air and then down again. I grabbed a diving rig and handed it to him. "Since you're doing so well, here, make it easier on yourself." No more words were necessary. He knew what to do now. He was back in charge.

As *Banshee* slowly backed up and slid away from her coral-studded grave, we could see another danger: that of slipping down into the deep blue of the abyss below.

"Putim anchor *antap long rip long nambis. Sapos bot pundaun?* (Put anchor on top reef near shore. Suppose boat falls down?)." *Yeah, good idea—we've got to be careful.*

The big Danforth stern anchor was still hanging in its chocks on the aft pulpit, easy to grab. Off they went with it, as far as they could go into the shallow water near shore. By placing it off *Banshee's* port side, it would act both as a pivot point and a safety stop should the boat start sliding on her own. Another guy got the idea and started turning the starboard cockpit winch. The force of both of these winches pulling on the anchors was easy to see, and *Banshee* moved as planned.

Yells came from the guys on the port side.

"Lusim, anchor no *pas* (not stuck). *Rop em i slek* (Rope is slack)."

The bottom leading up to the shore was mostly coral rubble, very poor holding for an anchor.

"No *pasim* (Don't move) *winis! Lusim* now."

With nothing to hold her to port, the danger was clear: she would slide off the reef into deep blue water if they continued to crank the winches.

"You *gat samting* (something) heavy? We need *planti* heavy chain and *bikpela* anchor," Paul yelled at me.

"Yeah, there's a heavy anchor right in front of the bow, and there's more chain in the locker—300 feet of it, okay?"

"Can you get it out *long no lektrik?*"

"Yes, I can do it. It's not easy, but I can do it."

"Gudpela! Get to *wok."*

Grabbing a rig with a full tank, I sat down underwater on the bow and started pulling out the rest of the heavy, 5/16-inch BBB anchor chain from the locker below. Each pull gave me about a foot of chain. My cut-up bare hands complained and my shoulders ached. I was so tired. The continued stress was getting to me. Somehow, I just kept going.

It took a full tank of air, but it was done. All the chain was out of the locker now.

Some guys in a speedie came round the bow and asked for the anchor. Paul shook his head, looked at me, and said, "You *putim* anchor *aninit* (underneath) *ol* chain, right?"

"Yeah, it's under there. First they'll have to pull up all the chain into the speedie. Then they'll find the anchor." I could see that no one was pleased with this concept.

Paul jumped in the boat and said, "Right, me *pulapim* (pull up). You *pasim long* me, Leslie."

"Paul, I can't lift my arms anymore. Help him, you guys."

Finally the guys pitched in and started pulling in all 300 feet of chain over the gunwale of the fiberglass speedie—one that I had recently repaired for them. They were not happy.

"Em i brukim (break) bot. You *mekim olrait gen* (make all right again)."

Sure, anything you say—just save my boat, okay?

The hidden anchor finally emerged from under its pile of chain and was loaded into their boat. Bob reappeared on the scene, this time in the loaded speedie, and took his usual commanding presence. *Well, at least he's the strongest one they've got and they'll need him.* Once the speedie reached shallow water, he hoisted that 35 lb anchor over his shoulder and walked it right up the reef, chain and all.

"Em i strongpela now. *Em i pas* (stuck)."

I believed them. *Back to winching. We're not going to slip now.*

The big Danforth and its rope and chain were brought back from the reef, thrown into an awaiting speedie, and set out to starboard for kedging.

The guys with the fuel drums were back at it again. This time they listened to me, and tied the submerged drums around the keel to protect *Banshee* from further damage and provide buoyancy. Bob had tied off the wheel, putting the rudder to port so it wouldn't be damaged. They also positioned the drums to protect the prop and shaft. They were sailors and knew the importance of a boat's rudder and prop.

Gradually, *Banshee* slid into position. The pivot point provided by all that chain and a solidly hooked-in anchor on the reef worked perfectly. They had her positioned on firm coral sand and gravel now, safely away from the coral heads.

I was ready to collapse. I was having difficulty concentrating and making decisions. My screamed-out voice was cracking and hoarse and my skin was burning from the constant immersion. I had to get out of the water, get some food in me, and take a break. I kept watching the speedies go back and forth with their *kagos,* and the urge to go with them was becoming stronger each time one left for shore.

The guys were working out between themselves how they were going to pull the boat upright now that they understood the magic of winches. However, the problem was made even more difficult by the fact that *Banshee* does not have a full keel. A full keel boat can stand on her keel with minimal support, and the rudder is protected by its structural attachment to the keel. *Banshee's* hull, however, has a cut-away forefoot and a very large skeg-hung rudder. *She sails like a dream—Herreschoff certainly knew what he was doing—but it isn't the greatest design for getting off a reef.*

They already had loops of our chain secured around the coral heads on the port side. Their plan was to tie lines to this chain at different points, lead them to and through the mast steps, and then down to the mast winches, which would provide a huge amount of leverage. They liked the way winches worked— *"mekim man strongpela."* They reasoned that cranking on the mast winches while easing out slightly on the starboard cockpit and bow winches would surely bring the boat upright. And at the same time, the keel would dig a trough in the sand, which would prevent further slipping downhill. I tried to explain that they would also need some props to hold her up once they got her standing. At this point they were so transfixed on their new skill of winching, my words probably were lost on them.

A sticking point for them was what to do with an anchor once it was freed and ready to be recovered; could our winches pull it onto the deck? And after the line came in and the chain came up, could you wrap the chain around the winch too? Could they just pull the anchor chain over the rail?

"Good grief, no!" I shouted. "You'll destroy my winches, the deck, and the rail. My god, those winches cost a fortune." I patiently explained again that the anchor lines must go through the metal chocks and not just straight over the toe-rail.

"Okay, okay, we *save*. We *wokim*. We do it old way from speedies. You no *ken* worry, Leslie." We *traim sananap* (try to stand it up)." Paul and Stanley's reassuring words helped to calm me down. I had to trust them. I had to believe they knew what they were doing. My respect for them had increased. They understood leverage and used it all the time to move large objects. Now we had given them "the winch." They didn't call it mechanical advantage, but they knew what to do with it.

"Go to it, guys, you've got a good plan." My strength was ebbing fast and I knew I had to get ashore. Half my life was here and the other half was with Joy on shore with all our things. I was torn in two and so very worried. *I'll just let them go along on this by themselves for a while. I think they've got it.*

An older man came climbing out of the cabin carrying my heavy tool boxes on his shoulder. As I saw him hand the boxes into a speedie, I saw my chance to leave. "I've got to go see Joy. Got to take care of my tools; we're going to need them." I jumped in and we sped off to the beach.

Joy

All morning I kept busy answering questions about our things and supervising the "controlled insanity" on the beach in front of Lynnah's house. I tried to keep my painful finger dry and out of things. *If it ever is going to heal, I have to.*

Small groups of friends sat on the ground, under the trees, chatting away as they concentrated on their tasks. There was the book salvaging group, the CD-cleaning *meries*, the chart-saving *meries,* the well-water carriers, the canned food cleaners, the tool-cleaning group of men, and the *waswas meries* doing the salt-soaked laundry. Many other groups were cleaning all the boxes of small spare parts, screws, nuts, bolts and assorted hardware—sorting them to their own design into bush-woven baskets. *Pikinini* ran everywhere, fetching this, carrying that.

I met Collen, who was described by his group as, *"Em i lektrisin* (electrician). *Em i gudpela."* Collen, I was told, could fix anything and was especially good with electric motors. *I hope so,* seeing all our salt-soaked power tools opened up in front of him on a piece of scavenged canvas. His mouth was stained red from chewing *buai* (betel nut). When I teased him about the SDA church's prohibition of this, he laughed, and his friends, with equally red mouths, grinned and yelled, *"Bekslaiders* (backsliders)*, planti bekslaiders hia.* No go church. You *traim* (try it). *Em i gudpela."* I made a face and declined. Having lived in Palau for years I knew all about betel nut chewing—more than I wanted to know about the disgusting habit.

Okip reappeared in his speedie bearing our precious solar panels. Crowds gathered as they were unloaded and carried ashore to be cleaned. Collen was particularly entranced with them.

"Tumas long wanpela. You *givim* me *wan—tumas,* you no need."

"No, these are ours. We need them, and we will keep them all, thank you. Let's all get back to work. I do need your help, and I thank you so much for all you're doing." *Better to just compliment them and get off this subject. I'm keeping all my panels.*

The wires were a mess—*Les must have had some trouble extricating them.* I fetched a pair of Lynnah's scissors and trimmed and tied off the wires to keep them from shorting. I supervised their cleaning and then got them discretely stored *"ananit long* house*"* as August directed. He would guard them personally, Lynnah told me.

Okip, his important delivery done, plopped his huge bulk down near Collen and tried to get his hands into anything that he could. I saw them take things away from him and politely give him some mundane cleaning chore. They knew—they had lived with this guy all their lives.

The village, it seems, is hard at work. I'm so grateful.

August, an older man, was the village policeman. He became a great ally. Although he didn't speak a word of English we managed to communicate, usually by gestures, and when necessary with Lynnah's translations. August had been given the job of keeping order among the beachfront helpers and of providing security for our things. He was great at organizing our cleaned items in neat piles under the house and up on the veranda. Things that he and Lynnah deemed "very valuable," including our salvageable food, he secreted away in the back room of the house, the only one having an actual door. My two diesel jugs of rum found a home there hidden under sail bags and cans of food.

Familiar shouts rang out from the beach—Leslie. *My Leslie's back. It's so lonely without her.*

"Joy, we moved her! We got her off the coral. The winches worked perfectly. She's in the sand now. They're trying to get her to stand up—damn that keel—makes it hard to keep her upright."

"That's great. Wonderful. Yes, yes, I know—the keel…really difficult—I understand."

"I'm so tired—just exhausted. All my muscles are cramped up. I've got to stretch out, maybe get some rest."

I gave her a hug—guess we were allowed that limited show of affection—and told her that Lynnah had food waiting. She didn't care what it was; she'd eat anything, she said.

After food, a bit of a wash-off, and some care of her festering cuts and scrapes, we sat down together and discussed the progress they had made and what we should we do for the rest of the afternoon. They were actually leaving us alone for a while.

BEACONS, *TOKSAVES,* AND THE MEN HAVE A PLAN

Joy

The long afternoon wore on. Les tried to sleep, but restlessness intervened, and I found her beside me as I wandered among the clusters of working villagers. She got the compressor started and began the never-ending job of filling tanks. As we sat next to it, we both kept glancing seaward, watching *Banshee*, but it was difficult to see much of anything from the shore. Occasionally, we thought that we could see the mast moving up and down.

"They must be trying to stand her up with the anchors, like I showed them,"

"Do you think they can do it?" I replied.

She shrugged and got up from the compressor.

"I've got to stretch my legs, take a walk for a while. I can't sit still any longer. You watch the tank, okay? Just cut it off when it's up to pressure. I'll be back to start the next tank."

"Fine, I'm sure you need it."

I watched her go. She was starting to feel discouraged as to how we were going to stand *Banshee* upright, and watching the continual up-and down-motions out in the bay was getting to her. *And she's exhausted and running on empty, too. You can't make decisions in that state.*

The compressor droned on, drowning out the villager's voices. I was left alone with my thoughts: *What if we can't raise* Banshee *and sail out of here, or the old underwater epoxy doesn't hold, or the attitude of the village turns against us? This is PNG after all, and we have heard many stories that clearly indicated that yachts rarely escape from strandings like this.*

What about the rest of our lives together if we lose Banshee—*would we stay together? Would there be another boat? Could we start over? In Hawaii maybe? At least it's modern America, not this insane time-warp we've landed in.* Looking at options kept me focused. I had to give her hope—she was doing all the work. I had to be emotionally strong for Leslie.

The irony of our situation kept coming back to me. These people, whose fundamentalist religion taught them that couples like us were wrong before God, were supporting and helping us. We had interrupted their lives, and all in all, they were kind to us. They were the key to the survival of our sailing lifestyle on *Banshee.*

Perhaps it helped that before our disaster we had done many things for the village. As many liveaboard dive boats visited Hermit and required local guides, Leslie had quite an interested group when she taught a class in diving skills.

While I helped out at the school, Les worked for a week repairing their beat-up fiberglass speedies—the very ones that were now rescuing our home. Many of them were sinking from mishaps with the coral. Happily donating our materials, our generator, and other equipment, Leslie repaired six of the 26-ft. boats, training others while she worked. *Perhaps this was a trade-off now.*

Shouts came from down the beach. It was Leslie, running toward me.

"Joy, the radio! They're talking about us on the radio!"

"What? There isn't a radio on this island, it's broken down. What're you talking about?"

"You know, the little portable receivers they have? They pick up Radio Manus with music and news. Let's get over to Namo's house and find out what's going on."

As we went along the path through the village, people smiled and nodded to us as we passed their houses. I heard them say, *"Toksave* come*, em nau"* and *"Yupela* (you two) go *long haus bilong Namo*—*long hap* (over there)." Slowly I was catching on to Pidgin. I really wanted to learn.

Fortunately, Namo spoke an understandable mixture of English and Pidgin. He explained that because many villages all over PNG are quite remote, the government radio stations with powerful shortwave transmitters are used to broadcast important news and messages (*Toksaves*) to isolated communities that listen in with inexpensive transistor receivers. The *Toksave* is the only way for small villages without a transmitter to keep in touch with the outside world.

"It PNG way," he said.

"Well, can I listen?"

"No, no, *em i pinis*, and it in Pidgin, *tasol*."

"Of course, but what did it say?"

It say, "A beacon go off *long* Western Islands group—*em i hia. Sapos sampela* (anyone) *save* information about two American woman on wrecked sailboat, call station or government office."

"Good god, they've heard our EPIRB! Oh no!"

I looked at Les. "Your mother is going to be so worried. She won't understand that we're okay, that we're refloating *Banshee*."

Les shook her head. If anyone knew Sue, her mother, she did. Although completely accepting of us, her way of life was so different. A worldly travel consultant with her own agency, Sue Brown Travel, in Boca Raton, Florida, she arranged exclusive travel for clients around the globe. *Yes, she'll be very worried, and I know she'll do something about it.*

Sue knew that we were on Hermit. Before the sinking, Les used her Magellan GSC 100 (a portable email device) to send short messages to her on a daily basis. She had also been writing regularly to her sister, Tammi, her father, Larry, and his wife Barbara about our experiences on Hermit during the twelve days that we had been there before the sinking. They had to know that we were still on the island and not lost at sea. But with an EPIRB transmission, people tend to assume the worst.

As for my family, I knew that my mother, even at ninety, would be able to handle the news okay. So would my brother. They were used to my sailing scrapes, near misses, and all those "adventures," as Mom called them. I had been doing this for over thirty years. She always told me, "It's your life, live it the way you want to. You've only got one chance at it." I appreciated her understanding and confidence in me.

"Okay, we've got to do something," I said. My mind was spinning, trying to figure out how to communicate with our families and the government. "There's no way we can radio from here to say that we're okay. Now that the beacon has stopped, they might think that we sank in the ocean and drowned. I've got to go back to Lynnah's and set off the beacon again. That'll give them an indication that we're still alive."

"You're going to do *what?*" Les exclaimed. A crowd was gathering around us.

"Easy, Les, let's keep this to ourselves. Let's plan this out and quietly walk back to the house and do what we have to do. This might even help our status here if they get the idea that there's an outside world out there who is concerned about us. Let me handle it, okay? You concentrate on saving *Banshee*. This is something I can do."

By the time we got back to the house, we had sorted out our plan. It was going to be a show, but a well-thought-out show. I quietly took Lynnah and Ben aside and explained about the *Toksave* and what we were going to do.

People were already hovering around, waiting to see what the two *waitmeri* were going to do next. I retrieved the beacon, screwed on its antenna, and deliberately walked out of the house and placed it on the *waswas* table outside the *haus kuk*. People stopped their activities and watched. The usual din ceased. It got very quiet. I pulled out the stop pin. All eyes watched. The beacon came to life, flashing its strobe light for all to see—*waitskins* magic on Hermit. *Such high drama. It serves two purposes: it notifies our world of our existence and position, and it might make an impression on the villagers. Maybe they'll stop acting like they're a universe unto themselves, doing whatever they pleased with us and our things.*

I followed up the "demonstration" with an explanation of how the beacon's message would eventually reach their authorities in Port Moresby. Lynnah and Ben quietly translated my words into Pidgin. My plan was to run the beacon for twenty minutes now, so the authorities could get a good fix on us, and then I would run it on a regular schedule at eight o'clock in the morning and again at eight o'clock at night for as long as necessary. *Good thing my watch still works. Hopefully, someone out there will realize that there is intelligent life operating the beacon and that we are still alive.*

For many of them, however, it was simply *"waitmeri mekim toktok long sky"*—just simply more magic. They didn't express their disbelief to me directly, out of respect for my age, but to Les someone said, *"Em i trikim,* true. *"Radio"* bilong Joy no *ken mekim toktok long* sky. *Lapun meri trikim* (She tricks us, truly. Joy's "radio" can't talk to the sky. The old woman tricks us)."

Drama over, everyone went back to work, and we returned to our endless jobs of filling scuba tanks and sorting our belongings on the beach. The long afternoon dragged on.

Both of us were still without shoes. They had simply disappeared and the situation was becoming serious. Our feet were chafed and cut up by the rough coral sand and rocks ashore. Sand fly bites became open infected sores. We tried diving booties, sea boots, socks, and rags. All to no avail. No one could or would confront anyone in the communal culture.

We kept watching seaward: *Banshee's* mast would occasionally come to vertical, hold there briefly, and then fall back down. *What were they doing out there?*

A speedie came zooming in with a load of men, including Paul and Stanley. Noting that tanks were being pumped, they said that after a rest break they would soon be back for them. Paul took off quickly in the direction of his compound on the opposite beach across the island's isthmus. We had been warned not to wander over there because of his "pets," the guard dogs. I didn't have to be warned twice. Once I had tried to speak to Paul when one of them was with him. The growling and barred teeth let me know not to come near.

We joined Stanley for a tour around the village and his pet followed us. Andrew was a delightful little parrot who would perch watching him in a nearby tree and then zoom in to land on his head. *What a wonderful free little friend he had.*

There were about forty houses situated along the two beachfronts of the flat isthmus. They were built around a grassy common area that doubled as a soccer field on Sundays. On one end of the grassy area was the cemetery with unmarked graves in the austere manner of the SDA church.

Some of the houses were occupied and some were deserted and falling down. All of the houses were built up on house poles, leaving space for storage and work areas underneath. The older ones were huge, where multi-generations could live together in one house. The newer ones were smaller. Young couples today wanted a place of their own—the culture was changing even out here.

As we walked along, Stanley told us about Hermit history, and Les and I bombarded him with questions. We were trying to adjust to this new place and time in which we had been marooned. Stanley had heard about my stumbling around in the dark after my *waswas* and not having a flashlight. When I told him we really needed a little kerosene lamp so we could move around after dark, he laughed and looked surprised.

"*Dupela* (you two) *save bikpela* things—world *bilong* you *save bikpela* things. You *lusin tingktingk* (forget) *long liklik* things—small things *long* life. Kerosene *lam* (lamp) *em i liklik* thing. *Mipela save* kero *lam*—no *havim lektrik, olsem* (like) you."

"Yes, Stanley, you are so very right."

Returning to our beach, we found the men were ready to go again. Les wanted to be out there on *Banshee,* even though she was so cut-up and tired. She gave Paul a look, grabbed some dive gear, and jumped in a departing speedie.

Leslie

The water around *Banshee* was still saturated with the brilliant fluorescent green dye marker; even the overnight tides had not removed it. The color permeated everything, including the workers.

A spider web of lines attached *Banshee's* port side to the shore-side reef. Lines went up the mast and down again, threaded through blocks and mast steps, and were tied and looped at every conceivable location.

"The genoa sheet car—not through that! No, it'll break! Paul, get that line out of there. That block cost hundreds. You can't do that." Once again, my screaming brought a stern admonition from Paul.

"You *laikim* save your boat, or no?" We do it our way now and it working."

"But Paul, I have to sail this boat out of here and I need that block for the sail."

"You *gat dupela*—one *long narasait* (other side), *samting* (same thing)—*movim* when you need. You *gat moa* (more) than one."

I could see I was getting nowhere and they were not about to move one line, no matter how loud I got. *Shit, they're really in charge now, aren't they? What a great beginning. Oh well, I suppose they're used to me by now.*

Trying to calm down, I focused on the anchors and lines and what they were trying to do to get *Banshee* upright. I noticed that two of the three anchors that had been placed in deep water off to starboard were now high up on the coral of the shore side reef.

"How did you get those two anchors up? It's over 100 feet deep out there."

"*Wakimap* (walk them up)," was Paul's reply.

"What? You're kidding!"

"We do it PNG way now. Bob and I go down, *painim* anchors, *putim long beksait* (back) *long* chain, blow up BCs, and *wakim* (walk) up *hia long wara* go down." A proud grin lit up his face as he described their efforts.

"Paul, you could kill yourself doing it that way."

"No worries. *Em i pinis,* now. PNG way."

Good lord, all that weight from 120 feet? Okay, enough of this. Time to go for a look around inside Banshee—*just want to listen to my bubbles.*

Descending into the cabin, the green gloom was still present, even though the offending source had been removed. *Well, no one was having any ill affects from it, so I assume it was harmless.* Fortunately, the waterlogged foam cushions had been taken out before most of the dye had seeped out, although when they washed them under the village's big well-water pump, green dye poured out with the saltwater.

I swam countless times in and out of the cabin, taking things out to awaiting hands. Getting the heavy things out was important, but sometimes the helpers got carried away, grabbing small items that could as well been left in the boat.

"Paul, *i tokim mipela kisim olgeta kagos* out *long bot. Ol kagos, tasol* (Paul tell us take everything out of boat. All cargoes, that's all)."

"No, these are my things and this is still my boat. Those are little things. Leave them alone, they don't weigh anything. Put them back, please."

Begrudgingly, they complied and stopped grabbing everything in sight, at least while I was staring at them.

Stanley had taken *Banshee's* "house batteries," (the batteries we used to run all of the electric items on board except the starter motor for the engine), but I now realized that he had unknowingly left the starting battery in the engine compartment. Leaving my tank and BC in the cockpit but keeping my reg in my mouth for breathing, I wedged myself down through the narrow hatch opening and freed the cables on the battery, motioning for someone to come pull it out. Then I swam back into the cabin for more things.

So much stuff—too much, really. We had so much and were so well-prepared for any kind of disaster, except this one.

I sat on the cabin floor resting, breathing from my tank. What a strange sensation. *Banshee* would rise up to an upright position, hover, and then fall back again. Winches would grind, lines and blocks would whine and groan, and then there was the heavy thump of fuel drums and the terrible scraping sound of coral against the hull. The din was insane. *A nightmare—*Banshee *is being torn apart bit by bit.*

The day moved on. Exhaustion crept over me. Going outside I asked, "Can I winch?"

"No."

"Pull lines? Set them?"

"No."

"Help move drums?"

"No."

"Can we talk about this? I've got some ideas about propping her up."

"Go away."

This had become their job now. A solid group of determined PNG men against one mere *meri*. *Forget it, they have me beat.* All I could do now was try to keep them from stripping too much off *Banshee.* I was afraid that I'd never see some of the things again.

"No, not the propane tank. Leave it. You'll open up the system and get crap in it." I knew there probably was water in the lines, but I didn't need them plugged with sand and muck. *Eventually we're going to have to cook aboard again.* I was quite worried that my tanks would disappear. Paul counseled me, saying, "Okay, you no *rausim dispela* tank *hia, em i gat* hose *long* stove, but *kisim dupela* tanks *long* deck (don't remove the tank with the hose to the stove, but take the two on deck)." I reluctantly agreed but insisted that they be stored under Lynnah's house with our fuel jugs.

Banshee's continual up-and-down motion was having another effect: the keel was digging into the sand. She was literally making her own grave, deeper and deeper. A little digging into the sand gave her stability, but too much and she would be too deep to bail her dry at low tide. Worried by this and frustrated by the futile efforts to get her to balance on the unstable fin keel, the "crew" became increasingly dejected and started packing up early to return to shore.

"Leaving already? It's still daylight," I questioned.

"Em i no *wok. Bot i* no *sananap* (stand up). *Traim tumas* (try too much). No *gud."*

Paul wouldn't even speak to me as he loaded up his speedie. I sat in the bow as we returned to shore. Frustration and silence hung over the returning boat like a pall. As soon as they beached the speedie, they all got out empty-handed and quickly departed, leaving me, the dive gear, and our things sitting in disarray amid the pools of oily, sandy water in the bottom of the boat.

Joy

On shore, I heard shouts that the speedies were returning—all of them it seemed, racing in together toward the beach. *They're early. What's happened?* Banshee's *still on her side.* I saw Leslie sitting in the bow of the last boat and I hurried out to meet them. Her thumbs-down gesture and strained, sad face said it all.

"Joy, it's not working. They can't stand her up. We're going to lose her. They won't listen to me at all; they've given up."

Her words tumbled out. She was in no shape to handle anything. She needed a bath, food and rest. Talk could wait till later.

"C'mon, Les, let's get you cleaned up and fed. You've got to stop this; you've done enough."

I put together a wash bucket of clean clothes and bath things and walked with her over to the shower area on the other side of the island. I tried to keep her off the depressing subject of raising *Banshee* and deal with her immediate needs. I knew she was near collapse. I could bathe later, even with one hand.

Later, after baths, clean clothes, and Lynnah's food, we sat near a sand fly-repelling smoky beach fire and surreptitiously sipped our evening rum disguised in soda cans. I listened as she related the day's depressing events.

Stanley sat down next to us and presented me with a small kerosene lantern. "From Paul. You *gat* kerosene? *Dupela* need light *long* night, and smoke *rausim san* fly. Paul say you *holim ol* time you need."

"Oh Stanley, how wonderful. You're right, it is the *liklik* things that are important. Thanks for bringing it." A knowing smile crossed his face as he walked away. He understood what we were going through.

As darkness approached, Les filled the lantern with our citronella lamp oil. "That'll keep those damned, biting bugs away, for sure. Now we can go where we want to at night." That little lamp became one of our important keys to survival in the days to come.

Sitting by the fire's warmth, far away from city lights and pollution, we watched as the brilliant stars covered the clear dark sky. Looking at my watch, I remembered my schedule with the EPIRB and went to go activate it.

When I returned from that task, Paul and Stanley appeared out of the nighttime shadows.

"We *mekim toktok* now, talk about *tumora*. We *havim plen*. You *harim* (listen), please." They sounded serious. This was their last tactic. It had to work.

"We *save dispela*. It *olsem wokim* house—we do it *oltaim*. We build house under *bot*. *Em i sanamap*. We *usim* logs and tie *olgeta—olsem* building house."

I smiled. "A cradle, not a house. We call it a boat cradle."

Confused looks passed between them.

"A cradle. You know, like for a baby," I said, holding my arms and making a rocking motion.

They grinned. "Okay, we *save*."

Laughing, they repeated their new English word, cradle, cradle *bilong pikinini*. "Okay. Cradle *bilong bot*. We *wokim bot* cradle."

"What a great idea. It'll work. I know it will."

"*Tumora* we go *long* jungle and *katim* logs. *Bringim bek* and tie up under water. Then, when we pull up boat, we *siuvin* log in. Just like house. PNG way."

Paul and Stanley, standing there in the firelight on the moonlit beach, wore big smiles from ear to ear. Leslie was grinning too, eager to be right out there with them.

"Um, one more thing. No Leslie. Men say Leslie *stap long nambis*. No come out. Men no *laikim* yelling. Leslie yell *tumas*. Men no work *sapos* Leslie come out. We do it PNG way. We *save*."

I looked at Les. She knew there was no other way—she had been out there. Her head nodded.

"Okay?" Hands extended to shake in agreement.

"Agreed," we both said, and we shook hands.

A Jungle Cradle for *Banshee*

Joy

We were both awake before dawn. Les came out and joined me in my veranda bed. Our resident family was still asleep. Only the ever-present crowing chickens were moving around this early. We furtively hugged each other and held hands under the covers.

One whole side of the veranda was now covered with our salvaged possessions. Soaked electronic gear, instruments, bedraggled charts, cameras, laptop computer, weather fax, radios, TV and VCR, strings of wire—thousands of dollars worth of equipment now reduced to useless rubble. Strange relics of a far-away culture. And two beat-up American women in a remote PNG island village, huddling under a small mosquito net, wondering if today would mark the end of their sailing life together.

We lit our new kerosene lamp, hoping its smoky flame would drive away the sand flies. Smearing Rid cream over our red, festering legs, we made the necessary trip down to the water's edge before dawn caught us.

Ben began chopping firewood, and Lynnah stoked and fanned the embers of last night's cooking fire. Soon we were standing on the beach with Paul and Stanley, drinking coffee, and drawing more pictures in the sand. I'd been in a lot of boatyards in the thirty-odd years *Banshee* and I had been together, and I'd seen a lot of boat cradles, but I had never had to construct a cradle underwater with my boat lying on her side.

The village crew seemed to take great delight in using the word "cradle" that I had taught Stanley the night before, smiling and joking a lot when they used the new word. They seemed confident about the work ahead and took pride in their ability to do it.

"*Ol* man *save* build *dispela, olsem* house—we *save gudpela,*" they told us.

I reminded Paul and Stanley that *Banshee* could not stand up unless her bow area was firmly supported—she would just fall over on her nose. I suggested using a forked log, with its base in the sand to prop up her bow.

"Okay, now we *gat narapela* (another) problem. Your *bot* hull, *sait* go up *isi*—*stret* up. No *gat hat* (hard) place *long sait long putim* logs (Your hull, the sides go up smooth, straight up. There is no hard edge to push in logs). *Bikpela heve* (big problem)—hull *bagarap. Sapos* we tie logs *long samting long* track?"

"No, you guys can't do that, you'll destroy the tracks and probably pull them off the deck," Leslie interrupted loudly.

Both men backed off with looks that confirmed why Leslie was banished.

"You're right, guys, we have no "rub rail" or a "hard chine" either, as we call them, but we do have a way to do it," I said, trying to calm everyone down.

Drawing more sand pictures, I explained that in making a boat's cradle the supports go up to the turn of the bilge, where the hull bulges out from the keel. Then wedges are pounded in at the top of the logs where they meet the hull, fitting them in firmly along the hull's curve. I drew a picture of a wedge, just to make sure they knew what I was talking about.

The light dawned. Smiles. Pictures really do speak a thousand words. *Of course they know; they probably use wedges all the time.*

"Em nau—watges."

"How're you guys going to cut down all these trees? With axes?"

"No, we modern man, *usim* chain saw—*olsem kain* (same kind) *wokim ol* house *hia.* You *gat* petrol *long* saw?"

"Sure, plenty, in the jugs under the house. Take what you need."

Leslie began filling scuba tanks as gear was collected and loaded into the speedies. By now, several of the men were well versed in filling tanks, although not always up to her specifications, especially when it came to draining the compressor regularly.

The work crew, equipped with long bush knives, axes, and the village chain saw, were soon speeding off to the jungle on a logging mission. Others stayed behind to gather diving gear and await the tanks.

We headed back to Lynnah's for breakfast and a more leisurely morning—one that we needed, especially Leslie. *Banshee* lay alone on the reef, still mournfully resting on her side, waiting…

Eight o'clock again, and I remembered to do the ten-minute beacon ritual. No one paid any attention to my efforts now. After filling tanks, Les took advantage of her time off and went back to bed for a nap.

The area around Lynnah's house soon became a noisy hive of activity again, with little groups sitting at their tasks and naked little *pikinini* scampering back and forth, in and out of the water. I practiced my newly learned Pidgin, mimicking Lynnah's phrases to everyone's amusement.

Yelling and waving came from the beach, and I looked out to see the men in speedies swinging by on their return from the jungle, laden down with logs, on their way out to stricken *Banshee*.

Several of the men who stayed ashore helped me sort through the piles of ruined electrical hardware and electronics stacked on the veranda. The mess was a nuisance in our crowded living arrangements. The cleaning *meries* would have nothing to do with it, calling it *kagos bilong* man. Sio, a tall, quiet, knowledgeable man from Hermit, was particularly helpful. He found our little Garmin 48 handheld GPS piled in with all the other salt-soaked ruins. *"Em i wok?"*

Sadly, I shook my head. "It couldn't possibly work; it was underwater for days, and I haven't got any batteries for it anyway."

He held it in his hand and stared at it. "You wait, *olsem* mine," he said, and disappeared. Soon he was back with an identical Garmin unit. *"Hia,* use my batteries, *traim* yours now." He opened our unit and exchanged the batteries with his.

"Oh, Sio, that's not going to work." I was so dejected, thinking of how much this stuff had cost and of all my work installing it.

"Traim, tanim (turn) on."

Impossible, but I'll try. I pushed the button. The tiny screen sprang to life. "Welcome to the Garmin GPS 48."

I was incredulous. "It works! My god, it works. Sio, look!" Leslie, hearing the commotion, emerged from her room. "Les, we've got a GPS. Now all we need is our boat."

Later, Les and Natalee joined me on the beach. They had a boxful of our shoes. Natalee explained how she got them.

"I got into some trouble for it," she said, "but I saw your suffering and knew I had to do something. So, I just went into people's houses and took them. It's not fair that they stole from you. You had to have your shoes if you're going to survive here. I've got *pebek* (payback) to do for this, but it's my problem."

We can walk with shoes again. It felt so good.

Our heavy house batteries had been brought ashore yesterday, along with the solar panels. Even though the batteries had been under water, I decided to try and salvage them. The guys lashed together a supporting structure for the solar panels. I replaced some of the salt-tainted water in the batteries with rainwater, and using salvaged wire, I hooked them up to the direct high voltage from the panels. They began to "percolate," and I hoped that they would equalize enough to provide us some battery power in the future.

During the day, we stared out at the reef, wondering what was going on. How were they doing? We kept seeing the same up-and-down motion of the mast. Every so often, *Banshee* would linger upright for a while and the crowd would gasp in hope, and then moan as she fell over once again. The suspense was killing us. The day wore on…

Namo's daughter scurried up to Leslie and me.

"A *Toksave* is on the radio. Come to our house. They've heard your signal."

Les and I stared at one another in surprise, then hurriedly followed her down the beach to Namo's house.

"Namo, what did they say? Have they heard us?"

"Yeah. The *Toksave* say, 'We *harim* your beacon. Please signal again to say you both *olrait.*'"

"You're kidding. Really?"

"Yes. You go signal again, now. Me *harim*, okay?"

Off we flew down the beach to Lynnah's house to switch on the EPIRB.

We watched the little beacon flash its bright strobe light, telling the outside world that we were all right. Our families would get the message soon.

Leslie

The up-and-down motions of *Banshee's* mast worried me. Depressing visions of the damage they might be causing danced in my mind. *She could be crashing down on the reef each time she fell—on her good side too, causing even more cracks. Damn, why did I let them talk me into doing this by themselves? I need to be there. I know what to do.* I hated the inactivity of just watching.

"Look, Joy, I could take our dinghy and paddle out there. I'll just watch."

"Get real, Les. You of all people can't 'just watch.' You'd be all over them in a second. You and I are not going to do this by ourselves. Get over it. Take a walk."

"Well, I could walk past August's house along the shore and watch from over there. It's closer, and I could see what's going on."

"Not a walk that way, silly. Leave them alone. They'll come and get you when they're ready," Joy replied, with a look that meant business.

Feeling very frustrated and inadequate, I took off through the village, keeping close to shore with one eye out to the reef. Finally, after wandering off by myself for several hours, I saw the speedies return and the men jump out. *Hey, I think* Banshee's *mast has stopped its waving. Damn, she's sitting still and…she's standing up! Is it possible?*

Happy yelling came from the crowd on the beach.

Hurriedly, I ran to Paul.

"It's up, Leslie. She stand up. Like I tell you—PNG way."

My heart raced. I grabbed him and hugged him. Joy came out from the crowd on the beach. People stood back and watched. Tears streamed down Joy's face. She couldn't talk—she just stood there holding him.

"Oh, Paul. You did it. You did it…My god…Thank you, thank you," I said.

"You come out now, Leslie. Now time *long* you *lukim*. You go swim down and look. You see PNG house *aninit Banshee* now."

The crowd was chattering and laughing.

"*Em i gudpela. Ol Hermit* man *wokim PNG* house *aninit* Banshee. *Em sananap* now. No *pundaun* (fall down), *tasol.*"

Paul was the man of the hour on Hermit.

"Paul, the anchors. Are they still set?" I asked, fearful that something might go wrong at this last crucial moment.

"You no *ken* worry, Leslie. All anchors still there, still set, even one on mast. We *holim* till we bail *bot* out *tunait* (tonight) *long* low tide."

I jumped in his speedie and watched eagerly as *Banshee* got closer. He couldn't get there fast enough for me.

There she sat, very low in the water, but standing upright, as she should be.

I couldn't stop the tears. Every time I spoke, I just cried. We were going to save her.

The speedie pulled alongside. *Banshee* was wrapped in a cobweb of lines, her decks awash with small wavelets from the lagoon chop.

Paul explained that we would be pumping and bailing her out tonight at low tide, about one in the morning. Hopefully, she would then float off her "*haus* cradle." But first, he wanted me to swim down and "check patch, *wan moa* time"—just to be sure. He also wanted to know where the bilge pump handle was.

He was talking about our big Whale Titan manual bilge pump bolted to the cabin sole crossbeams. Joy had mounted it there so that all one had to do, if the electric pump failed, was to open the bilge board, sit down on the floor, and pump. It was sitting there exposed and ready to go, with the handle, still tied by its string, lying beside it.

The underwater cradle was a work of art. *Banshee* was totally stable.

We headed back to the beach to find Joy.

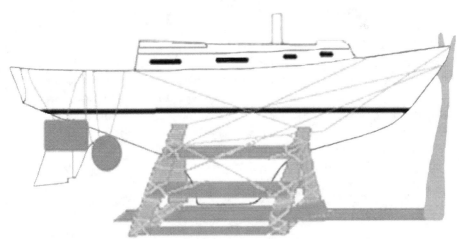

Eventually, we learned how these primitive island men had righted our boat and built "*Banshee*'s Underwater Jungle Cradle."

They found that they could easily bring the boat close to vertical by winching on the port anchor lines attached to the mast winch, which created a giant lever arm. In the jungle they had converted some of their logs into planks with their portable chain saw. Using the leverage of the mast, they inserted these planks between the keel and the coral rubble bottom as she rose. More planks and then submerged water-filled drums were shoved in each time *Banshee* stood more upright. The seawater from the drum was then blown out, imparting some buoyancy. As the boat's stern was the heaviest and flattest part, most of the drums were placed there. This also protected the vulnerable rudder and prop.

More planks formed a base for the two sides of their fabricated underwater cradle. These ten-foot planks were slid in place along the keel as *Banshee* came upright. The keel had dug such a hole in the rubble that they had to use shovels to partially expose it, allowing their long planks to fit in alongside the keel.

The sides of the cradle were constructed aboard one of the speedies. Each side consisted of two log triangles about four to five feet high, set at opposite ends of the long planks along the keel. The triangles were lashed together with our line and old fishing float cord. A diver would take a log from the speedie, go down, fit and mark it with an axe cut, and bring it back to be sawn to shape in the boat. Once the lashings were completed, they used some of their precious nails (reserved for house building) for extra strength and stability. As a cradle triangle grew too cumbersome and heavy for the speedie, they loaded it into the water and finished it as it floated by the side of the boat.

In the jungle, they found a stout tree with a natural fork in it. From this, they fashioned a forked support member for *Banshee's* bow. As the process of winching, lifting, and wedging planks under the keel continued, this very large forked log was wedged and lashed in place between *Banshee's* heavy stainless steel bow anchor roller and planks on the sand. Each time she rose up, this support log was moved along and brought up closer to vertical, a few inches at a time. The stern rose along with the bow, propped up by the buoyancy of the drums and wedged-in log supports.

As *Banshee* came upright, the finished cradle triangles were set in place, two on each side of the boat, just as a carpenter would build the sides of a house. The two cradle sides were lashed together across the bow and stern, and many, many other lashings were added for stability.

The cradle was so strong a storm could pass over *Banshee* and she wouldn't even budge. *Amazing, these guys.*

NIGHT WORK:
BANSHEE FLOATS AGAIN

Joy

After Les sped off to *Banshee* in the late afternoon, I sat on a log on the beach staring at the boat in the distance. *They've done it. How, I won't ask.* I was stunned.

For once, they left me alone with my thoughts. I couldn't stop the tears. My sailing home of 33 years stood tall and straight in the water, still and unmoving against the horizon.

Eventually, I shuffled off to the house, oblivious to my surroundings. The crowd had respectfully departed. *Had Lynnah sent them away?* As I came closer, Lynnah quietly appeared in front of me extending her arms in comfort. We didn't need to talk; words would not express my feelings. She sensed this and just hugged me, leading me up on the veranda to sit down. We sat there for a long while, holding hands.

I gradually came out of my fog, and grinning sheepishly said, "A beer. That's what I need now—don't even care if it's warm." Lynnah smiled back. She knew we still had some cans stashed in the back room. All she asked was that we be discreet and put it in a soda can so "boys no *gat* ideas." I followed the rules and went out to the shady beach to savor my prize.

Lynnah busied herself in the *haus kuk* as the dinner hour was getting near. Each day, near dusk, she would get everything ready for the evening: exchange her *klos wok* (work clothes) for a *laplap* and have her *waswas*—a beach swim and a rinse of well-water. Then she and Ben would put on *klos* church, fetch their worn, dog-eared Bible, and go off to the mandatory, twice-daily SDA prayer service. She never missed a service, morning or night. On her return, she would finish the dinner preparation over her open fire while Ben sat out with the men, PNG male-style, at the beach, awaiting the call to eat. The big woman worked hard. The house, the kids, the laundry, the garden, the food preparation, the cleaning-up—all were her responsibilities. At the end of the day, she looked like exactly what she was—a woman who had done a never-ending, hard day's work.

Ben's job came later: nightly spear fishing from his canoe to provide fresh fish for the family. Unfortunately, he had no diving fins. To show our thanks to him and "our family," we gave him a pair of long U.S. Divers fins, and his nightly catch improved rapidly. According to the strict SDA dietary rules, word for word out of the Old Testament, fish was the only acceptable protein available from the bountiful lagoon. We had been eating quite well lately, and Lynnah worked hard to keep us fed, using a lot of our salvaged provisions. We were happy to share, and everyone seemed to enjoy the change from their usual fare.

As dusk approached, Leslie and Paul returned. Her thumbs-up gesture and ear-to-ear smile said it all.

"Joy, they've done an unbelievable job. They actually built a house under the boat."

I hugged her and profusely thanked Paul and Stanley, who joined us on the beach.

"We wait *til* time tide go down *tunait*. I watch water *long nambis hia* (pointing with his foot to the incoming tide level on the beach)—we *save* time it go down. Then, long right time, we go bail out."

"How, Paul?" I asked.

"We *usim bakets long* bail out. You *gat bakets?* We *gat planti.*"

Later, after tank pumping duty, *waswas* time, and a meal, we retreated to "our back room", saying we needed to talk for a while.

Sitting back there behind the only door in the tiny thatched house, with our flickering kero lamp bouncing shadows off the woven walls, we held each other and talked. So much had happened in three days. Our former sailing life on *Banshee* seemed like a lifetime ago.

I dug around under the sail bags and found our stash of Philippine rum. The drink worked its magic, and we both relaxed. We both knew Les had a hard night ahead of her, but for now we had a small moment of togetherness and peace.

"Will she float, Les?" I asked.

She explained that while she was out there with Paul, she had examined her underwater repair job. The additional crack that Paul pointed out she felt was only a surface scoring and didn't penetrate the hull. She had reassured Paul about that and now me, as I was also concerned. I accepted her judgment—it would hold.

"Wish I could have done more to help. This damn finger is not getting much better. I don't even want to look at it. How am I going to help clean up the inside once she's floating? It's going to be a filthy mess."

"I know, but at least now we have a chance—more than we had before."

Her head started to droop on my shoulder. "Poor Les, you've worked so hard; without you, there would be nothing, nothing at all. C'mon, dear. Let's get you to bed. It's going to be a long night, but we're almost there, aren't we?"

After tucking her in under her net, I went outside and sat by the fire with the others, watching *Banshee* sitting still in the moonlight.

"You go *slip* now, Joy. *Mipela singaut wanem* time (call out when it's time)."

"*Lukim* you," I said, as I quietly padded off.

Leslie

I heard Joy saying, "It's time, Les. The guys are about ready. I've made some hot cocoa for you."

"Cold, it's so cold. I'm freezing."

"Get out by the fire. Move around, you'll warm up. I hated to wake you; you looked so peaceful under your net, snoring away."

"Please…"

"Well, at least you're up and laughing. That's good," Joy said.

I dressed and staggered out to the others sitting at the fire. The hot cocoa helped clear my mind for what lay ahead. It was a beautiful still night. The stars, the moon overhead, the warm breeze—*picture perfect.*

"Les, you always told me you liked night diving."

Joy's attempt at humor did little to cheer me, but in a few minutes, the men's enthusiasm for the "final push" was catching, and I was eager to go. They were fishermen, and reef fishing was night work. This night stuff was normal for them. *Although they did get to sleep and lie around all day—not exactly what I had been doing for the past three days.*

Piles of buckets sat near the awaiting speedies.

"Now, Paul? Is it low enough?"

"You no *ken* worry, Joy. We *save* right time."

Time passed. We waited patiently and started to doze off.

"Now!"

The one word command rang out and everyone fell to their tasks.

Off we went towards *Banshee*—plenty of guys, plenty of buckets, generator, lights, dive gear, and all.

This is it. The moment of truth for saving our home.

Banshee appeared ahead of us, a shimmering, ghostly shape in the moonlight.

We climbed onto *Banshee's* now dry cabin top. She was upright and rigid in her cradle, secured by anchors and all those cobwebbed lines. *So different from her unstable motion of the past three days.*

"Go *insait*, now. You *lukim*," Paul told me.

The water level was just to the bottom of the main companionway hatch in the cockpit; its higher threshold was dry. The cabin above this level was filled with air. *It's dry up there. I could stand up in the cabin and actually breathe, if I stood on my tip toes and pulled myself up.* I reached up and ran my hands around the cabin overhead. Little droplets of slimy water cascaded down the sides like a dirty fish bowl. I looked around and saw sand on every horizontal surface. *Yuck.*

Paul had stationed a guy in a canoe next to *Banshee* while we waited on the beach. His signal, a kerosene lantern, had alerted Paul to the water's favorable level as he watched the tide recede on the beach sand.

Water still flooded the cockpit footwell and seats, and flowed over the lower aft coaming and into the cockpit hatches around their hinged covers.

"Can you shut off *hasis* (hatches)? Water come in *hia*. And *hia*," Paul said, motioning to the aft anchor hawse.

"There's no way to close off the hatches, Paul. They go right into the engine space," I explained. "That hawse hole is small and it's covered. We can live with it."

The guys, not familiar with self-bailing cockpits, grabbed buckets and started bailing out the footwell.

"No, that won't do you any good. It'll just fill right up again," I said. "Look you guys, we've gotta do this fast and all together, so we can get the water level down before it fills up again. We have to pump and bail faster than the water can come in, at least at first. Then, once it's down and can't come in anymore, we can slow down."

In commanding, rapid Pidgin, Paul interpreted my plan, no doubt adding some of his own ideas along the way. The men fanned out armed with buckets—some poised inside under the forepeak hatch, some under the center hatch in the main cabin, and at the companionway. Others positioned themselves outside, ready to pull up full buckets for emptying. I put on a diving rig and sat down on the cross beams of the cabin sole and shoved the bilge pump handle into its hole. Looking around, everyone seemed ready.

From underwater, I nodded at Paul.

"*Bakets* now, *Hariap!*" he yelled. I started working the bilge pump. The men passed buckets full of water, dumped them, and handed them back for more.

"*Banshee's* Bucket Brigade" was in action.

From my underwater position, I pumped and pumped. It seemed never-ending: back and forth, pull and push. First I used my arms, then my legs, and then I alternated my sides—right, left, then right again. I could hear the noise of the bucket guys. *I know water is going out, but I can't tell yet; is it getting lower?*

I heard thumping. I paused and climbed up, looking at the guys in the cockpit.

"Leslie, *hul long wara* go out *long pam we?* (where is hole that water goes out from pump?) *Planti hul bek hia.*"

"The big one," I yelled to the guy at the transom and gave another shove on the pump handle with my foot.

"Oh, yeah. Me *lukluk long* bubbles. Yeah, *wara em i* come out. Me *pilim* (I feel it)."

A stretch and then back to pumping and bailing.

Endless pumping. It seemed to take forever. Everything hurt.

I looked above me. *Is it really going down? It does look lower.*

Slowly, gratefully, I stood up and looked at the water level. Paul was smiling. It *was* going down—down along the bulkheads, down past the cockpit coamings, down below the cockpit hatches—down and down.

It was working.

Still, we had a long way to go—back to pumping and more pumping. I heard the mast rigging groaning and realized they were easing off on the attached anchor line. *Good idea. I'm sure they can handle it after all this.*

I didn't need a regulator any more; my head was actually above water as I sat at the pump.

More noises: loud cracking, lines, bulkheads creaking.

Thump, bump…Movement… I could feel the hull moving in the water. *Are we afloat?*

"My god, she's floating. We're coming up."

Some guys had come below and were sitting around me on the cabin benches; the water was up to their waists. The bailers had stopped. More guys came below. Out came the *buai* and they just sat there, staring at me, chewing and chatting as I continued to pump.

It's like, okay meri, we've done our job, you've got a boat again, you finish it off. They seemed to be quite happy to just sit there, inches away, and watch me pump. *Well, I'm not going to complain, not now. I've got a boat.*

Paul settled in with the rest of them sitting inside the wet, sandy, slimy cabin, laughing and joking.

"You *wok* now, Leslie. *Mipela pinis wok. Bot* okay. Time you *wok.*"

I kept pumping. *They've done their job, it's my turn now.*

The cabin brightened with the approaching dawn. I wanted to get enough water out to see if my repair patch would hold. I kept pumping, then looked for incoming water.

No water was coming in. We were floating.

"Time to go, Les," Paul announced.

I crawled out into the cockpit and daylight hit me in the face. *Banshee* was floating on the little waves of the early morning breeze.

I was so exhausted I could barely stand. I had been pumping for hours.

"Is she anchored? Don't want her to float away, not now," I joked with them. We were all tired, but we were all very happy.

When we arrived back on shore, the village was slowly coming to life. I pulled up a few buckets of well water, threw them over me, grabbed a towel off the clothes line, and staggered up the steps of the house. For a moment, I sat on Joy's bed.

"She's floating."

"Oh, Those Ninigo Boys"

Joy

The words "she's floating" roused me from my early morning dozing.

"Oh, Les, you really did it?" She was wet, cold, and shivering, sitting there on my bed. "Go get in your bed and cover up. You're so cold. I'll come in. You've got to get warm."

I followed her into her room and piled blankets on her. She was shaking now, her teeth chattering. Strain, exhaustion, and possibly hypothermia. I rubbed her arms to help her circulation. *She sure was cold, poor thing.* I stayed there until she gradually warmed up and fell asleep. *I couldn't have done it. I know I couldn't.*

It was dawn, but for her it was still the dead of night. I pulled the curtain across her doorway. *Let her sleep.*

The village was awakening. I smelled cook-smoke and motioned to Ben and Lynnah to let Leslie be. They didn't have to be told. One look at *Banshee* floating high on her lines told the story of her night's work. *Les could sleep for two days straight now if she wanted to.*

Soon the work crews settled into their little groups under the trees and on the grassy area in back of the house. *Same people, always in the same places. Do they stake out their little turf? Oh well, none of my business; the job is getting done.*

I wandered among them, helping out, focusing my attention on the jobs at hand and, for once, gratefully letting thoughts of *Banshee* pass for a while. *She was anchored and safe. Les and I can discuss the next move when she gets up.*

Loud shouts came from the beachfront.

Everyone dropped what they were doing and raced to the water's edge. *What now?* I followed along with the crowd.

Banshee! What in hell? Terror gripped me. I stood there dumfounded, staring at the scene out on my boat.

Rudely awakened by the yelling, Les pushed through the crowd, staggering to my side.

"What the f...?"

"Les, I don't know, but we're here and they're out there. Just be calm and watch. We don't need to rile them up. Look around you, we're surrounded."

We watched the activity on our boat, a half-mile away.

Banshee was moving. *They're unrolling the damn genny!*

"They're sailing her. Oh, no, please."

"Joy, they're trying to sail her. Look, they've let go the anchors and she's moving. Someone's up the mast as a lookout."

Cheers came from the crowd.

"Those Ninigo Boys, oh, those Ninigo Boys!" Frida cried out. The crowd picked it up.

"Ninigo Boys, Ninigo Boys. *Gudpela* sailors, true," the crowd chanted.

It was out of our hands now—beyond anything we could do. Events had to take their course and we'd pick up the pieces later.

Quite a few of the villagers were immigrants from neighboring Ninigo Atoll, a much larger island group forty miles to the west. They were descendants of Micronesian seafarers, now intermarried with Melanesian PNG stock. To this day, the tradition of building and sailing sea-going sailing canoes on Ninigo still carries on. The "Ninigo Boys" are famous for racing their fast sailing canoes in their large, open lagoon.

There is no doubting their sailing ability, but with Banshee? I assumed Paul was aboard, and probably Stanley, who is half Ninigo Boy himself.

Banshee's large genoa slowly unfurled and caught the light breeze. Doing what she was designed so to do well, she effortlessly followed her helm and sailed away from her gravesite and into the wind.

She seemed to hover there, pausing between turning right and away behind the headland or left back into the village bay. *Where are they going?* Banshee, *please come back.*

Now she was getting smaller on the horizon. The crowd held their breath.

Gradually, she turned. The crowd roared. The genny rolled up and then came out on her other side, a perfect jibe with the magic of modern roller furling. She coasted along on a beautiful reach, then headed toward us, hardening up to the northwesterly headwind blowing across the isthmus.

A beautiful sight.

"Bikpela bot, em i sel isi (sails easily)," the crowd sighed. Their appreciation of sailing boats was obvious. The entire island's population was transfixed on a boat now raised from her coral grave and sailing, with dignity, into their harbor.

The Ninigo Boys were on stage and they knew it. Their tacking maneuvers up-wind with only a foresail were flawless. She came closer, and with each tack, the crowd gave their approval. As they made their final approach, bow-in to the beach, I heard the stern anchor pay out. At the same moment, they expertly headed her up into the wind, luffing the sail to stop her. A guy dove off the bow with a line in his teeth, and swam for the giant anchor embedded in the coral rocks along the shore.

Banshee swung to her anchor in front of the village. Oh, those Ninigo Boys.

Leslie

As soon as I saw *Banshee* tie up in front of the village, I wanted to go aboard. *Okay, they've given her back to us, now she's ours again. Where's our dinghy? I'll swim if I have to.* I scurried to our tiny fiberglass dinghy and started dragging it down to the water. The crowd gave way as I pulled it along. My back to my job, I didn't see Paul step in my way—I practically backed into him.

"No, *Leslie*, not now. You *stap hia*. You no go out," he commanded. "You wait for church meeting. Guards go out now."

"What? Paul, get out of my way. That's my boat and I'm going out there."

What the hell is he doing? He can't keep me off my boat. Just 'cause they saved it doesn't mean they can tell me what to do. Dammit, it's ours. He's got no right. I was boiling. As I squared off to face him, I saw the remaining crew jump off *Banshee* into an awaiting speedie. One guy was lugging one of our large, black duffle bags. It was obviously heavy and stuffed full.

"What's he got in my bag?"

"Look, Leslie, *lusim*. He takes the last of your *kago* off so we can clean. They take down to my place. *Isi, Les.*"

"Paul, get out of my way—I'm going out there if I have to swim, and you can't stop me."

Paul continued to block my way and the crowd was gathering. Their mood was turning ugly. *It's like…shit, like it's their boat now. I've got to get Joy. They'll listen to her.* I left the dinghy at the water's edge and ran to get her.

"Joy, Paul won't let me go out to *Banshee*. He says we've got to wait until after church tomorrow. You've got to help. Come on."

"Hell, I thought he and Stanley were out on *Banshee*," Joy said, as she hurriedly pushed through the crowd surrounding Paul.

"What's going on, Paul?" Joy towered over him, her voice icy calm.

"I post guards *long bot* and *bot* off limits to all now, you too. We have meeting *afta* church *tumora, afta* Sabbath. *Yupela* wait. Then, we decide—church decide."

"Paul, that is my boat. It is a documented U.S. vessel. I am the captain, a U.S. citizen. We thank you for what you have done in returning our boat to us. Now, I am asking Leslie to go out there by herself and check it out for me. She is going, Paul. Do we have a problem?"

Silence. You could have cut the tension in the air with a knife.

Joy paused, still glaring down at Paul. He was speechless. He had never seen Joy like that. I had, and knew when she meant business. She turned to me and said, "Les, please get in the dinghy and go out to our boat and make a survey. Now go."

I got in the dinghy and started rowing towards *Banshee*.

Yells came from onlookers on shore.

"Leslie, you no go. *Village councilor tokim* you; you no go out. You *stap long hia."*

I stopped rowing and looked back at Joy. She said, "Keep rowing," and motioned me to move on. I kept on going, blanking out the unpleasant scene on the beach.

I climbed aboard. Sand, salt, coral grit, and rubble covered everything. The boat smelled like a dried-out reef baking in the sun. Diesel fuel and oil residue coated the walls and dripped into pools. Rotting food and unidentifiable gunk was in every corner and cabinet. My family's Yiddish word, *dreck,* came to mind. *Now I know why people just walk away from disasters like this.*

The teak ladder had been torn out. I lowered myself down over the oily, slippery cabinets into what once was my comfortable home. It was so empty, a smelly, damp, empty cave. Tears came quickly and didn't stop The pent-up pain of many days flowed out with the tears.

I sat there, alone in my private space, my world, our boat, and sobbed.

Gradually, I came back. *Got to get in gear and put this back together. It's a boat and I know how to fix boats—damned well. First, the engine. Got to save it; we'll never have the money to get another.*

Opening up the doors to the engine space, I saw our once clean and shiny red engine was now covered with rusty, oily streaks. Saltwater was pooled in every crevice. The foam sound-proofing insulation was torn and sagging from the walls and overhead, completely saturated. *Okay, what tools do I need? Got to drain the engine and get the water out, flush it with diesel and oil. Where's a knife and a bucket? I could cut the sump drain hose if I only had a knife. My beautiful ever-sharp Myerchin rigging knife that I had hidden behind the fuel tank—they even got that. Shit, when does it end?* I tried to concentrate and mentally made a list of needed tools and supplies. *What a mess; what I'd give for a hose and running water.*

Finally, I jumped back into the dinghy and rowed ashore, full of determination for the job ahead. *This is something I can do.*

Joy

Wow, what a shock. Usually Paul is so calm and reasonable. What's this all about? After Les rowed away, I turned and walked back to the house, saying nothing, letting the crowd settle. *Let him cool down, then we'll talk later.* I chatted with Lynnah for a while on the veranda, and then a little later, when everyone had returned to their jobs, I started mingling again, helping and answering questions as usual.

I saw Les return from her survey of *Banshee,* and quietly headed her off before there were any more confrontations. *Don't know exactly what's going on here, but something's up.* Joining me, Les spoke of tasks and tools. *Always good with the practical stuff, that's Les. "Just get me going on a job and leave me out of the emotional shit," I could hear her saying.*

As we were talking, Namo's daughter, Noly, shyly approached us. "Another *Toksave,* Papa say you come. Important."

Dropping our plans mid-sentence, we dashed off to Namo's. We didn't talk and anticipation hung in the air between us.

A crowd hovered around Namo's broken down hut. Namo limped into the scene and said, *"Toksave* come *long* radio, you *gat bikpela* message now. *Em i* say: We *harim* signal you are okay. No signal anymore. The American representative comes on Hermit shortly."

Dumbstruck, we stared at each other.

I looked at Les and said, "The American representative? The U.S. Embassy is sending someone to Hermit?

She snickered, grinned, and said two words: "My mother."

"Les, you're kidding. What's your mother got to do with this?"

"Trust me, I know. It's my mother. She's behind this, you'll see."

I still couldn't believe it. "Namo, how is he getting here?"

"Police boat. *Wan bilong* Lorengau *long* Manus. Very fast. *Em i* come *hia* many times. Ronnie Knight *draiva* (driver). Take only five or six hours, *tasol."*

"Namo, today's Friday. Did they say when?"

"Mande night—*em i* come, true. *Yupela lukim."*

"Who's Ronnie Knight?"

Namo laughed and rolled his eyes, as did the other men standing there. "Ronnie, *em i bikpela waitman bilong PNG. Em i* come *hia oltaim. Em* white *autsait,* black *insait.* Ronnie *i* born *hia*—PNG citizen, true." From the nods, covert lewd joking, and assents of the crowd, I figured this Ronnie guy was a local hero to the men.

"Okay, guys, *inap* (enough). I got it. Monday night it is. We'll see what happens then."

We left Namo and his ribald cohorts and slowly walked back to "our beach." My head was spinning with the day's events, especially this morning's confrontation with Paul. *Where are we going with all this? We just want to save our boat.*

"Well, if the U.S. embassy rep is really coming to Hermit, it might give us a bit more leverage with Paul and the rest. Maybe they'll think twice before they mess around with what could become a high profile case for PNG."

We went back to the beach work groups. They all seemed to be in full swing now in preparation for this evening's Sabbath. Everything, we were told, must be cleaned up, covered, and put away by sundown.

The SDA church in PNG conforms to their interpretation of strict Old Testament Sabbath rules. Like the traditional Jewish Sabbath, there was no work, no play, no machines, just religious services and prayer from sundown Friday to sundown Saturday.

The church's attitude on Hermit was strict: either participate or stay quietly inside your house. Friday afternoons were to be spent tidying up one's house, the church and the village. Even food had to be prepared in advance.

At five o'clock every Friday evening, the gong tolls and all activity ceases at Luf village. At first we tried to be very respectful of their Sabbath custom, even participating in it a bit. But after our disaster it became, as Les put it, a "big pain."

Among the villagers there were many *bekslaiders*, mostly men in their twenties and thirties (easily identified by their *buai*-stained mouths) who should have been the backbone of the village. Church attendance was low: women and babies, a handful of men, indoctrinated church elders like Paul and Stanley, and the few remaining old folk. The *pikinini* had their own SDA "Saturday School," complete with a teacher and help from some of the mothers.

It was obvious that the austere and strict rules proscribed by zealous early SDA missionaries and the long-ago writings of Ellen G. White, the sect's founder, didn't have much appeal. The prohibitions were all-encompassing: no secular or traditional music and singing (only gospel); no jewelry or body decoration; no decorative handicrafts; no traditional tribal dancing or dress; no *buai* chewing or alcohol consumption; no pigs; no and more no's. The mandatory twice daily attendance at church, plus evening "Bible study" sessions, didn't leave many individual freedoms left. The church, which should have been the center of village life, was losing its grip and not meeting the needs of much of the village population.

Take everything away from a primitive, spiritually animistic and traditional people and fail to replace it with something meaningful that ties in with their local culture, and what is left? Even their own unique *tok ples* language, normally a point of great local pride, was extinct. No wonder resentment seethed just beneath the surface of so many.

Still, to live here and accomplish our goals, we had to go along with it, even though much of our visible compliance was only lip-service and dreary play-acting. It became sheer drudgery.

The drowned engine required immediate attention. If we were going to have any hope of salvaging it, it had to be quickly drained of corrosive saltwater and then repeatedly flushed with a mixture of engine oil and diesel fuel. We knew we had no time to waste. Our precious engine could not sit one more day or a seizure would be imminent. Paul and his lofty admonition of "no one on the boat until after tomorrow evening's close of the Sabbath" could go to hell for all I cared. We had to save what was left of our engine—now.

Les began looking for her tools and supplies and I puttered about, trying to be useful. My finger was not getting any better, even with Lynnah's twice-daily dressing changes and iodine soaks. She convinced me to apply aloe to aid in the healing. I was skeptical but went along with it. There was nothing else.

"Joy, where's the socket extension bar? I've got the 9/16" socket and the rest of the stuff, but not the extension. I saw it earlier, but now it's gone. I need it to remove the starter."

That two-foot long extension was absolutely essential to remove the poorly-located starter motor in our cramped engine space. *Shit, not more missing stuff. Are they taking our tools? We've got to have them to fix everything. Good grief.*

Our frustrated conversation was overheard by several people, including Ben and Lynnah, and a small group gathered around us.

"*Yupela* need mechanic. *Mipela gat* mechanic *hia*—diesel mechanic, true," someone said.

"What, there's a diesel mechanic in this village? Who is he?"

"Oh, *em i* no *hia* now. *Em go long pisim* (fishing). Go *long* Maron *ailan. Nem bilong em,* Bill. *Em i* come *bek afta Sabbath,* you *lukim.*"

Lynnah chimed in. 'Oh, yes. We *havim* mechanic. Bill, *brata* (brother) *bilong* me."

I looked at Lynnah. "Why didn't you tell me? Of course, we need a mechanic. Lynnah, your own brother?"

"Yes, true *brata. Havim* same mother, same father."

More voices—"*Em i* go Madang Technical College. *Em i gudpela* mechanic."

What's a mechanic from a respectable place like that college doing out here in the bush? Jobs are scarce in PNG and anyone having qualifications puts them to use in towns—one doesn't usually find them hanging out in remote villages. I was dubious about this guy. *We'll see.*

"Anyway, we've got to have that extension back, wherever it is. Someone has it and we've got to have it back," Les implored the crowd. "Please get it, please guys, help us."

A dejected Les slumped off to a beachfront log and sat down, shaking her head. A few minutes later she found me again, this time near tears.

"Those damn guys, Okip and Bob. I just wanted to cool off for a while, and they showed up with their useless buddies. They just went on and on, saying things like, 'You are not our culture. You put your ways on us. You put your things on our beach, then you want them back and tell us we steal. We don't want you here. You two *bagarap* life in our village. You leave, go home.' They wouldn't shut up."

"Take it easy, Les. Okip's crazy. They know he's a nut case, but they've got to put up with him. And Bob, c'mon, everyone has told us to stay away from him. Ignore them both, okay? I know you don't have the extension, but it'll turn up. Go on out there and get going with the oil change. Just forget those guys. We've got bigger problems than their stupid ramblings."

She gave a weak smile and trudged off to our dinghy and her beloved boat. *Les is much better when she's doing something; got to keep her busy. These guys can sure bring her down.*

I continued roaming around looking for the all-important extension. Bob and Okip had settled in with the guys cleaning up our soaked power tools. I approached the group, ignoring the unpleasant duo, trying to find out if any of our 110-volt tools could be salvaged. Bob confronted me with an official-looking notebook and waved papers in my face.

"You *lukim hia,* Joy. Your *bot mekim planti* damage *long rip. Dispela rip bilong* Hermit. You *kilim* coral; you *kilim pis. Dispela rip* our life. You *putim badpela* poison *long wara. Olsem spik hia* (like it says here) you *mekim* 'environmental damage.' *Dispela pepa* (paper), *gavman pepa.* You *rit* (read) *planti."*

The others stared in amazement at what he was doing. People gathered. What was with this guy? Bob was not a favorite with them, particularly among the women whom he harassed. He was from Ninigo—"not one of us," they would say, and back off.

I took the papers thrust at me—*my goodness, carbons too—very official looking. What the hell is this?*

"You no *havim* 'tour guide.' You no *ken draivim bot.* You *stupid.* Me 'tour guide' *na* 'reef warden' too," he said, holding a metal badge that looked like it came from a kid's toy shop. The words "Warden" stood out in bas-relief. Okip, seizing the opportunity, smugly waved a similar "Magistrate" badge under my nose. *Good grief, what idiocy have I gotten myself into now? This is so pitiful, it should be laughable, but it's not—these guys are for real. Damn, where is Paul?*

"You pay *planti bikpela* fine—*planti kina.* 'Compensation'—you pay 'compensation.' You *givim* money now—me *kisim.* You *pebek* Hermit."

Not seeing Paul or Stanley, I was feeling very alone and compromised. I couldn't believe that after all we had been through that this was actually happening. I had heard tales of PNG compensation or "pay-back" monies—a cultural norm for transgressions such as killing someone's pig, trespassing, raping a woman, or…*damaging a reef in a shipwreck? Surely they realize it was an accident, don't they?*

When we first came to Hermit, I had told Paul that, as we had just come from Palau, we had no *kina,* the PNG currency, and so would be happy to barter for anything that required payment. He had said, "No problem, most of us prefer that anyway. *Kina* doesn't do us much good out here—no place to spend it." So, in our carefree days before the sinking, we had joked about existing in a "cashless society." *But now, it seems they are actually demanding some kind of payback. Or is it just Bob?* I had heard that some of these PNG compensation claims can get pretty outlandish. As someone had told me, "it's never enough."

The situation with Bob and Okip was getting heated, and I didn't want to make it worse. I took Bob's papers, stuffed them in my pocket, and left. *I've got to talk to Paul about this and soon.* Retreating to Lynnah's safe veranda, I watched the beachfront and awaited Leslie's return from *Banshee.*

Sometime later, an oily, grubby Les pulled her dinghy ashore. As I greeted her, my worried demeanor told her something was amiss.

"Okay," she said. "My good news first, or from the looks of you, your bad news?"

"Go ahead, Les. Mine can wait. I can't find Paul anyway and it's his problem now."

"I flushed the engine, Joy. I'll have to do it several more times, but for now it's done. Gallons of water came out, but the engine turns. I found the big breaker bar and the engine crank socket, and used them. The half-inch drive handle would have helped, but I can't find it either."

She had cut the engine sump hose off the oil change pump, leaving its shut-off valve for future flushings, and drained all the water and oil into a bucket. She repeatedly flushed the engine's oil passages with a mixture of diesel and oil, and left them topped up with oil until the next time.

She also drained the expansion tank and the engine block's water passages, using rainwater to flush and fill them, adding coolant to prevent rust. She was very concerned about polluting the lagoon with more oil and had dutifully brought all the "oily stuff" back ashore.

"They can tell me what to do with it. It's their lagoon—we've done enough damage already."

"Yeah, the damage—that's the bad news. It's Bob again," I said, as I showed her his papers and related my story.

"Shit, that jerk again. When's he gonna quit?"

"When he and his buddies get what they want, Leslie, and not until then. Remember, when we sank, they said, 'Why don't you just leave? You're American—you're rich—all Americans are rich. Just take off now and collect the insurance. All you people do that.'"

"But, Joy, we told them we didn't have any insurance and that we certainly aren't rich."

"You think they believed us? What is "rich," anyway? Look around you, they have so little. All this 'cargo' they've been pulling off *Banshee*—that's rich to them. They see stuff like this and to them we're rich and you can't tell them otherwise. I'm very happy that you, at least, were successful. But, c'mon, you're a mess as usual. *Waswas* time, dear."

Les meandered off to the shower and I, as time was growing close to the dreaded gong of the impending Sabbath, pitched in with the crowd that was hastily cleaning up our work area on the beach.

I tried to help pick up as best I could using only my left hand, but much of my efforts were futile. The *meries* said, "You no *usim han*, you *stap hia. Mipela* come *long askim* you—*dispela gudpela, holim, o dispela badpela, putim long paia.*"

"Okay by me."

I noticed Bob getting increasingly agitated and directive as I stood there answering questions from the *meries*. *He's really putting on a show.* I tried not to look at him as he kept glaring at me. *Excuse me; I have a right to talk to these ladies, you know.* One woman ran up to me with our tattered, soaked engine parts manual, rescuing it from the trash fire.

"You *laikim?*"

"Yes, yes, thank you so much."

"*Em i bilong* engine, *samting* true? (important?)" she said.

"Yes, please." I grabbed it and took it to Lynnah, telling her to put it somewhere safe where it would dry out. "We can't fix the engine without it. So glad it's been found." *God, what would we have done without it?*

Bob was in his element—directing women. For the Sabbath, all our stuff, from tiny spare parts to large items, had to be piled discretely underneath the house and completely covered. Not only was it wrong to work on the Sabbath, it was wrong to look at *"wok"* on the holy day also.

Seeing me alone, just standing there, Bob attacked: *"Wokim,* lazy *waitmeri.* You no *sanap* (stand up), *mekim nating* (do nothing). You stupid *meri tasol.* You *pikimap pipia* (pick up trash)—*meri wok.* You *wokim olsem ol meries bilong* Hermit. *Ol ples mas* (must) clean *long* Sabbath. *Hariap, waitmeri. Movim."*

His words stunned me and everyone in view. *Meries* rushed to my aid, hustling me away from the unpleasant scene. *"Mipela save Bob.* You go *long* house—*em i* no come *antap* (up there). Go now."

Shaking with fury at this grossly arrogant man, I got out of there fast and said nothing. *Anything I say now will only make it worse. He knows he's wrong. He's just so dumb, that's all.*

Leslie returned, clean clothes and all. One look at Lynnah and I knew the best thing for me was to go off to the shower and quickly. Later, when I returned, peace had seemingly been restored and Lynnah was preparing for church.

"Yupela come *long* church too. You *mas. Bot* up now. You go *givim* thanks. People *laikim* see *yupela long* church. *Sindaun* (Sit down) *long* me."

"Lynnah, do we have to?" *It's bad enough on Saturdays, but Friday night as well?*

"Yes, you have to—people *mekim toktok.* This *bikpela* Sabbath—*bot* come *bek."*

Appropriately chagrined, we draped our *laplaps* around our shorts and dutifully fell in line behind Lynnah's ponderous, proud bulk, heading off to church.

"Sure would rather go to the "back room rum bar," I whispered to Les.

"Happy Sabbath"

Joy

"Happy Sabbath, Happy Sabbath!"

With pasted-on smiles, we shook hands and dutifully mouthed the now-standard Sabbath greeting as we followed Lynnah into the small village church. Sympathetic nods came from the parishioners as I awkwardly proffered my left hand and held the bandaged one close.

"You *olrait?*" accompanied the handshaking and greeting. The devout, seemingly genuine villagers raised a deep feeling of gratitude in me, despite my cynicism. Quite honestly, I was very thankful, for our situation could have been so much worse. I resolved to make a public statement of our appreciation.

The church was a simple thatched building with a floor of soft, dry sand, a welcome cushion for repeated kneeling and standing. The *meries* of the church kept it raked and had decorated the ceiling, walls, and altar with freshly cut flowers and palm fronds. Numerous strands of brightly colored cloth hung from ceiling rafters and waved in the breeze, adding a cheery effect to the solemnity of the church service.

A large table seating the elected church elders faced the pews, which were roughly hewn benches. Women, many holding small children or nursing babies, sat on one side, and the few male attendees sat on the other. The vacant rear pews of the men's side took up the overflow of *meries* and latecomers. The few remaining oldsters had honored spots in the front. Some pre-teen males like Bently, Lynnah's son, having graduated from the *pikinini* Saturday School, sat solemnly in the front, eager to take their place as "Christian Men" of the village.

Unfortunately, many of these youths lost their piety when they came under the influence of the rebellious single male *bekslaiders* in their late teens and early twenties. Chewing *buai*, smoking tobacco, and acting tough was infinitely more appealing than church. Wearing large, black o-rings on developing biceps was a signature of this childishly idolized group, called *raskals* in PNG.

Behind the elder's table, a revered wooden carving of a huge open Bible adorned the altar. For a while I thought it was an actual Bible and wondered where they got it. With missionised Pacific island cultures, the Bible is taken as the actual spoken word of God—fundamentalism to the core—and not as selected writings by various ancient authors subject to different versions and interpretations. No wonder the large carving occupied such a position of honor: its advent had liberated them from what the missionaries called the "shameful paganism" of the past. With this attitude taught to them by passionate SDA missionaries of the fifties, one could understand why their traditional culture had been so completely banished.

A door lead through the side of a dividing partition and gave access to the back of the altar and to the outside. This provided privileged "back-door" access for the various preachers of the service. The whole thing had the effect of a window-like stage for the various "players" in the church service, who popped in at various moments. It was very confusing to us as everything was, of course, in rapid-fire Pidgin.

A black chalkboard giving notice of the hymns and prayers of the day hung behind the altar. It also served for notices of donations, elections, Bible classes, and church business. My recall of the church's environment was rather detailed owing to the unusually lengthy time I spent dutifully sitting there.

Church attendance had never been a regular part of my adult life, being delightfully freed of the dreaded duty upon leaving home at seventeen. However, after our disaster, I felt obligated that we should put in a regular appearance out of respect for the "village culture," as they called it. It seemed to help keep the peace, and at least then we couldn't be criticized for living there, accepting their assistance and not participating. Trying to convince Leslie of this was a little more difficult—my Jewish friend had never attended a Christian church service and had rarely set foot in a synagogue. I envied her blissful freedom from the dogma I was forced to learn as a child and the time later spent unlearning and dealing with its entrapping web of guilt.

We sat down in the pews next to Lynnah amidst smiles and approving nods from the congregation. Ben and Bently went over to the men's side. *It's like they're honored that we are here, but how strange that a family can't sit together.*

Lynnah fell to her praying, and we sat there respectfully quiet.

I whispered to Les, "When the time comes for announcements, I'm going to stand up and give a few words of thanks. We do owe it to them."

She eyed me suspiciously and nodded. "Better you than me. I don't do speeches."

The brief evening service began. Someone put a hymnal in my hands for us to follow along in the singing. None of the hymns or prayers were familiar. After many ups and downs of kneeling, standing, and sitting, the service mercifully came to a close, and I made my speech of thanks to the congregation. Paul and Stanley at the elder's table seemed particularly appreciative. *Well, I meant it from my heart—can we go home, please?*

We exited the church through the line of handshaking elders. There was so much I wanted to confer with Paul about, but I knew the Sabbath rules, and his officious demeanor told us that we had better comply.

As soon we got back to "our beach," off came the church-going *laplaps* and on went the Rid cream. We poured warm beers into soda cans in the back room bar and found an isolated log to perch on and enjoy the rest of the sunset.

"Do you realize it's only been five days since we sat in that nice, quiet anchorage around the corner? You know, Joy, we went over there last Friday just to get away from all this Sabbath stuff and now we're right back in the thick of it."

"Yeah, and a helluva lot more, unfortunately. Just endure, Les, and we'll make it."

After dinner, Les talked about progress on the engine. "Shit, I didn't drain and flush the transmission. Bet it's full, too. I gotta go do it, right now."

"Now, Les? It's so black out, and it's the Sabbath."

"That's why I've got to do it now. No one'll see me. I'll be real quiet and keep low. Besides, tomorrow we've got to do the church thing again and we can't let that saltwater sit in there. We don't need a destroyed transmission too."

Well, she is right; it's just the awful timing. "Up to you, Les. I'll wait up for you."

Before I knew it, there was Les, stealthily paddling out to *Banshee* under cover of darkness. *What do I do with her? She's going to do her own thing, no matter what.*

Leslie

I knew I had to do this quietly; fortunately the moon wasn't up yet. *Damn, how stupid not to have flushed out the transmission earlier, and we've got plenty of fluid for it—even found the little pump.* Slowly, I paddled out to *Banshee's* ghostly shape and crawled aboard, not even turning on my flashlight. *Really dumb, this Sabbath nonsense, secretly running around in the dark, on my own boat yet.*

Keeping low, I opened the cockpit hatch and stepped below. I slid feet first into the engine room. "Ow, my feet! What the f…?" I reached down to feel my feet, and my hands came up wet. Clicking on the flashlight, I found blood all over my hands. It never occurred to me to wear shoes—we never wore shoes on the boat. I propped up the light and looked around. Glass—brown beer bottle glass was everywhere. Small shards stuck in my feet.

I stopped most of the bleeding with a rag, and picked out the tiny glass shards with an old knife. *The rest will have to wait until later.* The bigger pieces of glass I threw in my bucket—*they'll never believe me. I'll have to show them something.* The rest I swept out of the way, so I could reach the transmission without getting cut further. *Who in hell could have done this? Sabotage, plain old sabotage. They really don't want us to fix this, do they?* My feet, still bleeding, hurt terribly. *Shit, there are still glass pieces in my feet but I can't see to get them out.* I made some bandages out of the dirty engine rag and went at the transmission with a vengeance.

I pumped it out with the little hand pump, and lots of oily, red fluid-laced saltwater spurted into the bucket along with the broken glass evidence. Several flushes with new transmission fluid, and I was satisfied—*okay for now; time to get back. Hope nobody heard me yelling. Paul's got to do something about this. Someone did this deliberately.*

Wincing in pain, I climbed out of the cramped engine space and sat down in the cockpit. "Ow, more glass!" I muffled a scream and discretely turned on my light in the footwell. Glass was everywhere—the footwell was covered with broken glass shards. *Wow, they really mean business.*

I was absolutely fuming as I paddled back to shore. How I kept from having a screaming tirade, I don't know, unless it was because, deep down, I understood the serious consequences that it would create. Joy met me as I pulled the dinghy up. My feet, still not recovered from the coral cuts and insect bites, were a miserable bleeding mess.

The light from her lantern shone on my sandy, bandaged, and bloody feet.

"What the hell? Les, what happened?"

I related my unpleasant story and could see anger rise in her face. She, even more than I, knew we had to be very cautious in handling this new development. We were on very shaky ground.

"I'll get Lynnah to boil some water," she announced. "You'll need to wash and soak them and get the rest of the glass out. Ben's pressure lamp will give us some bright light. Go sit up on the veranda and stop walking around, you nut."

Docilely, I followed her instructions and limped through the sand up to the house.

Joy

"She do what?" came Lynnah's incredulous reply when I told her of Leslie's escapade. "Me *tingkim* (think) she down *long paia long* you. Me no *save*. Why Leslie do *samting* stupid *oltaim. Em i* no *tingktingk.*"

"Lynnah, you are so right, but she did save the boat, and she works so very hard. She just has her own way of doing things, *tasol.* C'mon, let's clean her up."

Motherly Lynnah was at the ready. "You go *long* now—you no *ken halpim*, not *long pinga.* "I take care—no *ken* worry, Joy."

Politely dismissed, I retreated to my log at the fire, after covertly pouring a stiff rum into a soda can.

Eventually, when people started turning in for the night, I meandered in and found Leslie safely tucked under her net in her room.

"You okay, dear?" Les mumbled assent as she rapidly fell asleep. I padded off to my net-covered bunk on the veranda.

RELIGION AND POLITICS
HERMIT STYLE

Joy

Saturday, the Sabbath. The clanging of the village gong awakened us to the tidy, clean village of Luf, with *Banshee* serenely anchored just off the beach. A view from the air would show nothing but a peaceful island village with a yacht anchored in its placid bay—how enticing.

The horror of the past week was now covered by the tides, and the ensuing mess created in its wake was discretely hidden away. Even the ingenious cradle, the savior of *Banshee*, was on its way to becoming a hidden underwater monument. The trauma's remaining evidence was the burnt charcoal of the rubbish fires and the charred, water-logged remnants of our possessions.

The morning church service didn't begin until nine o'clock. I anticipated a slow, peaceful morning. Sleeping out on the veranda, I always awoke early to the ear-piercing crowing of the roosters that preceded the inevitable gong. Leslie's room was shaded by trees and darkened by a curtain pulled across the door. I went in quietly and straightened our stacked clothes and belongings while she awoke.

"Oh, my feet, my legs," she moaned. "Joy, how am I going to walk like this? God, it hurts. That glass...the cuts, they're infected and we've no antibiotic pills. Dammit, this is awful. What are we going to do?"

I looked at her legs and feet. Each nasty slash was red and swollen and her feet and ankles were all puffed up. It doesn't take long in the tropics for a small cut to become a big problem.

"Okay, we deal with it the old fashioned way. Hot soaks—hot as you can stand it—in soapy water with bleach. Lots of iodine and antibiotic cream. We've still got some. I'm using it every day, though don't know that it's doing me much good."

Off I went to the cook-fire for the water kettle. The soaking and other ministrations seemed to help, and after bandaging her feet and ankles to keep off the flies, she began moving around.

"Not the church, please. I'll just stay here, okay?"

"No way, Paul's got to see you, and if you limp into church like that I'm sure he'll take notice. Someone put that glass in there, Les. It didn't get there by itself."

"Okay, okay. I'll go, but Joy, let's face it, there are people here who want us gone, and they're not going to quit. They'd love to have *Banshee* all to themselves. Haven't you heard them talk—that stuff about 'two *waitmeri* can't sail a boat, and just go home and collect the insurance?'"

"Home, Les? Home is 34 feet, right out there—that's what I told them—and somehow, we're going to sail her out of here. They heard that too. As for the insurance issue, I've explained many times that we don't have any. Now let's stop this and do what we have to do."

Eventually, we followed dutifully along to the morning service with the family. After our first Sabbath on Hermit, we had learned that the nine o'clock service was the one to go to—it was much shorter.

As we entered the church we shook hands with Paul. His eyes dropped to Leslie's bandaged swollen feet as she limped in.

We persevered through the long morning's service, rising and kneeling by rote now. The swarms of flies were particularly bad in the church with all the people and lack of breeze. Flies are a serious problem with cuts and sores in the tropics, and a small uncovered wound can blow up into major proportions in no time when it is attacked by just one fly. The only bandages we had were what we had scavenged from *Banshee*, along with some non-sterile gauze that Lynnah offered us. Band-Aids did not exist, and in the tropical humidity the plastic ones are useless anyway. Masking tape sticks well, but we didn't have any of that either. So, we had a rather rag-tag look with pieces of gauze tied around our feet and legs to ward-off marauding flies.

The service over, we went back out along the handshaking line, and I waited alone for Paul to come over. I wanted "special dispensation" for us to attend only the nine o'clock service.

"Leslie's feet, Paul, they're badly cut up and infected, and my finger is not healing—my whole arm is aching. You know we have no antibiotics. There was broken glass in *Banshee's* cockpit and engine room last night. She had to do something out there and didn't use lights so to keep it quiet. You know, being respectful and all."

"Yes, I hear about glass. Why she go out? You *save* Sabbath rules. But, I am sorry about her feet."

"Paul, she had to check the patch to be sure there're no leaks. *Banshee's* anchored in

50 feet of water now, you know. Don't want her to sink in that," I said, giving him what would become our standard excuse for spurious boat visits. "And, she had to get the saltwater out of the transmission—waiting would destroy it."

"Right. That had to be done. Me *save*. Stanley and me talk *afta* Sabbath. You come *long* too—we talk. Okay?"

Kind words. Maybe he feels guilty.

For Leslie and me, the rest of the Sabbath day was spent being discretely busy at cleaning and organizing. Les wanted to go out and clean *Banshee*—the broken glass mess particularly infuriated her.

"I've got my boat back," Les said, "and now I want to get it ready for us to move back aboard. I can't stand this communal living here one minute more."

I wanted so to help, but this injured right hand of mine made it impossible. We agreed that she would collect all needed equipment and supplies in a bucket, put her tools in her old messenger bag on her back, and then make an unobtrusive dash for the boat.

"One trip only," I cautioned. "No back and forth stuff. Remember the only activities permitted are church, eating, and sleeping, Bible reading, and praying, so stay inside, keep a low profile, and don't come back until sundown."

"Happy to do just that," she grinned. "See ya."

When I returned to the house, Lynnah queried me as to Les' whereabouts.

"The boat. Where else?"

"Oh, but that not allowed and..."

"Lynnah, please." I cut her off. "*Maski,* okay?"

Worriedly, she looked at me. "No service *long* eleven?"

"No service at eleven. I'm going to do my own cleaning in the back room where no one will see me; I'll even put down the windows. I want to get some of this stuff off the veranda—*tumas* temptation for loose *hans?*" She agreed and smiled knowingly. "Don't worry, dear. If I go out on the veranda, I'll check to see if anyone's looking." The idea of being co-conspirators appealed to her, and she went away, chuckling.

Leslie

I was so happy to be out on *Banshee* doing my own thing: *Like being let out of prison— free—how good it feels. Our boat again.*

My first concern was to get the starter off the engine so we could save it. I found my 3/8" drive ratcheting wrench handle and 9/16" socket, but the long extension, adaptors, and ½" drive handle were all missing. It was obvious that someone had taken them.

I must have spent the better part of the afternoon lying behind the greasy, filthy engine wrestling with the starter bolt. I tried loosening it from every conceivable angle, even attempting to tap the edge of the bolt-head with a hammer and chisel, thinking that might turn it. Nothing worked—that bolt was not going to budge without using a handle to provide leverage and an extension that reached beyond the confinement of the engine space. Joy and I had known that; that's why we were prepared with the right tools. Now they were missing!

Frustrated, there was nothing else I could do except clean. My knuckles and hands were bruised and bleeding from my attempts with the starter bolts—*sort of matches my feet now.* I busied myself with scraping up the sand, rubble, and *dreck* in every corner. I filled our salvaged garbage bags with the burnable stuff and dumped the rest over the side. Cleaning out the refrigerator's rotten remains was another smelly horror. *Just look at my hands—what a mess—cut, bleeding, and filthy with embedded crap.*

The village gong sounded and saved me from my self-imposed exile at hard labor. *What I'd give for a hot soak in a perfumed bubble bath.* I was exhausted as I dumped my donations into the evening's rubbish fires on the beach. All I could think about was a wash, a plate of food, and sleep.

"Have you talked with Paul yet?" I asked Joy.

"Just about to go down there. Go take care of your cuts and I'll come in and tell you what happened later. Get some sleep, please."

Joy

I had my mental agenda and I hoped to find Paul and his "lieutenant" in a receptive mood. They seemed so when I respectfully entered the meeting room, illuminated by a flickering kerosene lamp. This meeting time at the close of the Sabbath was a village routine. People awaiting audience stayed outside for their turn with the leaders. When the seat in front of Paul was vacated, I was motioned to sit down. Stanley sat respectfully to the side.

I had been granted an official audience with the "Chief."

I addressed my concerns: Bob's presentation of the reef-damage citation with the threat of unspecified fines; his bullying treatment of me on Friday afternoon; the broken glass sabotage on *Banshee*; our need for free access to our boat—our home; the missing tools; our increasing medical problems that could only be alleviated with antibiotics; and the impending visit of the U.S. embassy representative and the police.

I had brought him quite a full plate. Should I leave Hermit with the embassy representative and police to seek hospital treatment for my gangrenous finger? I also needed to check in with the PNG authorities in Lorengau, now that they knew we were in the country. We had visas in our passports but had not yet cleared-in with customs and immigration. Legally, they had to be informed of our disabled situation on Hermit and what we planned to do, especially if we wanted their continued cooperation. Also, we needed supplies if we were ever going to sail *Banshee* away from Hermit.

Decisions and responsibilities—a lot for one elected village councilor on a small, remote island.

I finished my speech and respectfully waited. Paul had had a tough week. Without his able leadership we would not be sitting here having this conversation—we both knew that—and it weighed heavily on him. His first responsibility was to his people, the small band of the extended Hermit family. Then it was to visitors, "our guests," he called them.

"We of Hermit have reputation of saving boats, not destroying them. That *mas* continue. We *halpim* you until you can leave."

He politely addressed all my concerns. Stanley got a little defensive about the glass episode, saying that he had personally investigated, and that it was done inadvertently by a *pikinini* throwing a bottle. A child was blamed. He had been dealt with, *tasol,* and there was nothing more to discuss on the subject. *"Thrown" under a hatch into the engine space? Sabotage, if it had occurred, was an embarrassing concept not to be dealt with in front of "guests."*

I could see Paul's blood boil when the subject of Bob came up.

"Not one of us," he made it clear.

I had been told that Paul, when provoked, had a fierce temper and would never run from a showdown.

"*Sapos* I am there when he *givim* you disrespect, I take him down, right there."
Brave words for a little guy half Bob's size.

He quickly negated the reef damage citation, saying it doesn't apply to a shipwreck.

"Where he *gat pepa?*" He shook his head in disbelief that Bob would do such a thing. "We *mekim* him 'Reef Warden' to *givim samting* to do—so he no bother us. I am very sorry he did that. Please, I take *pepa,* and you owe *nating.* We handle Bob. Stay away from him. I tell him stay away from you."

"The embassy visit, Paul. Do I go back with them in their boat?"

"Yes, absolutely. *Dupela* go, check in with authorities, call your families, and take care of your medical problems. I post guard on your boat. It will be safe until you return."

"What? Leave the boat here alone?" I interrupted, my voice rising. "No way, Paul. That's asking for trouble. We do not leave our boat alone in small places like this."

Stanley and Paul looked at each other as if to say my objection wasn't exactly in the plan.

"Now, Joy, you trust us. We save your boat. We responsible for it."

"Absolutely not. Either I go back with them and Leslie stays here to guard the boat, or we both stay and the police boat leaves without us. I will simply tell the police that I refuse to leave and that Leslie will not go without me. I guarantee that. I trust her completely, and she owns half of *Banshee* anyway. She is perfectly capable of handling anything that may come up."

"Leslie own half the boat?" They both stared at me. "We think she is, you know, crew—your helper. We didn't really believe when she told us."

"She is a full co-owner of *Banshee, tasol.* I go—she stays. Do we agree?"

"Okay, okay," they reluctantly agreed. "But there must be a guard. Two are out there now and they sleep there tonight."

"That's fine, Paul. Now, how will I get back to Hermit from Manus?"

"You can put out *Toksave long* Radio Manus. We come fetch you when you ready. You *mas* pay for petrol; already we *usim planti* from village *stoa* to save your *bot.*"

I agreed that we certainly had to pay for the gasoline and asked them to figure out what we already owed. Stanley was the keeper of the village's stock of precious gasoline. Without it there would be none for the outboards and generators—a serious consequence for the village. Their only protein source was fish with scales. Everything else was on the SDA prohibited list, including the PNG staple, the pig. Everyone, particularly the men, had to fish regularly. Without outboards, they were limited to dugout canoes, and in those they could not venture outside the encircling reef for fear of being swept away to sea. While the night fishing in the lagoon was good for small fish, the larger, meatier ones were to be found outside along the ocean-facing reef wall. For this their speedies with 40 hp outboards were required.

In addition, Stanley had to put aside a very important supply of gasoline for emergency transport off the island. Should anyone need lifesaving medical treatment, the only hospital was at Lorengau, and it usually took twelve hours to get there by open boat. With no paramedics, no 911, and no radio to call for assistance or advice, they were incredibly isolated and alone, a fact of life for so many remote PNG villages.

"Joy, we talk *moa tumora*. We *save* you go *long* police—you prepare *long* trip. Tomorrow is "Games Day" and people volunteer to go clean your boat—they *givim* up games for you. In morning, we talk *moa*. You go now, we *mas* talk *long* others—*em i* wait *autsait.*"

I ambled back down the beach to the fire, feeling the soft sand and lapping waves at my feet. *Banshee* was beautiful outlined in the moonlight. *We've come a long ways but we've got so far to go. I'll have to talk to Les about my leaving and her staying here alone—that's a big one, but not now; tomorrow when she's rested.* I didn't want to end the evening just yet and I savored it as I sat alone in the firelight.

My peaceful solitude was interrupted when Stanley appeared beside me.

"*Hia, bilong* you. You, Leslie, *usim* now—get *moa long* Lorengau."

Puzzled by the plastic container he had thrust into my hand, I started to ask what it was.

He said one word: "*Amox.*"

"Oh my god, Stanley, thank you, thank you. We'll be all right now. I was so worried leaving Leslie—her feet, the cuts…"

"And *pinga bilong* you. From Paul. *Lukim* you *tumora.*"

I sat there speechless. I had just been given a full bottle of the lifesaving antibiotic, Amoxicillin, called *Amox* all over PNG. The standard 500 mg capsules would cure almost any tropical infection.

I hurried to the house and grabbed a cup of drinking water. I peered into the brand new bottle—100 of them, just like it said on the label. Taking out two for each of us, I went in and awakened Les.

"Les, Les, wake up." As she came out of her sleep, I said, "Gold, Leslie. I have gold. Look in my hand—*Amox.*"

"Where did you get it?"

"Shh, quiet. It's from Paul. Here, take two. I've taken mine already. And hide the bottle, Les; they'll steal it for sure. Don't talk about it to anyone, understand? Believe me, this stuff is pure gold here."

She greedily gulped down the two capsules.

"I'll explain tomorrow. Let's go to sleep now. Everything will heal up quick, you'll see. I guess Paul keeps it for serious emergencies."

Amazing he had these antibiotics. It's a long way to the nearest pharmacy.

THE BIG CLEAN-UP

Joy

It was Sunday, "Games Day" on Hermit, the villager's sanctioned outlet. Hotly contested soccer and volleyball games, with both men's and women's teams, went on all day. Men we hadn't seen on the Sabbath Saturday came out of their home seclusion and joined the *meries* and the rest of the village. Decked out in team uniforms, they played and watched with a fierce involvement and concentration. The happy, cheering crowds on the village green, watching and covertly betting on the potential wins of their favorite team, and the laughing and comradery of the day were such a contrast to the serious, somber mood of the previous day's Sabbath; it felt as though everyone had broken out of their shell with reckless abandon.

On this particular Sunday, though, we were amazed that a group of volunteers was willing to forego the first rounds of their beloved games to devote time to *Banshee's* nearly impossible clean-up.

Paul and the all-male volunteer clean-up crew arrived in Paul's speedie, minus the outboard motor. *Banshee* was anchored about fifty yards offshore, but most of that was shallow coral reef. Boats with outboards had to be poled over the fringing reef every time they approached the beach, while an engineless speedie could float in.

The plan was to fill up buckets with well water, set them on top of *Banshee's* cabin, and use siphon hoses to clean the inside of the boat. To facilitate this, they put one of their plastic 55-gallon catchment drums in one of the speedies and used it to cart water from shore.

Leslie, eager to accompany them, was quickly rebuffed by the men.

"Wok bilong man, now. You come *long ol meri afta."*

"Not that shit again," she said quietly to me as we fetched buckets, hoses, and soap.

"You'll never change them, dear, no matter what you do, so just ignore it and be glad they want to help."

The antibiotics had made a dramatic improvement in Leslie's legs and feet, and mine too, although my finger still looked and felt terrible. *Maybe it'll slow down the infection.*

Close to noon, the men returned to the beach, eager to get back to the games. We were given the use of the speedie. Some *meries* volunteered and two young guys, Peter and Danny, were detailed to Leslie's "crew." Paul and the men had made it clear that they had done their part, and the rest of the water hauling, poling, paddling, and cleaning was up to *ol meri*, although Peter and Danny would, if asked, *"upim bakets."*

Leslie

The first job was the water. A contingent of kind-hearted *meries* joined me at the well—*women's work, of course.* Dip down, fill up, pull up and lug out to the speedie, a procedure they knew too well. Peter and Danny waited, male fashion, until they were called to move the speedie. They, of course, handled the poling and paddling. *Such ridiculous regimented division of labor.*

I climbed aboard *Banshee* and lowered myself down the slippery walls and seat benches. My helpers worked at positioning the full buckets on top of the cabin, ready for siphoning.

What the f…? Gooey white powder was everywhere. *Was it corrosion, salt? Wasn't here yesterday.* I stuck my finger in the mess and tasted it.

"Soap! Shit, there's soap powder everywhere," I shouted. "Those damn men didn't clean; they just threw our soap all over everything and tossed in some buckets of water. Those stupid jerks, they wasted our soap and made an even bigger mess."

Hearing me, Natalee and Hedis peered inside and started giggling. Natalee jokingly tried to soothe my anger. "Men, they can't clean, we know that. That's why it's women's work. They'll just make a mess and leave you to pick up after them. They don't know how to dissolve the soap in water first. Little boy *pikinini* don't do laundry, their mothers do."

Hedis chimed in, "You no *ken* worry, Leslie. *Olgeta meri hia halpim* you. *Mipela save* clean-up. *Dupela* boy *stap autsait, wokim* hose. *Ol meri* come *insait na* clean *long* you. No worry, Leslie."

"Okay, okay. Me *save*," I said. I could catch the drift of their Pidgin; Hedis didn't speak a word of English.

For the rest of the afternoon we scrubbed, sprayed, and washed, trying to get rid of the slime and green dye that permeated everything. Then I would brace myself in the all-too-familiar position on the cross timbers of the open floor and pump out the over-flowing bilge, which acted as a catchment for the cleaning water. The soap helped to emulsify the oil, diesel, and sludge. The only problem was that the cleaning water was slightly brackish and full of suspended sand particles. As it dried, a residue of fine-grained dust remained. We learned to live with this brown, gritty powder. It coated everything: the decks, the cabinets, our dishes, our clothes, our nails, skin, and hair.

As the water supply buckets emptied, Natalee and I dispatched the others to get more. We waited patiently, but they had departed for the lure of the games, leaving the speedie beached and alone. It was useless to call after them. They had left, and the din of the crowds made it impossible for anyone to hear us.

Jumping in together, we swam for shore. *It's just Natalee and me now, I guess.*

"I'm sorry, Leslie. Paul asked for volunteers this morning and all of them agreed. It's not very fair of them to leave, but there's not much I can do about it. I'll still help you. Let's use your dinghy, though. It's easier for us *meries*. Paul's speedie is much too heavy to pole out."

Dear sweet Natalee, my friend.

Alone now, the two of us made water-runs. We continued the scrubbing, rinsing, cleaning, and pumping until our arms and legs ached. Natalee, quite a bit taller than I, was particularly helpful at scrubbing out the backs of lockers and high shelves, all beyond my short reach.

"Time to go," we agreed, and in the fading light, we paddled ashore.

"What can I say, Natalee? Thank you so very much; *Banshee's* so much cleaner. I can handle it from now on."

Now I could work on bringing *Banshee* back to life; I was beginning to call her home again. Overwhelmed by tears, I cried all the way back to the beach. *What would I have done without Natalee?*

Joy

"Leslie, they're coming tomorrow—the embassy rep. There was another *Toksave* while you were out on *Banshee*. They should be here tomorrow night. Can you believe it? They say it'll only take them five or six hours from Lorengau."

My words tumbled out as I saw her come ashore in our dinghy. I knew she was tired, but I was so excited—*an American coming here, from the outside world.*

"You've been crying, Leslie, What's wrong?" I asked. Stopping my excited monologue, I looked at her as Natalee departed.

"I'm just happy, that's all. Joy, it's clean now. Well, almost."

"Oh, Les, that's great. Perhaps tomorrow I can go out and look."

"Of course, I want you there. I've missed you. You said there was another *Toksave?*"

"Yes, the police boat is arriving tomorrow night. Les, we've got to talk—this is serious. I'm going to Manus with the police boat and the embassy guy when they leave here. I've got to check in, see the authorities, and do something about this damn finger."

"You're leaving? I'm going to stay here alone?"

Her voice was incredulous. I knew this was going to be hard for her, but I knew, deep down, that she could handle it.

"Someone's got to guard the boat. We can't both leave—we won't have a boat to come back to."

"And Booby—someone's got to look out for him. Oh Joy, I'm scared, but yeah, I've got to do it—there's no other way."

"I've talked it over with Paul and Stanley. They weren't exactly happy about it, but they agreed to come to Lorengau in a speedie and pick me up, as long as we pay for the gasoline. This embassy visit is a big deal. Everyone's talking about it. It has never happened before—no one comes to Hermit. Oh, and Bill just got back. You know—the mechanic? Don't get your hopes up, though."

"When can I talk to him, this Bill guy?"

"Tomorrow, Les. They tell me he's sleeping. I'm sure you'll find him tomorrow, I know you. C'mon dear, clean-up time. Look at you."

Bikpela day tomorrow—we both knew it.

A U.S. Envoy Comes to Hermit

Joy

The long awaited day arrived. The first-ever ceremony of state on Hermit.

Behind the scenes, meetings and preparations had gone on late into the night, and everyone rose to their tasks at sun-up. We, however, were mostly unaware of all the goings-on—an intentional omission.

As the star attractions, we were now "guests" and so were politely excluded from the preparations. Food-sharing was so communal that Lynnah and her special *meries* thought nothing of availing themselves of normally unobtainable goodies from our salvaged stash in the back storeroom. We had no idea that dishes for a lavish feast, featuring tasty exotics from *Banshee's* galley, were being prepared in the many *haus kuk* of the village *meries*.

Confrontations of the past week were glossed over and seemingly forgotten, and everyone was on their best behavior: the *Gavman* was coming. Another *Toksave* informed us that the police boat would leave for Luf at noon. The 22-foot boat, equipped with a Hamilton Jet-Drive, could make the trip in six to seven hours, while a normal island speedie with 40-hp. outboard took about twelve hours, weather and seas permitting.

For Leslie, the search was on for the floorboards that had been *Banshee's* cabin sole. She was eager for me to go out to *Banshee* and have a look, but knew I was only able to balance with one arm—an unsteady condition in a boat that lacked a cabin sole and was still slippery with diesel residue. She found one section of the floorboard in Ben's woodpile ready to go into the evening's fire, and then she created a stir trying to find the other pieces. Her accusations about firewood even upset August, the unflappable policeman. He gruffly pointed them out under the house. They were being used as storage bases for our numerous cans of paint and epoxy.

Then Leslie started trying to find Bill, the mechanic. All morning she pestered Lynnah about her brother Bill, eager to talk to the engine man about our engine. Finally, Lynnah gave in when she spotted Bill next door.

"Em i stap long haus boi. You go *painim,"* she said, dispatching Bently to go with her.

No one had mentioned to Leslie that the *haus boi,* or "men's house," was off-limits to women. However, no women on Hermit dealt with engines. To Leslie, sex-role rules were meaningless; she was interested in engines, so off she went to find Bill.

Leslie

"Em hia, Bill," Bently mumbled as he left me standing alone in front of his uncle.

A thin, round-faced man in his mid-thirties grunted at me between spits of betel nut juice. His sole attire was a pair of ragged shorts that barely hung on his gaunt frame, and a woven "purse" for his *buai.* Bill's bare-chested and unkempt appearance was unusual on Hermit, where covering up with "Christian" clothing seemed to be so important. Bill, obviously, was a devout *bekslaider.*

"Bill, they say you are mechanic. I wait for you long time. My boat out there sank. I need mechanic. I need you to help me with my engine."

Silence.

Deadpan face, chewing and spitting.

Rapid Pidgin between the men.

Deadpan again.

"Bill, when can you come out to my boat? I need your help. Will you help me?"

"They tell me your story. You no have to tell me. Me *save* everything."

The man's icy pomposity and the glares of his buddies were intimidating. Bill considered himself the heir apparent to the traditional chiefdom of Hermit. He didn't have to do anything for his position; he was born to it. Paul, in contrast, was elected to his salaried government position.

"You wait till Ronnie come. I go out *long* men. We fix your engine. I no go *long* you. I go *long* men, not *meri,* you wait, *tasol.* You go now," he said, and dismissed me with a wave of his hand.

Not this stupid meri shit again—I've had enough. Was this guy a real mechanic or not? What a pompous ass.

To calm myself, I focused on my immediate problem of the missing extension bar.

"Look, someone's taken my two-foot extension bar that we need to get the starter off. We've got to find it. Can you ask?"

"You *lusim long* sand like everything."

"No, it was on the veranda with the rest of my tools and now it's gone. I've got the socket, but not the bar. Please help."

"Okay, okay. But I no come out till Ronnie come. We *wok* together *long* men, not you. We decide *sapos* you need extension. Now you go—time *bilong* man *hia*."

Joy

"Please, Les, I want to see the boat with you—just you and me—before all the others come. Okay?"

With her assistance I climbed aboard and sat in the cockpit for the first time since that fatal day exactly one week ago. I was speechless. I grabbed her hand and just held her. We were finally alone together, back in our home.

Getting down below was no easy task. The ladder was gone, torn off by Bob and stashed under the house. The bare cabin benches had an oily slipperiness to them, making footholds difficult. Les eased me down the four-foot drop and again we just sat, alone in our world. *Thank you, dear Leslie, you saved her. You brought her back from the grave. She's definitely your boat now.*

The afternoon dragged on. A short *Toksave* confirmed that the police boat had left Lorengau bound for Hermit. Twilight came, then darkness.

Everyone watched for lights on the horizon. They would be coming in through the reef-strewn eastern entrance. "Ronnie *save* way *long rip, long nait,*" they said.

Shouts came from the beach.

I couldn't see them at first, but, yes, there they were—flashlight beams.

It would take a while before the boat reached the beach. The only way in was through a shallow passage in the fringing reef down by Namo's house at the other end of the bay.

We stood there with people who had become our friends and family as the lights got closer, waiting for our *"wantok,"* the American from the outside world. They didn't need guiding in, I was assured. "Ronnie *save.*"

The police boat's lights searched the beach and then fell on *Banshee*, starkly illuminating her in the black night. The police boat turned and headed toward her.

"No, no, come *long hia*. Come *long nambis—meries hia,*" the crowd yelled. *What were they doing? What the hell is going on?*

"Hey, get off my boat!" I yelled as it pulled alongside *Banshee* and men climbed aboard. *What the hell?*

"Les, look, they're inside. They're poking around inside. What are they doing?"

Someone next to me said, "Police checking property. They think maybe village take boat. People steal things."

"What? You guys saved it. That's my boat. I don't want them in there."

Finally, they moved their boat toward the landing area.

The small police boat came in close and guys took lines ashore to tie her up.

The crowd hushed.

A tall white man rolled up his pants, stepped over the bow, and waded ashore.

The village's generator roared to life and bright fluorescent light flooded the beach landing area.

What a show.

An elderly village man dressed in his best *laplap* stepped out of the crowd and walked toward him, hand extended. *Must be James, Lynnah's father, the traditional chief of Hermit.*

"Apinun (good afternoon)," the white man said as he shook hands. *"Tenkyu,* true."

The *meries* that we were standing with pushed us forward. We probably looked just like one of them, standing there in our own dignified *laplaps* draped over our shorts.

"I'm Mark Prokop, the U.S. Ambassador's representative. Are you two all right?"

The glare of the bright fluorescent light held over us made one feel as if on stage. "Oh, we're fine," we chorused, "and *Banshee's* floating as you can see. It's been quite a week."

"I can imagine," he said with a smile.

We moved with the crowd down the beach. Kero lamps replaced the glaring fluorescent and its noisy generator. I really had no idea where we were going but we just went along, tailing behind the men. Paul was explaining the week's events to Mark. It felt strange, walking behind in the crowd while someone else told "our story" to our own representative. *Doesn't he even want to hear it from us?* We looked at one another and shrugged. *Oh well, Paul's in charge—PNG way, again.* Mark was quite attentive and ignored us like recalcitrant children.

When we reached "our home" at Lynnah's, it was lit up with the fluorescent. We were seated at a long table set up between the veranda and the *haus kuk.* It all seemed so contrived, as this was where we lived every day. Now we were suddenly "guests."

I noticed the policemen were all carrying loaded handguns on their belts, and one had bandoliers of bullets across his chest. A tough-looking, heavy-set white man with a shaved head and big belly hanging over his shorts was clutching a high-powered combat rifle. His scruffy, unshaven appearance, along with numerous tattoos, gave him the look of some macho bad-guy in a B-grade action movie. *What is going on? This is a peaceful little village.*

The white man was introduced as Ronnie Knight. He gave a grunt, then continued speaking in high-speed Pidgin to the attentive men of the village. He seemed to be Australian, but his Pidgin was very natural and local.

Leslie listened avidly to Mark as he spoke of her mother's efforts to get him here. I just sat patiently. *None of this "rescue" stuff, as Mark called it, would have happened if it were up to my family.* Didn't bother me, I was long used to it.

An elaborate dinner of several courses was served. *We'd be quite fat if we ate like this everyday.* Ronnie held his rifle as he ate.

What's a political guy like Mark going to do for us in this situation? I was more interested in finding a diesel mechanic. Eventually, I voiced my concerns about our engine.

The gun-toting white man across the table from me finally spoke to me.

"I'm a diesel mechanic."

"You are? We could sure use your help."

"Bill and I will have a look tomorrow. We brought a fresh battery and a pump. We've been inside—not much in there."

"Well, yes. We pulled everything out to float her. Why go inside? No one was there; we were all on the beach."

No response—he just stared through me. He turned to his friends and continued in Pidgin. Not a bit interested in our female version of rescuing our boat. *A Papua New Guinea white man, all right.*

After the elaborate dinner, Mark asked if we would like to talk with our families— he had a satellite phone. "Your tax dollars at work," he said with a laugh.

What a scene, two bedraggled white women, standing in a light rain under the palms, calling home to mother half a world away.

"Mom? Mom, it's me, Leslie. Oh, Mom, you found us—I knew you would."

She and her mother gabbed just as though they were on the phone together back in the states. *It's wonderful to be loved.*

When it was my turn, I got the usual answering machine. *That's okay. It's nothing new for me.*

"And now, if you will just sign these "Privacy Act" papers, I'll take your pictures— digital camera, of course. And, may I see your passports? You do have them, don't you? I'll need to photo them also—have to document everything, you know. I'll email them to your families with pictures of you two as soon as I get back to Morseby."

Les and I tried to get more personal with him, joking about our salty passports and the U.S. "privacy" papers and how far removed we were from a society that was concerned with such things. However, our rep remained detached and aloof.

He's very quick and professional, but doesn't he want to personally hear our story? We were both still in shell-shock and really could have used a friendly ear. Later, Les went over to the guest house where he was staying, but was told to "see him in the morning," that he was tired and was going to his room.

The policeman with bandoliers across his chest and gun at his hip stood guard over our possessions under the house. *Interesting, all we had for a guard before was August. Now we need an armed officer?*

GOOD-BYE, JOY

Joy

When I awoke I had no idea that today I would be leaving our new-found home on Hermit, leaving *Banshee*, leaving Leslie, journeying to an unknown town on a distant island, and not returning for three lonely weeks.

Surely the visitors will stay more than one night—we have so much to talk about. Leslie must have had the same idea as we sat around drinking our morning coffee before breakfast.

"Uh, Mark," she said quietly, trying to get his attention away from the English-speaking village men he was avidly conversing with. "Can we go somewhere and talk privately for a little while? There are several things that we'd like to discuss with you."

"What? Oh, yes, Leslie. What was it that you wanted?" he asked distractedly. The men stopped their conversation and stared at her, the unexpected silence putting her off.

"Uh. we'd just like to talk with you, that's all—anytime you're free," she said hesitantly.

"What about, Leslie? I'm sure we're all friends here. You can talk in front of these guys, can't you?" he said, nodding to the surrounding men for approval. "They've filled me in on everything that happened. Did a great job, these guys. Real seamen, they are. You were definitely fortunate to have them here."

The male bonding ritual had set in; we had become minor players in the drama.

"It's not important, Mark. Some other time, perhaps. Sorry to bother."

What more was there to say? Looking back on it, both of us were still very much in shock from the sinking. Having someone from our own culture to talk to would have done wonders for us. Emotionally, neither of us was functioning very well. Now I understand why counseling is given at disaster sites.

Ah, breakfast, and it smells heavenly.

"Wow. You two certainly eat well around here. No problem about food, as I can readily see," Mark exclaimed heartily as he sat down to a four-course breakfast complete with scrambled eggs. *Eggs? Where did these come from? I've seen plenty of chickens, but never an egg. And fresh flowers on the table. My, my. And that lovely aroma. Baking? A cake in the oven? Mmm. The usual fare of a piece of smoked fish and left-over boiled tapioca has certainly been upgraded.*

They were really trying to impress the *"waitgavman bilong* Moresby." Carolyn's apt description of all the "put-on" fancy food preparation fit quite well—"acting-white," she kept saying as her *wantoks* laughed. Practically all of it came from our salvaged stores. I didn't mind the sharing, but I really would like to have been asked.

A big golden cake appeared, smeared with jam from *Banshee.*

Big smiles. "A pan-cake," announced Joen, Okip's daughter and the village's temporary schoolteacher.

"Pancake?" Les and I looked at each other, wondering.

"Oh yes," another *meri* chimed in." Leslie *tokim mipela olsem plaua em* mix *pinis.* You *putim wara, tanim tasol. Mipela kukim* 'pan-cake' *long bus-aven.* (Leslie tells us that it's like a prepared flour mix ("mix *pinis"*). You put water in, stir it, that's all. We cook the pancake in bush oven)."

"You used the whole bag of mix in this cake?" we both asked at once.

"*Oh, em nau, isi long wokim. Gudpela? Planti swit* (sweet). You *laikim? Ol meri traim. Em gudpela* true. *Laikim tumas.*"

"Great. Just delicious," I assured the proud women. *I've just never had a cake made with pancake mix, that's all. How inventive. I guess we can forget about having pancakes, though. We figured we had salvaged enough to last for quite a while.*

After stuffing ourselves with unaccustomed amounts of food, we waddled off to find a comfortable place to sit. The *meries* wouldn't think of us doing anything to assist, and it seemed like this was not exactly a work day. *What is the plan?* I wondered. *I still want to talk with Mark, but now he's gone off with the men somewhere.*

"Look, Joy, they're out on *Banshee.*"

"What the hell?" I cried. "This has gone far enough. They just step aboard our boat when they get here, and now there they are again. Doesn't anybody ask permission around here?"

"C'mon. Let's go," Les yelled, as she pulled the dinghy down the sand and into the water.

The police boat was tied alongside. Ronnie, Bill, and Okip's son, Dougie were aboard *Banshee* and some of the other policemen were sitting on their boat. They were all completely engrossed in working on our engine. Bill was below in the engine space, and they'd rigged a direct gravity feed to the engine from one of the diesel jugs.

"Sort of a make-shift day tank," I quietly explained to Les.

Looking right through me, Ronnie asked Les about the starter wiring. She laughed, shook her head and pointed to me.

"Been hers for thirty years—she's the electrician."

Closing my eyes, I visualized *Banshee's* wiring and related it to Bill. He and Ronnie traced out the wires and hooked in the spare battery they had brought. Amazingly, the missing extension bar had been mysteriously "found."

"We've got a spare starter, if you think it'll have a better chance. I can get it," Les volunteered.

The men agreed and dispatched her to fetch it, along with some tools and one of our big five-gallon buckets, leaving me to continue with my verbal wiring diagram. Big Dougie hung around in the cockpit; his hands seemed to grab at anything loose. *Haven't met him before. Strange guy—kind of shifty and hostile. Definitely makes me feel uncomfortable.* I tried to ignore him and kept talking about engines and wires. His voice was aggressive, loud, and intimidating as he tried to order me around, making comments about "stupid *meries*." *Who is this guy?*

Les quickly returned with her prize, the spare starter. Jim, our expensive American mechanic in Palau, had assured us that "it was fixed and good to go" when we stored it away. Although it had been sunk, at least it hadn't been connected to the shorted-out wiring when the engine went down.

"Great, but we'll try the one that's on there first; then, if it doesn't go, we can use the other one," Ronnie directed.

The starter switch became two positive wires touched together—primitive, but effective.

"Ready…Hit it."

Sparks flew, and the sodden engine turned over rapidly, spewing seawater and diesel from every orifice. Then it died.

"Em bagarap."

"Okay, okay. Next one. Where's that extension?"

Bill unbolted the spent starter, and a guy in the police boat tested the spare one with the boat's battery. The reassuring clunk and whirring noise made us all smile.

"Good idea, having a spare," I heard someone say.

"Just had it rebuilt for too much money," I said.

Rapid Pidgin and several "shits" came from the engine space. Bill crawled out with the starter in his hand.

"So, this is your great American mechanic? Can't even get the splines right when he rebuilds a starter?"

"I can't believe it. You mean it doesn't line up?"

"Not in a million years—wrong spline—doesn't even fit your flywheel. You paid a guy to do this?"

"Yeah, too much. Way too much," I said, as my heart sank.

There wasn't much more that could be done; they poured the engine full of oil and instructed us to rotate it twice a day, no matter what. The botched starter job from Palau had such far-reaching consequences. If only we could have gotten the engine running immediately, so many things would have been easier for us in the weeks ahead.

"I can take the starter with me and see if I can find another spline in Lorengau. They're pretty standard types for a Delco like this. I'll take the alternators, too. We'll see what we can do," Ronnie said.

He's truly trying to help even though he was so gruff at first.

"Thanks, Ronnie, and you too, Bill. Guess I'm going with you to Lorengau. I've got to get this finger fixed."

"Yeah, not much more we can do here. We'll be heading back around two o'clock this afternoon. You packed?"

"Today? You're leaving today?"

Les and I both stared at each other. *Now? So soon?* Everything was happening so fast. There was seldom any time to talk, to be together, and now we would be pulled apart, each to go our separate ways on our separate missions. For how long, we had no idea.

Back to the house to plan, to pack, and to say good-bye. How do we say good-bye to each other, after all that has happened here?

"Joy, make a list of things we need. Do we have any paper and pencil?"

"No, try Joen at the schoolhouse. I gave her some before we hit the reef."

Nodding, Leslie went off in search of what are probably some of the most common items in a western household, but definitely not on Hermit. Bush knives, yes; writing equipment, no. Lynnah and I settled down to discuss the finer points of traveling on speedies and staying in guesthouses, PNG style.

The trip to Lorengau, she told me, takes a normal speedie about twelve hours, but the police boat makes it in about five or six, depending on wind and sea. For the guest house in Lorengau, I would need to take a pillow and sheets.

"Sometimes not so clean," she advised. *Mmm, sounds lovely.* "There is the hotel, but '*bikpela* money,' and you no *ken* cook food there. The guesthouse has a community kitchen." Mark, of course, would stay in the hotel, but he was a *gavman* and no doubt it was paid for.

What about the toilet on the boat?

"No problem. You *tokim draiva* you need toilet now. *Em stap. Ol man tanim* round. You *ken* go *long sait*—you 'member *tekim pepa. Manmeri* do *olsem long bot*—PNG way, you see," she said, smiling.

They've got it all figured out, don't they? Guess they have to.

Les returned with the writing valuables. Lynnah also had a shopping list for me:

flour, sugar, yeast, baking powder, rice, tea, cooking oil, etc. No mention of payment, of course—who had *kina*? We had enjoyed her hospitality, and now it was "time *bilong pebek,*" as the PNG expression went.

Les and I put together quite a lengthy list of "necessities" for our continuing survival and comfort. A Chinese two-burner propane gas stove. A good-sized battery, matches, lots of rice (tapioca and I definitely were not friends). A kerosene lantern was high on the list, along with kerosene. A voltmeter to fix anything electrical or test batteries. Some knives. All of ours had developed "feet" and left. And battery acid. I wanted to drain out the contaminated stuff and replace it with fresh. The list went on and on.

Les mumbled something about that old Z-spar underwater epoxy she had used to patch the hull—she wasn't too pleased with it—but I admit I didn't give it more than a passing thought. There was so much else to think about, and truthfully, I was still in shock and not at all emotionally prepared for leaving.

"Joy, did you notice that my Gerber stainless multi-tool is missing from the toolbox? The sheath was hanging near the companionway, and now the sheath's gone too. It was there last time I was out there alone, but since the guys went aboard, it's gone."

I just shook my head resignedly. I had grown too used to occurrences like this. My head was spinning. Les was excited, full of questions, lists, and things to do. For me, the fog was rolling in: *Where am I going? How am I going to handle all this?*

"How long, Joy? The guys say they'll come for you when you send a *Toksave.*"

"A week, maybe a little more. Depends on what they want to do with this finger."

"I'll be okay. I've got a lot to do here. It'll keep me busy."

Tough little Les—never a quitter.

"I'm depending on you, Les. Keep them away from the boat. Remember, it's ours, no matter what they say."

Some activity around the moored police boat caught my attention: people were calling to me.

"I think I've got to go, Les. Where's Mark been? I haven't seen him all day. Sure would have liked to talk with him. He's hardly had anything to do with us."

Grabbing my bag, I gave her a lingering hug—*guess that's allowed under the circumstances.* Mark appeared out of nowhere and stepped aboard.

The engine roared to life. "Got to go, dear. Please, please take care of yourself."

"And *Banshee*, and Booby, right?" she grinned.

"I'm coming, I'm coming," I yelled. They were pulling the boat out into deeper water.

I couldn't look back. My whole life was there on that beach.

OUR SEPARATE WAYS

Leslie

Things were moving too fast. One minute we were talking about Joy leaving and mak-ing hurried lists and the next minute she was vanishing over the horizon.

She's going. She's really leaving. They left so quickly. Ronnie was driving and the little boat was pulling out. Laughing, yelling, waving—*so many people.*

"Here, Leslie," Ronnie shouted as he threw a package ashore. "Have some apples. We don't need them now."

"No, no, give them to Joy, for the trip."

Ronnie had an entire package of our salvaged Handiwipes tied around his head and his wrists. He was tossing them like confetti at a send-off celebration, yelling and waving as the boat sped away.

"Joy, don't forget the underwater epoxy! We've gotta have it. This stuff isn't going to hold. Find some, no matter what." *Shit, did we talk about that? Did we write it on the list?*

I jumped in and swam for the apples and grabbed all our carefully washed Handiwipes as they sank around me. *What's this all about? Why'd he take them? Damn, we just cleaned all of these.*

I watched until the police boat faded into the distance beyond the reef and then turned back to reality: the house, Lynnah, our stuff, and *Banshee* still sitting quietly at anchor. *Up to me now. Want to get back to living aboard where I belong. No way am I going to live in that hut one minute longer than I have to. Going to need a stove so I can at least make a cup of tea. The propane barbeque should work. Just got to clean out the lines with fresh water. There's plenty of gas in the bottles.*

I climbed up on the veranda and told Lynnah my plans.

"*Maski* that, Leslie. You stay *hia* til Joy come *bek*. It no right you go out *long bot*. You *yangpela* woman alone now. Not right you be out *long bot long* no man. Woman no *wok long bot; wok bilong* man *tasol*."

What a load of shit. That's my boat. I've fixed it before and I'm going to do it again. Man's work—crap. Where's she living? Unfortunately, I knew very well the answer to that question.

"Lynnah, that's my boat out there and as soon as I can get things together I'm moving out there. I want to have *Banshee* livable for Joy when she gets back. I'm not waiting, that's all there is to it."

Lynnah looked horrified, sat down in stony silence, and took up her sewing. *Acceptable women's work, of course.*

"Look," I said. trying to be reasonable after my outburst. "I need to be able to cook, and I think I can get the outside barbeque going. The gas bottle is still hooked up."

"You wait, Leslie, you wait. You no *ken usim* gas bottle without man. You no *save*— you *pairap* (blow-up) *bot. Planti paiawud* (firewood) *hia*. You *ken wokim paia, isi*. Maybe Namo *wokim* stove *olrait. Em i save* stove *long* gas bottle. You wait, Leslie."

That controlling, demeaning command of "you wait" became a standard reply (especially from the men) to any of my requests. I just stood there in stolid acceptance every time I heard it.

"Lynnah, I installed that stove, and built the whole propane system, and a lot of other things, too. C'mon, let's go have a cup of tea and I'll explain things to you."

Hand-in-hand we walked to her *haus kuk* for what would become a regular ritual for us. Cups of tea solved so many problems. As time passed, she became my emissary to the church elders—all male, of course. Through her I found a way to communicate what I wanted to do and thus received their tacit approval and protection. She was amazed to find out that I was a single-hander before my partnership with Joy and was used to doing everything by myself—an unthinkable concept in her culture.

"No man, Leslie? No *wan halpim* you?"

"Alone *tasol,* Lynnah."

My tool boxes and propane plumbing parts were piled in total disarray under the house. To find the tiny bronze fittings that I needed to re-configure the system for a single burner, I had to laboriously paw through the collection, making more of a mess. To my horror, when I opened the tool boxes I found them full of diesel oil—the men had poured it in as a preservative. The oil, along with the pervasive sand that I inadvertently added as I searched through the parts, created a gooey mess.

Full of plans for my first project toward my goal of returning to proper boat living, I filled a bucket with everything I could think of needing, and along with a jug of rainwater, grabbed Booby from his daytime hideout and hopped into the dinghy.

"Remember this, Boo-Boo? We're home again," I called to my furry companion as he eagerly jumped aboard *Banshee*. Everything had to be thoroughly sniffed and scented as he roamed through the empty boat trying out each open locker and shelf. *Does he remember? He sure acts like it.*

When I went below, the reality of the sandy, oily mess, made worse by peeling paint dropping from every surface, confronted me again. The bulkheads and overheads all resembled a bad case of leftover sunburn. *More water, more cleaning—it's going to be a long drawn-out process. Depressing and sad, yes, but fixable.*

After a rainwater flush, I used a scuba tank to blow out the hoses to the propane tank. *Now I just need tea, sugar, a cup, water, and my old pot, and I'm ready to turn it on. Then I'll be set.* I hurried ashore for my tea-making paraphernalia, telling myself not to forget some of the closely-guarded matches from Lynnah's stores.

"Leslie, you no go out again. We have tea *hia*. Me *gat paia*. You *stap hia*."

"No, Lynnah. This is important to me. Just let me have a few matches and I'll be fine, you'll see. And I need more buckets of well water. The boat is still very dirty."

"What? *Ol* people *tokim* me *bot* clean now. No true?" she asked.

"Lynnah, they did a good job. It's just that it's going to take so much more cleaning. Remember it's not just a boat, it's my home too."

Kindly, albeit a bit begrudgingly, she doled out the valuable matches while I pulled up more bucketfuls of well water, and then I was off to my great experiment.

It all worked perfectly. I was so proud as I sat there on my own boat again sipping hot, sweet tea in the late afternoon. Booby came to sit next to me, rubbing up against me as if to say, "it's nice to be home."

For the remainder of the afternoon and long after darkness fell, I worked in flickering kerosene lamplight making plans, cleaning, assessing what I would need, and fixing things. *I don't want to leave—I'm home now.*

The sound of Ben's voice from his canoe alongside brought me back to reality.

"Leslie, you come *bek* now. Guards come *long bot*. You no *ken stap hia*. Lynnah *wokim kai long* you. You come. You *slip*. *Tumora* you *ken* come *bek*. *Em i olrait*, Leslie. Lynnah wait *long* you."

"Yes, Ben. You're right. We'll be there, Booby and I."

As we reluctantly departed, I knew it wouldn't be long now. We had a home again.

Joy

As I left, I saw Les standing on the beach, waving. She was yelling something at me, but I couldn't quite make it out. The engines of the powerful "jet drive" started rumbling and kicked into action. It was smooth at first, and then I could feel the g-forces pulling me back. *This is no ordinary 22-foot boat.*

Ronnie was talking to me, but it was hard to hear him above the engine noise. He motioned me to a seat at the stern where there would be less pounding. *Sure glad I brought a cushion. Lynnah had said I would need one.*

Two long seats lined the open boat's sides and several battered 55-gallon diesel drums were wedged between them. A tiny closed cabin covered the bow. Ronnie, in well-stretched swim briefs, perched his heavy, near-naked bulk on the little driver's pedestal behind the wheel.

"This baby gulps a lot of fuel," Ronnie announced in a commanding voice. "We'll have to stop about halfway to refuel the tanks under the seats."

It was sort of like riding a wild horse—a very small boat with a ton of power on a big, open ocean. As we sped through the pass to the open ocean, I watched Luf village recede in the distance. *Strange to be going out to sea without* Banshee's *comforts and safety.*

Mark made a place for himself forward near the cabin. *Still wish I could talk with him. Every time I try he just puts me off with some comment. What's the big problem?*

As we hit the open sea, Ronnie opened up the throttle and the little boat plowed through the waves, throwing high white spumes of water and spray on either side. At the stern, the noise was deafening and the g-forces intense. Standing up to stretch took effort, and with only one useful hand, it became difficult.

Okay, five hours, and we'll be inside the long reef of Manus. I settled down as best I could for the bucking, roaring ride. *Just endure—it's all one step at a time.*

Hours passed. The little boat pounded through the chop. The guys had it easy for toilet necessities; "turn and look out to sea, okay?" But Ronnie never slowed down. Finally, I succumbed to nature's call and was told to just hang over the stern and hold on tight. It was like a salty, high-powered bidet.

I was glad I had remembered to bring my yellow PVC foul weather jacket. With spray flying everywhere, I would have been very, very cold, without it. I was rapidly becoming a sodden, uncomfortable mess.

I caught a whiff of diesel. With each passing wave the pungent, irritating odor was becoming more intense. I looked down at the cockpit floor and saw the oily sheen on the water sloshing over my feet.

My questioning look at Ronnie brought a disgusted look in response.

"Yeah. With all the pounding, one of the drums sprung a leak, but we've got enough to make it. Just watch your step; it's all over the place, and it's damn slippery." *And rapidly getting all over me and my poor finger. Not much I can do.*

Finally, we stopped to refuel. While the boat rolled in the open swells and the guys did their job shifting fuel on the slippery, oily deck, I huddled forward next to the cabin door, sitting near Mark. I was determined to make some kind of personal contact with him. "Have you been with the Foreign Service very long? And where's home?"

Under the circumstances, I guess he couldn't ignore me since his male "pals" were temporarily occupied. I found out that he was from Connecticut and had been a stock-broker before entering the Foreign Service, his last posting being Zimbabwe. *Well, at least we had a talking point now.* I quietly inquired if it would be possible for him to make a sat phone call to my brother, since we had been unsuccessful before.

"Oh, no need for that. You'll be in Lorengau and can handle that yourself. I'm sure there are lots of phones around."

Well, so much for that. Guess I'm on my own now. He seemed happy to tell me all about Africa, but much of PNG was unknown to him as he had only recently arrived. This trip out to locate us, he said, was a good opportunity for him to see the country. He had had a great morning doing all the sights on the island, even going deer hunting with Ronnie. *So that's where he's been—playing tourist and sightseeing on Hermit. So much for us, I see.*

Maron Island, one of the islands in the lagoon, supports a healthy herd of deer brought in long ago by the German former owner of Hermit, back in the days when all of Hermit Atoll was a huge copra and cocoa plantation.

Copra, the husked dried meat of the coconut, was once a profitable cash crop in the islands of the Pacific. Processed, it provided coconut oil to world markets. Now vast commercial plantations of palm oil trees replace the large copra plantations of PNG. However, the groves of coconut trees remain, now self-perpetuating and tangled with undergrowth.

Hermit's herd of red-tailed deer peacefully lives out its existence on the little island surrounded by the lagoon. Left to themselves, with a fresh water spring and jungle forage, they appear to do very well.

Noticing the rack of antlers protruding from the cabin's forward hatch, I now realized what the men had been doing this morning. *Aha—the intended target of the high-powered rifle Ronnie had been clutching was deer, not pirates.* The smell of fresh kill emanating from behind the closed door added to the stench of diesel fuel.

Mark said that he had spent a blissful morning speeding around the lagoon in the police boat with Ronnie, the guys, and Natalee, one of the tour guide girls. They had visited the remains of the old German castle, hiked up to a peak for a panoramic view, and topped it all off with a bit of hunting. Using the boat and the high-powered rifle, they were able sneak up on an unsuspecting member of the deer herd peacefully ambling along the shoreline and "bag" him with a single shot. *I see, two "boys" on the government boat, with fuel paid for by the disaster victim's mother, enjoying their "rescue" mission to the utmost. No wonder I couldn't find him.*

Fueling completed, I retreated back to my oily, wet rear seat and endured the remainder of the pounding part of the ride. It was actually a beautiful day, and it was great to be off that damned island and out to sea.

The afternoon sun finally lowered in the sky and with it the wind and sea, until a glassy calm replaced the pounding waves. For some time we had been able to see the peaks of mountainous Manus as we drew closer. I had assumed we would turn inside the reef surrounding the north coast, but, no, we continued on the outside. The boat slowed and a lookout climbed on top the cabin, searching the waters along the outer reef's edge.

A yell, a rev of the engines, and the chase was on. *What are they after?* Then, I saw them: a beautiful school of marlin leaping playfully out of the sea. *No! Please, no more hunting. Not these beautiful, free animals. C'mon guys, you've all got enough to eat; leave them alone. Run away, beautiful fish.*

Ronnie's fishing line was paid out and the boat circled the pack.

"Go for the big male there. Cut him off from the females and young ones. That's how to do it—he'll try to circle back."

I cringed on the seat near the cabin door while these bloodthirsty men focused on their prey. *If there is a spirit that protects the creatures of the sea, please help them now.*

"Damn. Too bad. We missed them. They're spooked now. See them following the male?"

Flee, beautiful beasts. Escape to live another day, on another reef where the hunters have long gone home.

Homeward bound now, in darkness, the lights of Lorengau town shown ahead.

Soon we were pulling into a dock and the guys made the boat fast to the pilings. I saw trucks, buildings, and lights. "The Knight compound," I was told by a voice in the darkness.

Mark, his voice brusque and matter-of-fact, said, "I'll be going to the hotel, and then tomorrow around noon I'll catch a flight back to Moresby, so I won't be seeing you again. I can now report to your families that you are both okay. I think someone here has made arrangements for you to stay at a guesthouse. It's a lot cheaper than the hotel. Guess they'll give you a ride there. I've got to go now, the car's waiting." He hurriedly leaped up to the wood slat walkway overhanging the berth. *Sort of acts like he's trying to get out of here as fast as possible.*

Crash, thump, yells in the dark. "You okay, Mark? You hurt? There's a loose board there, mate—guess you found it."

"Yeah, right. Don't worry, I'm fine," he said between groans as he extricated his leg from the hole in the walkway, grabbed his bags, and made a hurried exit to the safety of land. That was the last I saw of Mark Prokop, U.S. Embassy representative.

We all climbed out of the little boat, offloading bags and belongings now thoroughly soaked with oily saltwater. At Ronnie's urging, I had brought with me our starter motors, alternators, and our little Honda generator. Ronnie professed to be able to "fix anything," and we were happy for his offer.

I stood there waiting in the darkness, surrounded by my first "semi-civilization" in what seemed an eternity. Tin-roofed ramshackle buildings, fences, and what looked like an open-air workshop faced me as I stood on the shore. Vehicles, wreckage, and heavy equipment in various states of repair littered the area fronting the buildings. Old World War II wreckage, scoured and washed up by the surge, covered the shoreline. The war had left its mark on Lorengau. Many rusty relics, pock-marked with barnacles and coral, rested on their sides along the beach.

Where do I go from here? My safe, secure little world was now turned completely upside down. I've got to be so careful of what I say and do. One misstep, one wrong word, and I could blow the whole thing. These people seem to want to help me, and I certainly need all the help I can get. Endure. Just one day at a time.

Ronnie directed me to a yellow Jeep driven by a one-armed guy.

"That's Job. He'll take you to John Akau's guesthouse now and get you to the hospital in the morning for that finger of yours. Just ring him here when you're ready to be picked up. You got my number?" Ronnie had it covered, but all I wanted now was a bath and a clean bed. *Food would be nice too. I haven't eaten since Hermit and it's getting quite late.*

I had no idea where I was going but was too tired to care. At least it was civilization and I was off Hermit. *Oh, Leslie, you're still out there. Take care, dear.*

Job turned out to be a great guy and seemed to be able to answer all my immediate questions. As we drove down the dark, wide street, I peered out trying to get my bearings. Set back from the street, John Akau's was a two-story affair with a small grocery store in front on its lower level, still open at this late hour. Betel nut sellers, taking advantage of the covered location and its blazing lights, camped on the cement walkway.

We pulled up to a stairway leading to the rooms over the store. This was it—my PNG home for the duration of my stay in Lorengau. I clambered out of the Jeep and Job grabbed my smelly bag. I was so soaked with oily saltwater that I left a dripping trail as I walked.

A woman greeted us inside and introduced herself as Lois, John's daughter. Several guests (both PNG and expats) in the "common room" welcomed me as I was shown around. I joked and apologized for my "smelly, drowned rat" appearance, telling them that after a shower I would definitely be more human. My PVC rain jacket was so filthy that I wore it into the shower with me.

Showered, changed, and with a stiff glass of rum in hand (I never travel without my stash), I sat down on a soft sofa and had my first civilized conversation in months.

"Where did you say you came from?" Jaws dropped and incredulous faces stared. "And the other one, your partner, she's still there?"

"Yeah, right. It's all too true, unfortunately."

And now for another shot of the "Spirit of the Philippines" and some well-earned sleep.

LESLIE ON HERMIT
MOVING BACK ABOARD

Leslie

That first night with Joy gone there was no way I could sleep. I kept waking up and padding out to sit by the shore. *That is my boat sitting calmly out there. People are on it—I can see them, but I'm not "allowed" to go out. Crazy.*

As I sat there, the first rays of dawn finally appeared. Booby sat next to me making passes at the clucking, crowing chickens. *Not much I can do: they have my dinghy out there. Swim maybe?* I settled for yelling at them to come in. I had great plans for the day.

"Leslie, why you yell? Boys come in soon. They come *long* church. You wait. Come *havim* tea. People no *laikim* you yell," Lynnah admonished as she escorted me off the beach. I guess I was becoming a public embarrassment, but I had got myself into a furious state.

Lynnah gave me the routine: because I was a *yangpela* single woman, the church must set rules for me and I would obey

I told Lynnah that I had a boat to fix and wanted to get out there living aboard independently as quickly as possible. My response, of course, brought tears. Why couldn't I just obey and be a *"gudpela* village *meri?"*

The boat guards, my friend Peter and a swaggering, irreverent teen-aged boy by the name of Johnny, finally came ashore, and I pounced on my dinghy. Peter was willing to help me with work on the boat, but he kept evading the issue of assisting me towards living aboard again and especially about cooking my food there.

He muttered, "You *toktok long* Paul."

I began to load possessions that directly influenced my boat-living needs into bags and started dragging them down through the sand to my dinghy. The constant harassment of the village men while I labored in the hot sun, getting the damn sand all over everything again, sapped my energy. *Why are they being so tough on me?*

Lynnah was adamant that I not touch a single one of my salvaged food cans.

"Paul say you *kaikaim* (eat) *hia long mipela*. The church say *meries* with families *wokim kai long* you—they *bringim hia* —*tripela* time *long de* (day). You no cook. You *gat wok*. Church decide, *tasol.*"

I was only to load tools, diving gear, charts, navigation equipment, paint cans, fishing gear, sails, books, small boxes of hardware and parts, and other items directly specified by the church. I was prohibited from loading any food, clothing, cleaned and dried mattresses, bedding, cooking equipment or anything else that would enable me to live aboard.

Madness. Utter madness. Where the hell is Paul?

Again I heard the familiar, "You wait, Leslie."

Eventually, when Paul returned from the morning church service, I vented my frustration on him.

"What's with these rules about what I can take back to my boat? Why are you and the church telling me this? I am not a child; forty-three is old enough to be a grandmother. I'm not a member of your church or your village; I'm not even Christian. I simply want to go live on my boat."

He listened patiently, but I saw him wince when I made the remark about not sharing his beliefs. *What the hell is an independent Jewish woman doing in a place where one's every breath is controlled by this church of his?*

Standing there, sweating in the hot sun, I listened as he authoritatively described the church's position, and therefore his, as its leader. I was a "young" single woman without a man to care for me, and so the church was now in charge of my care. All my living arrangements would be handled by Lynnah and Ben, and I would be ashore by dark and stay in the house. The church *meries* had been instructed to feed me three meals a day and I needed to show up and be appreciative. Did I have an objection? If so I should let him know now and he would call a meeting of the church elders. They, not me, would decide.

"*Tasol, em pinis*. You wait, Leslie."

"No way. Not okay." My objections were numerous and vocal.

"You wait; we talk tomorrow, *afta* church meeting."

This is going to be one helluva long uphill climb.

I spent the rest of the day hauling stuff out to *Banshee* and surreptitiously hiding prohibited items, including food. I felt very sneaky and this only increased my frustration level. *If only Joy were here, this stupidity would never happen; she would put an instant stop to it. One word, one look from her, and they would just slink away. I've seen it happen too many times.*

Many of the items I brought out to the boat were still salty (everything got the "lick test" and not much passed). A routine took shape. I'd make a couple of trips ashore to haul well-water out to *Banshee* and fill containers. Then, after letting the fine sand settle out, I would dunk the various items not passing my test in successive washes and then dry them on deck in the sun.

I resolved to simply ignore the restrictions of the church, placate Lynnah and Ben, make respectful requests to Paul, and basically go about my life as if Hermit had ceased to exist. For my own sanity I had to get out of their constant influence.

I wanted to get as much of our stuff back on the boat as possible, so we would be ready to sail when Joy returned. We had talked about having a crane haul us out at the old Lombrum navy yard on Manus, an idea she was going to investigate. We knew the hull was weakened, but if the winds were light and we could get a tow, maybe we could make it there.

The next day, Booby and I were ready to go at dawn, but we had to wait for the boat guards to come in with my dinghy. *This nonsense is going to end very, very soon—early morning in the tropics is the best time to work.* When I saw Paul pass by on his way from church, I asked if I could borrow the wheelbarrow. My back was killing me with all the lugging. This was one item I was determined to have.

"*Wilka* (wheelbarrow) *bilong* church. You *painim* there. Okay, you *kisim,* but watch it, lock it, and keep *pikinini klia* (clear or away)."

In my zeal to get the wheelbarrow, I made a pest of myself to everyone around the church. However, it was locked. "You wait, Leslie" rang in my head. Figuring I had made my desires well-known, I retreated to *Banshee.*

At about mid-morning, I heard Bento's yells from the shore. *My wheelbarrow—oh, you sweet man.*

The advent of this wonderful carryall simplified my tasks no end. I watched it like a hawk; no *pikinini* were going to harm my new "truck." Of course, the inevitable did happen and I almost flew to the beach, screaming at them, as scared little naked beings scattered away from the *longlong* (crazy) *waitmeri* and her *wilka.*

From early morning to evening, the log seats in front of the *haus boi* next door to Lynnah's were occupied by lounging males who seemed to pass much of their time chewing, spitting, and gossiping while their women labored all day. Pushing my heavy wheelbarrow, it was hard to pass by them without encountering their stares and jeers. A few church men came and went, but the *bekslaider's* group seemed to hang around all day. This was accepted PNG village custom. The men had done their one "job," fishing from their canoes at night, and now nothing more was required of them. The mothers and wives did everything else. The inequity of many young able-bodied men just sitting around doing nothing while I lifted and carried in the hot sun was very discouraging. I had never experienced this kind of male disregard before.

So, I simply asked for help, choosing Bill, Lynnah's brother. Would he help me carry things out of the back storeroom and load them into the wheelbarrow? One motion from him and all his friends followed—PNG men do not do things alone. As I led Bill and his friends into Lynnah's house, I thought—naively—that I had finally secured some help. I just kept handing items from the storeroom to all the smiling male faces, assuming that they were loading my stuff into the wheelbarrow. When I thought I had enough for a load, I cheerfully thanked them all and went out to cart it away. I looked down at the wheelbarrow. It was empty. The men, including Bill, had vanished along with everything I had handed them.

When Lynnah returned to the house, she was aghast.

"What you do? You *brukim ol* rules. You *mekim toktok long ol* man *long haus boi?* You no *ken*. You *askim* come *insait* your bedroom and you alone *hia?* You no *ken*. Then you *givim* your things? Women no *ken*, Leslie. You stupid. You *longlong meri*. Of course they *kisim* things."

"Lynnah, he's your brother."

"Leslie, grown man *bratas* do not stay in *haus bilong sisa* (sister)—*tasol*. They no come *insait, sapos* husband no *hia."*

"Oops."

"Leslie, you no listen. *Tunait*, Ben and Paul *mekim toktok*. Problem *bilong* them now. Men take care of it. *Aidono* (I don't know), maybe August *painim* your stuff again."

I felt really stupid. *I don't want to wait for tonight. I want my things now—they're mine, dammit.* Impulsively, I ran over to Paul's compound, completely forgetting to heed his dogs. As I came yelling into his compound, his dogs ferociously chased out at me, teeth gnashing. I quickly backpedaled and fell over in the process. There I lay, spread-eagled on my back with three or four growling, barking dogs slavering over my face until someone came out and chased them away.

The next morning after church, Paul paid me a visit to settle the impasse of my living situation and to deal with the question of which things I may or may not be allowed to return to the boat. With Lynnah's permission, I invited him in to view my salvaged belongings.

"You take this, this; and this," he said, as he strode into the storeroom, "but not those," he said, as he pointed to the food cans. *"Ol* things *bilong* bedroom stay *hia*. Take nothing in question—*olsem* fishing lures—things you say people take. You *mas* leave those alone so church *ken* 'stock take'."

"But, Paul, they took lots of tools; I can't leave my tools here. How will I work? And there are many things in my bedroom that I'll need for working on the boat. I can't just stop what I'm doing all the time and run back here just because it's not on the allowed list."

He was becoming frustrated by the ridiculousness of the situation. *He's probably never experienced this from a woman.* Eventually he tired of the game and said he had to return to his compound. *And to his much more compliant wife.* From that point on I simply ignored the childish situation and did what I had to do.

By the fourth night I was ready to do a "sleep-over." I had my wok and spatula, plates to eat on, and plenty of canned food. I'd moved the cockpit cushions back aboard, but not the actual foam bunk mattresses, thinking that would be too blatant.

I felt like making a stir-fry with the *aibica* (a spinach-like vegetable) that grew so profusely by Lynnah's *haus kuk* and had even salvaged a bottle of soy sauce. My first night on my own; I felt like a teen-ager again, moving away from home.

Lynnah was tearful, and Ben admonished me about my safety. The church, the rules, what will people think?

I tried explanations. None satisfied. I continued to pick my *aibica*, grabbed some salvaged onions and rice before the family gobbled them up, kissed Lynnah good-bye, got in my dinghy, and left. *I'm leaving "home"—such drama.*

Booby greeted me as I came aboard. "We're home, Boo-Boo. We live here now. I've even got your favorite cat food."

The only downer was my unwanted guards. I set immediate rules for their movement around the boat. "Go up there, on the bow. I'll be in the cockpit. You stay there, and I'll stay here. Yes, I'm sleeping on board," I replied to their questioning. "No, I don't want to sit and talk with you. What? No, you can't come inside if it rains; you may sleep in the cockpit under the roof while it is raining. Of course, you could always just go home anytime you like. I really don't want you here, you know. I'm just fine without you."

They retreated, dumfounded, to the bow. Never in their wildest imaginings would a *meri* speak to a man like that; furthermore, staying out on a boat by herself at night was unthinkable.

The night was uneventful except for a short rain shower, when I had to reinforce my "no men inside" rule again. Did I want any company? Certainly not.

"No, thank you, and good-night."

I wanted to deal with the issue of "the men" in my life, but since it was Friday and preparations for Sabbath Eve were in full swing, I knew full well that I would get nothing out of Paul about the guards until Sunday. I planned to get everything I needed aboard by dusk and hide out on the boat until their Sabbath was over.

Namo still had two of our propane tanks, along with our ruined 3-burner cook stove and oven. I had surveyed the damage to our stove, and there was no way he was going to resurrect it. Patiently, I tried to explain this to him, but he would not budge. I figured what he was after was the untouched propane stored in the two 20 lb. tanks. He had a simple little gas stove, and after cooking over an open fire with Lynnah, I knew why gas was much preferred.

I drove my dinghy down to his beach to fetch the heavy propane tanks. Namo greeted me dressed in his customary *laplap* and bare chest, dripping red *buai* from his mouth.

He would not accept any explanation as to why the stove would never work again—all he needed was *"moa* time and spray lubricants.*" Enough of this nonsense, if I'm ever going to get these tanks back it's now.* I grabbed them and marched them down to my dinghy. *One more day and he'll own them—standard PNG practice.*

By the time I heard the gong announcing the beginning of the Sabbath, I was mentally prepared for my two "on stage" appearances at church. Freshly showered and draped in my *laplap*, I appeared at Lynnah's on time and ready to accompany her to Friday's evening service. She was beaming with pride and relieved that I was being so cooperative.

Everything happened just as scripted and the church elders were pleased, faces were saved, and too many "Happy Sabbaths" for my liking were smilingly said. *Not bad. One down, one more to go. Anything to be alone and have my home back.*

At the appointed hour, my two unwelcome guards approached in their canoe.

"You go home now. I thanked everyone in church—you heard me. Thank you too, but I don't want you here anymore," I said as they came alongside. Johnny jumped aboard and ran forward. I cornered Peter, and he was quite cooperative. It was all relatively painless with him. If I wanted him to leave, he would do so. And so he did. Tasol. *One to go.*

Johnny, however, was impossible. *How do you discuss this difficult subject with an immature teenage brat, overflowing with male hormones, who has decided that it is his god-given duty to care for you?* "Just stay at your end of the boat," ended my side of the conversation. But not so his. Rain provided another venue.

"Me *gat wara* (wet). *Ren* (Rain) *i* come down. Me come *insait?*"

"No. This is my bedroom. Go home!"

"You *laikim pren* (friend)?"

"Aaaah…Get out!"

I had so much to do that I forgot about my unwanted visitor until he reappeared after Sabbath closing. I had done a beautiful repeat performance of publicly thanking everyone at the 9 o'clock service and then scurried off to *Banshee* to work and hide out the remainder of the Sabbath.

Staying down below, I flushed the saltwater out of the engine. Every time I did a flush, more came out. I was religious in my duty, rotating the motor morning and night. I drained the fresh water side and refilled with salvaged coolant to stop the rust, flushed the transmission, washed away the salt grime, and hoped for the best. *We'll never have enough money to buy another engine.*

Occasionally, Bill would stop by on his way to go fishing and help me turn the engine. One time he offered to "check injectors." Not knowing very much then about bleeding injectors, I was elated. "Oh yes, fuel come out *isi long* injectors. Now you *mas putim planti* oil down *ol hul* (all injector holes)." At the time I didn't know of the destructive bending he had done to the high-pressure brass fuel lines, but his advice to pour my oil and diesel mix down the injectors made sense, and it did turn easier.

When Johnny arrived, I just glared at him and pointed to the bow. When he left early the next morning, I noticed that my lovely black coral and turtle shell necklace, along with the matching bracelets, had vanished from the bulkhead shelf. *Only you and me, Johnny, on this boat now. I know where they went. It was only an arms-length reach from the outside.*

My confrontation with Paul and Stanley, at Sunday's "Games Day," was a pushover. They knew they were beat, and after my church appearances, they accepted that I now dwelled exclusively alone on my boat. Johnny would be reprimanded and told not to return to *Banshee.* My jewelry would be returned.

My home was mine again.

Days of cleaning, scrubbing, sorting, and stowing passed. Joy had been gone a week now, and I thought of her often. *Is she okay? Did she contact my family and ease their worries? Did she hear me yell to her about the underwater epoxy? Why haven't we heard from her on a Toksave?*

I tried sleeping on the washed foam mattresses, but they were still salty and wouldn't dry out in the boat. Each morning I'd awaken damp and salty. Lynnah visited several times and just shook her head at the mess I was living in—*and this from a woman who lives in a bush hut.* She agreed with me that the mattresses had to be hauled back ashore and washed thoroughly this time.

Finally, about mid-week, came the promised *Toksave.* "Come and get me."

Gossip flew around the village. Who would go? A free trip "off the rock" was a very big deal, and Joy was buying the gasoline. Joy's agreements with Paul and Stanley for only the two of them to go (less weight, less fuel) were instantly forgotten. The *waitskin merie* was paying and half the village was vying to get aboard the 26-foot speedie. "*Wan gudpela* time *long pebek.*"

When I saw the little speedie leave with both 40 hp Yamahas on the back, loaded to the max with all those people, I hoped they would have glassy, flat seas. It resembled an overfilled teacup. Paul came alongside as they were leaving to collect fuel jugs for Joy to fill. I handed him a sealed note for Joy. As I passed him the jugs, I looked down, saying, "Where, Paul, will you ever put these?"

The day after the speedie left, the wind started shifting, and a swell began to come around the headland and into the bay. The men had anchored us bow-in to the village, tying to an old World War II ship's anchor close to the beach, and carrying out a long stern line to one of our CQR anchors set on an underwater reef. As the waves slapped up under the flat stern, I thought, *I should be taking this on the bow.* Although protected by the reef, the seas could build up since there was quite a bit of fetch out to the reef's edge.

I went to Ben with my concerns and endured the usual questions: "Do you really know how to turn your boat around? Shouldn't we wait for Paul? He knows how. Are you sure?"

"Trust me. I've been doing this for years, but I do need your help."

I also wanted to dump the 300 feet of bow anchor chain into the water to get the weight off the bow deck. There is much less corrosion and loss of galvanizing on steel chain if it is underwater due to the lowered oxygen content in seawater relative to air. Ben and Bento came to help. It took a while with much untangling of lines, but the end result was quite satisfying. *Banshee* now rode normally to the incoming swells, and I felt much more secure. Just for good measure, they helped me set the Danforth as an additional stern anchor, doubling up for safety.

By late Friday, the wind was really whistling across the isthmus, and I was quite glad for that double stern line. As we were very close to shore, there was no wave fetch, but the wind was howling. I felt I still needed to make one further change for safety. When they tied us up to that old beachfront anchor, they did it in standard island fashion with just a line tied directly to it. No chain, no thimble, no chafing gear. It could wear through at any time.

Damn, and it was almost the Sabbath too. Better make arrangements and excuses now for any prohibited working and absence from services. Lynnah was not pleased. I listened to a recitation of "The Rules" and "God will protect you on our special day." After all this was finished, I collected my supplies, picked my *aibica* dinner greens and retreated to the boat. *So nice to have a private home again.*

The Sabbath dawned windy and full of squalls. I donned a diving rig, secured an extra stern line to the old war relic of an anchor and then proceeded to do a bit of underwater mooring maintenance. The surface chop was unpleasant, but underwater it was much better. Every so often I would surface to see people's hats and Sabbath religious tracts flying off into the wind. *Meries* grabbed at their flowing white church dresses in efforts to retain their proper Sabbath dignity; men glared at me. It was really blowing, and I was working on the Sabbath.

Where was Joy? No Toksave—nothing.

Finally one came through on Monday night during the customary evening message hour. There was a fuel crisis in Manus. The fuel tanker had broken down in Lae (the closest PNG mainland city), and Lorengau had no gasoline; the storage tanks were dry. The returning speedie with Joy would be delayed until an alternate supply ship could deliver emergency fuel supplies—maybe a week. She'd notify us with updates. She had to buy two drums as per our agreement: one for the trip and one as payment for all the fuel consumed during the rescue.

The waiting continued, for both of us.

I kept busy and tried to stay out of trouble by rarely visiting shore except to get my evening dinner *aibica*.

Something had to be done, though, about the solar panels. The array was becoming too much of an attractive nuisance. I was happy to charge villager's batteries as I had plenty of power, but the incessant "Me *traim wan long haus*" or just plain "You *givim* me—you *gat planti*," became wearing. With Paul and Stanley gone, the village was settling into minor anarchy and squabbles were developing. Collen did make away with one of the solar panels, as he was the self-proclaimed local *lektrisan*. With Ben's help I retrieved it, but not before I saw crossed wires and sparks fly. *Shit, he could easily short the thing out with his bumbling.*

Ben and I disassembled the array, stored the old and hopefully equalized Trojan "house power" batteries under the veranda, and moved the panels to safety inside their house. Lynnah felt much better, and a property war was probably averted.

As the third Sabbath approached, we heard again from Joy that emergency fuel had finally arrived and that they would be returning on Sunday.

Joy was coming home, and I had a home to offer her.

JOY IN LORENGAU TOWN

Joy

Daylight and unfamiliar noises startled me from a deep, exhausted sleep. *Cars and road noise, people talking, doors shutting, and, oh yes, chickens. Where am I?*

I gradually came out of my stupor and looked around. The expression, "the first day of the rest of my life," came to mind as I mentally surveyed my tiny room. Two single metal beds with sagging springs, a water-stained ceiling, walls of cheap plasterboard, a fan and table lamp, and a knocked-together clothes cupboard shoved in the corner completed the inventory. My filthy clothes and bag littered the floor.

Printed cloth curtains hanging over screened-in louvered windows blocked out the early daylight. Grabbing a robe, I pulled back the curtains to view my new world. *Hmm, pleasant second story view of grass, waving coconut trees, thatched houses, and larger permanent buildings set back from the wide paved street. And a nice cat.* I watched him wash contentedly on a nearby rooftop.

Coffee. Maybe I can snitch some instant from a cupboard. Would anyone care? The common kitchen was furnished with basic utensils, a tiny fridge, a two-burner stovetop and sink and, of course, no soap. The one-stall flush toilet was a great improvement over the early morning beach or the old ladies' pole-and-plank walking. *Is that me in the mirror? Where in hell have I been?*

Priorities for today: local currency—that's kina at the bank; the hospital for the finger; food; the local authorities; families; Ronnie....one thing at a time. Just be careful of what I say. I don't want to tick anyone off...Got a long way to go.

The *haus meri* (cleaning lady) arrived and asked if I had any laundry, frowning at my smelly, oily bag and clothes. The answer was obvious and the price was cheap. I tried to make myself as presentable as possible for my public debut, then phoned Ronnie's house and made arrangements for Job, the driver, to pick me up. I really had no idea of where I was. Soon the yellow Jeep arrived and we were off.

The Australia-New Zealand Bank across from the Lorengau public market had customers in lines out to the street. Job figured about an hour's wait, so we agreed to meet then. My stomach was growling, but again, no *kina*, no food. A single banana since noon yesterday was not much to go on.

The U.S. dollar-to-*kina* exchange rate was quite favorable, *but would my credit card work? Please, no banking system entanglements now,* I thought, as the heavily barred teller's window got closer. Uniformed security guards armed with billy clubs were everywhere, inside and out.

Amazingly, everything worked, and I walked out of the bank with 2,000 *kina*, a princely sum. *Not bad for 500 bucks. What will it buy?* I had to start thinking in *kina*, my new currency.

The hospital was somewhere up a hill and the fee to be seen was 20 *kina*. I sat with the sick, the injured, and the young mothers holding irritable, crying babies. The general ambiance was one of neglect and disorder. An air of poverty and hopelessness hung in the room. One look told me it would be quite a wait.

Eventually the triage sister interviewed me, the lone *waitskin* in the room. "You no *gat dokta?*" By now I had the explanation for my presence in Lorengau down pat. She winced while peering under my makeshift bandage. Would I prefer an M.D. to a Medical Officer? I nodded yes as she filled in my form. More waiting ensued.

The doctor was kind and empathetic to my tale and amazed that I was sitting in front of him to tell it. He cleaned and trimmed as I looked the other way—local anesthesia wasn't even considered. I clenched my teeth as he worked. My injury was minor compared to those stoically borne by others in the waiting room—untreated bush-knife wounds and infected accidental amputations. At least I still had a useable finger, only slightly shortened.

Infection in the tropic heat and humidity and unsanitary living conditions were the biggest barriers to healing among the local population. Their decisive method of dealing with it was to simply cut off whatever was infected. Before I knew it he had me scheduled for the operating room at eight o'clock tomorrow morning for nail removal and amputation of the fingertip.

Whoa, slow down. I knew my thinking was still a bit muddy, but this radical approach threw me. "Can we try antibiotics by injection first, a big dose? I'm staying in a clean place and certainly can be trusted to use sterile wound healing supplies and techniques, now that I can obtain them."

"Well, if you wish, but for most of our patients that is impossible, so we just remove the infected part, sew it up, and send them home."

I assured him that I would behave and that I had some knowledge of what I was doing (my degree in biology, perhaps?). He listened, and I happily accepted some rear-side shots and a course of heavy-duty antibiotics, with admonitions for a follow-up visit in a few days. He added some anti-dysentery worm pills as a consideration due to "where I had been living." *What a charming thought—poor Leslie, she's still there.*

Job collected me once again, and this time suggested that I be left at the Knight's place to meet Valerie, Ronnie's mother. Perhaps then I could organize the rest of my immediate needs.

Fine with me. Great progress. I'm clean. I've got money, a private room, medications and a treated finger—more than I had yesterday. And tonight I may even have clean laundry.

Picking my way through various discarded vehicles, heavy equipment, rusty machinery, and a wrecked boat or two, I followed Job's directions and arrived at the open door of the sprawling, ramshackle house described as "the Knight's." A *haus meri* busied herself in the kitchen, the TV blared, and Ronnie lounged on a sagging sofa. A dog and a couple of cats sniffed at me as I hesitantly entered the dimly-lit enclave.

"Hello, Ronnie, you there?"

After a mumbled acknowledgement and an offer to fetch "Mum," I hung at the doorway and peered inside. The room had a "well-used" appearance of several generations of living, with piled-up reminders of another time long gone. The stale odor of burnt-out cigarettes and empty beer cans permeated the closed-in atmosphere; heavy curtains and shutters defied any sunlight and breeze from entering. *Depressing.*

"Yer mus' be Joy. I've so wanted to meecha'. What'a time yu'v had, luv. C'mon in, c'mon in," said an Australian voice with a country twang.

A tall, thin woman in her late sixties, with a nervous but friendly manner greeted me and offered tea. The TV blared and Ronnie disappeared. I settled on a propped-up old sofa and found space for my tea mug among overflowing ashtrays and empty drink glasses. Rumpled, raggedy pieces of stained carpet littered the painted and cracked cement floor. Two big teen-aged girls of mixed ancestry passed through from rooms in the back, nodding to Val's introductions.

"Me girls. Well, Ronnie's, but they've been w'me since they was lil' babes."

A lighted cigarette balanced between her shaking, arthritic fingers, badly twisted by the disease. We chatted and shared personal accounts about our lives far away from the modern world. She was comfortable to talk with, and I felt I had found an ally.

I learned that "her Ron" had been in the Australian Navy and was stationed here in PNG for many years during his military career. Young Ronnie and his sister were born here and PNG was their life. When Ron mustered out, they didn't want to return to "Oz" (Australia) and so became copra plantation owners in the colonial style when PNG was still a territory of Australia. As the world price of copra dropped, Ron and Val moved into shipping and settled in Lorengau.

Manus, a large isolated island north of the PNG mainland, transports the majority of its supplies and products by ocean freight. Today, Knight Shipping is the primary cargo shipper and supplier for Lorengau and all of Manus. When Ron died, Val continued to run the business, assisted by Ronnie's national wife, Angie.

"Without 'er, there'd be no business at all. Thet Ronnie, always got 'is head in other things. He doesn't give a stuff fer th' biz'ness, neva' has."

When PNG became an independent country in 1975, resident expats and others born in PNG were offered citizenship, a choice Ronnie accepted when he turned eighteen. Val laughed when I asked about her. "Nah, I'll always be'n Aussie. Couldn't do thet. Got family "down south." Me Mum's still goin' strong and in 'er nineties, too."

I was getting rather shaky from hunger and inquired if there might be a sandwich available. She was shocked. "Yer haven't eaten? Ronnie told me there's a *kai bar* (food counter) out at Akau's. No dinna' afta yer got in? Why didn't Ronnie tell me? The house-girl certainly coulda' fixed yer a meal. Yu'v got *kina* now?"

Something edible appeared in front of me and I stopped feeling dizzy. Val was kind and kept muttering about her careless son. When I finally left, I was armed with a pencil-drawn map of town showing shops, government offices, and the two local "supermarkets."

Val heartily recommended the buffet lunch at the Harborside Hotel, where she met "her bunch" each day—only ten *kina* for a full plate. The exchange rate made it about $3. She told me there were evening meals at a hotel near where I was staying, although one did have to make arrangements ahead of time. All I wanted was for someone to put a big plate of meat and potatoes in front of me and let me dig in. I was still suffering from shock and fatigue, and knew I had to eat regularly to get over it.

Map in hand, I thanked her profusely and took off on foot for town. *Tomorrow I'd make a good breakfast, and tonight I'll try a meal at that hotel near Akau's—two normal meals under my belt should improve things a lot.*

I checked out the local public produce market, but it seemed a bit lacking in vegetables that I could recognize. Lots of very wilted and unknown local "greens" littered the stalls and floor mats, but I did find some bananas and one head of cabbage. As I strolled among the stalls, I saw that *buai* and *daka*, the long green seed used in the "chew," seemed to dominate the produce on sale. In back, I noticed everything was stained red with the spit from the disgusting habit.

The two grocery stores, "Best Buys" and "Papindo," were better stocked, but I had been warned—"If you see it today, buy it, 'cause it won't be there tomorrow." Supplies came in from Lae once a week, courtesy of Knight Shipping on the *MV Manus*, but by the end of the week, anything edible or useful had vanished from the shelves.

I wandered around the town, map in hand, checking out the various shops and familiarizing myself with landmarks and buildings. So many of the buildings were either falling down or boarded up. The abandoned ones that still had some importance were securely chained. Graffiti interspersed with the spit stains of red *buai* graced most vacant walls. Lorengau, it appeared, had fallen on hard times; the Australian colonial era seemed but a dim memory reflected in the graceful bay-front park and what was left standing of a few stately old houses.

My backpack full, I began the three-mile trudge to Akau's. The walk in wasn't bad as I was rested and the last part was downhill to the grassy park fronting Lorengau's wide bay. However, going back up the hill laden with heavy bags was a killer.

The nearby hotel was happy to accommodate me and promised a hearty dinner of chops and potatoes at 7 pm. *Time for a drink, a bath, and a change before a civilized dinner.*

Later, as I walked back to Akau's, I reflected that today was certainly an improvement over yesterday. The meal had certainly lived up to expectations, although it appeared that I was their only customer. Aside from pain from the doctor's slight surgery, I was actually beginning to feel a bit more back in control of my own life. *Oh, please take care, dear Leslie.*

On the second day I was up early making lists and plans. The other guests had checked out, and I had the rooms on the upper floor all to myself while I fixed a one-handed breakfast. Lois Akau, an educated, attractive, and friendly woman in her early thirties, came up for a chat. She managed the establishment for her father and lived with her child at the rear of the property. The guesthouse was actually the second story of what used to be their large extended family's home. Nowadays, their small counter grocery occupied the front of the lower floor, and what used to be a restaurant was in back. All that remained now were the remnants of a broken down *kai bar*, old assorted tables and chairs, discarded display counters that had seen better days, and a continually blaring TV set that seemed to be the major attraction. Lois pointed out that there wasn't much tourism left on Manus, or PNG for that matter. "Too many *raskals* and corrupt government officials that just don't care," was her take on the depressing downturn of the country.

I nodded as I listened to her. The water stains from the leaking roof and the threadbare furnishings of the place spoke for themselves. At night I had heard the busy scurrying and scratching of the rat population in the attic overhead. At only K50 (about $12) a night, it was fine by me.

My first mission that day was to check-in with the provincial bureaucracy, and I arrived before many of the offices had opened. I had our salt-soaked passports and ship's papers in possession and I felt ready to answer questions and fill out all the usual forms (I could still grasp a pen and write in a limited fashion). The embassy rep had told me that the officials had been notified of our predicament and were expecting to see me.

The government offices were located on the main road to town, right at the turnoff to the Knight's. *Best looking buildings I've seen yet. One can sure see where the money is spent.*

I wandered among a maze of pigeonholed offices filled with scurrying male officialdom and female clerks who looked right through me as they chatted away at their own conversations. Desks were piled high with stacks of papers; filing cabinets overflowed and thumb-tacked bulletins covered any available wall space. Typewriters and log books adorned sagging desks and counters—a time-warp of bureaucracy seemingly untouched by the computer age.

My repeated queries eventually got me directed to the office of the Provincial Administrator. I stood at the counter, cleared my throat, and attempted to announce my presence. People pushed past me. It was as though I was invisible, a non-entity, a strange *waitskin meri* who had wandered unknowingly into their Pidgin-speaking community.

I stood my ground and became more persistent. A woman at a nearby desk stopped her chewing and chatting and directed her gaze at me, speaking in the Melanesian-accented Australian English of educated nationals.

"Whom do you want to speak to?"

"The Provincial Administrator. I was told to see him."

"You want to see Wep Kanawi?" The room fell silent as all eyes turned to stare at me. "What about, may I ask? He's very busy."

I had come this far and certainly was not to be put-off by an office clerk puffed up by her own self-importance. As we faced off at the counter, I calmly and slowly recited a shortened version of our saga, throwing in the mention of "U.S. Embassy representative" for good measure. Somewhere in the midst of my story she abruptly turned away and motioned to another to announce my presence to the esteemed Mr. Kanawi. *Guess I got her attention*, I thought as I stepped back a few paces.

A thin, vigorous, grey-haired man bounded up to the counter. "It's Joy, isn't it? Come in, come in. You have quite a story to tell, I'm sure."

The Provincial Administrator, Mr. Wep Kanawi himself, stood in front of me, and it appeared I was expected.

Silence and stares emanated from the stony-faced office inhabitants as he ushered me into his large, well-appointed private office. *How nice to be treated with kindness and respect again.*

Wep turned out to be a charming man, well-educated, knowledgeable and helpful. I felt comfortable in his presence as I related our story. And he asked if Leslie was indeed safe back on Hermit, and I assured him that that certainly was true—I never would have left her otherwise.

As I was sitting there, he put through a phone call to Susan Jacobs, our U.S. Ambassador in Port Moresby.

"Yes, Mrs. Jacobs, I can definitely report that one of them is now actually sitting in front of me. And Leslie? Joy says she's safe and well on Hermit. They felt it very important that one of them remain with the boat."

Passing the phone over to me, he indicated that she wished to talk with me. Mrs. Jacobs—"call me Susan, please"—was equally gracious and concerned for our welfare. She assured me that her next phone call would be to Leslie's mother in Florida to pass on my good news. *Guess this whole rescue saga of ours has become sort of a high-profile case here in PNG.*

The routine forms were a breeze, and we joked about my salt-soaked passports and ship's documents. Then he asked how else he could assist during my stay. Noticing the computer terminal on his desk, I asked about Internet access so I could communicate with our families. It appeared one had to be this high up before modern technology was provided.

"Yes, I'm sure our diplomat will be able to help you out. Please come this way." Wep introduced me to an older, well-spoken man, Thomas Polume, a diplomat and former ambassador to several neighboring countries.

An actual government diplomat no less. My goodness, I'm certainly moving in high places—from Hermit to the aristocracy. Besides that, he was a truly nice person. For the next few days, Thomas, a gracious gentleman, became my ally, advisor and confidant. We had wonderful conversations, and his Internet connection and phone were generously provided. He told me his wife was Australian and showed me photos of his beautiful family—all "down south." Originally from a small village on Manus, he been a minister in his local church before joining the government service. Now he was on leave between ambassadorial appointments. *What a treasure I had found.*

My first objective was to compose a long letter to our families giving them a detailed explanation of what had happened to us and what we planned to do. I wanted them to know the facts to stem any misinformation and worry. For this Thomas generously offered a computer terminal and left me alone to work in the quiet of his small, air-conditioned office.

He also wanted to be sure that I spoke to all family members by phone. "A letter is needed, of course, but just a short phone call is very important at a time like this." *With Leslie's family I could agree, but unfortunately, I already could guess my brother's response.* I assured him that Leslie had already spoken to her mother by sat phone on Hermit, but that I couldn't get through David's voice mail at his office. At his urging I tried again, with the same dead-end results. *No complaints. I know the drill.* I would have loved to talk to my mother, but in her nineties she was frail and resided in an assisted living facility. I feared a long-distance phone call might upset and confuse her. My sole link to her was Dave, and that could become rather tenuous at times.

Keeping my thoughts about family dysfunction to myself, I turned my efforts to "the letter." It wasn't easy to write. I tried to cut through all the pent-up emotion and produce something that would not only be factual but would clearly state our plans, feelings and why we wanted to salvage our boat and the lifestyle it provided. When I finally pushed "send", I felt emotionally exhausted.

"More writing and try again tomorrow," Thomas said as I went out into the fresh air. A long walk and then that buffet lunch Val told me about at the Harbourside.

Val was ensconced alone at "her table" and already into her second brandy and water. In my usual open American manner I inquired if I could join her and meet her friends; she had been so friendly the day before. Her reply took me by surprise. "Well, ach'ly no. Waitin' fer me bunch. We always do lunch t'gether ev'ryday. There're plenty of tables."

Rebuffed, I wandered away and found my own seating arrangements. I watched her friends arrive and sit down. *Definitely a closed circle, I see. It's okay to be friendly within the confines of her home, but here, she's onstage—the owner of Knight Shipping holding court. Anyway, the food sure looks great and I'm starved.*

Shopping and searching out information occupied the rest of the afternoon. As I could only buy what I could carry on my return hike, each day's load had to be adjusted to fit.

I had heard that there was a crane across the bay at the Lombrum navy yard. Could they haul out *Banshee?* Les and I had discussed this as a possibility; now I needed an answer. And rumors were beginning to be heard that the town was getting low on gasoline—something about the Shell tanker having broken down in Lae. For first hand information on the fuel situation, I trudged out the dusty dirt road to the Shell tank farm outside of town.

"Yes, stocks are getting low, but the tanker is now under repair, you no *ken* worry. They get petrol to us—they have to. *Nogat* roads *long ol liklik* villages along coast. Only way is by speedies and they've *ol gat* to have petrol for their outboards."

Just the same, I went ahead and paid for two drums of gasoline, plus the oil for the 50:1 outboard mixture. I assured the Shell office that "my guys from Hermit" would bring in their empty drums for filling when they arrived so there wouldn't be any need for a deposit charge on the drums. As I safely tucked away the receipt, I had no idea at the time just how important buying that fuel in advance and having that little verifying slip of paper would become.

The next day, I timed my visit to Thomas' office to coincide with what I thought would be a good time to catch my brother at home and connect with a phone call. LA was six hours later (and a day behind), and I took the kind gentleman's word that a call would be okay. I placed the direct dial number and, of course, got the answering machine. Ignoring the canned message, I spoke right over it hoping someone would hear. It worked, and Christine, Dave's wife, answered. She was surprised to hear from me, but I heard some hesitancy in her voice.

"No…Dave's not here. He…ahh…went to a meeting and won't be in until late."

Not to be put off, I persisted, saying it was early here and we could set a time when I could call again—when she would be sure he would be home. She agreed and we left it at that. For the next three hours I busied myself at the computer answering emails from Leslie's relatives. Their wonderful concern consoled me, and I felt happily adopted into the family.

Financing the salvage of our former lives was my big concern. My damage estimate ran to around $20,000. Quite simply, we didn't have the money. The stock market crash had left us with very little contingency funds. I had my little Social Security pension and had never had a problem finding teaching jobs in the Pacific. I was mobile and happy to go where a job was offered. And Leslie, a PADI dive instructor, was equally willing—give her a job in a warm ocean and she'd happily go at it. We certainly had the ability to repair the boat ourselves and the ability to earn money after our home was restored. But right now, we had a desperate need for immediate funds to carry out our plan. We needed family to believe in us and our abilities, and help us financially.

By my calculations, my brother should be home by now and the time that Christine and I had agreed on had arrived. Thomas was insistent—"Please ring him again. You two need to talk—you're brother and sister." *Right, in normal families, I'm sure. You just don't know this one, and I'm definitely the odd one out.*

Again, the recorded drone of the answering machine, but as I spoke, Christine picked up. "Aah...He's not here yet—just don't know where he could be, must be a very late meeting. But Joy, I did want you to know...Umm...we did tell your mother. We hesitated at first, but when we thought you were really gone, we told her. She's okay. She took it quite well."

"Gone? Chris, we were never 'gone,' not even lost. We were on an island and the EPIRB verified its location. Whatever were you two thinking?"

My question went unanswered as she assured me that Mom now knew we were okay and they had termed it "another of Joy's adventures." But as for Dave..."Well, he's a very busy person and sometimes quite hard to catch. Why don't you just email him?"

"Sure, Chris, like I always do."

I turned my attention back to our strapped financial situation. *I will just write and be honest with them all—where else have I got to turn?*

The result of all this was that within 24 hours, Leslie's family had generously pledged loans in immediate deposits, and my family, via my brother, had turned us down. "Sinking?" he said. "Sort of goes with the territory of living on a boat, doesn't it?" If that was an attempt at humor, it was lost on me.

Oh well, nothing new about that. We had the security of knowing that funds were available, and now all we had to do was to get *Banshee* away from Hermit.

Days passed full of lugging supplies up the hill to the guest house. It was hot in the tropical sun and my back and legs ached from the effort. The midday lunch at the Harbourside broke up the day nicely and kept me going. After the fourth day of having my evening meal at the hotel near the guesthouse, they inquired re my choice for the next day. I requested fish for a change, thinking that this was a seaport town. What a mistake that turned out to be.

During the day of my ill-fated dinner, I ran into one of the waitresses from the hotel's dining room. She appeared to be doing her shopping and showed me a strange-looking river fish she had bought. I thought nothing more about it until it appeared in whole form—skin, head, fins, and all—on my dinner plate that evening. *Yuck*—this was not what I had in mind when I ordered a fish dinner. The smell even put me off, but I did make an effort to eat some of it as I was the lone guest and all the kitchen help seemed so pleased with "their fish." Big mistake.

In the middle of the night it hit me and I barely made it to the restroom in time— one big, bad case of tropical dysentery. Whatever was wrong with that fishy creature continued to haunt me for the next month. The medical people were impressed that my finger was healing so well. Maybe I did know something about self-treatment, and they laughed at my fish story. "Please be more careful. Cleanliness standards in this country are quite limited," they admonished. As my finger was better, I resolved to fix my own evening meal in the communal guesthouse kitchen.

One day, my friend from the provincial government pulled over his car as he passed me on one of my "walkabouts." His sad face told me of two defeats. Alas, his Internet connection, along with all the others at the offices, had been disconnected for lack of payment. "A sad comment on PNG" was his take on the situation. He also said that there was no longer an adequate crane at Lombrum, so hauling *Banshee* out of the water there was out of the question. I thanked him profusely for all his time and effort and wished him well on his new diplomatic mission. A great citizen of his country, whom I never saw again.

Where could we haul-out for repairs?

Ronnie provided the needed advice: Lutheran Shipping in Madang, located 230 nautical miles to the south of Hermit on the north coast of PNG. *Could we do that under sail alone, without an engine, electrics, charts, or autopilot, and with a severely weakened hull?* The thought of our damaged hull haunted me; a boat sunk on a reef can be refloated as we had done, but sinking in mid-ocean would be the end of the story.

I had numerous talks with Ronnie about Madang and its facilities when I visited Val, usually in the mornings at her house ("jist not at lunch, please"). On one of my visits, following behind Ronnie out to his boat pontoon, a familiar-looking knife sheath on the back of his belt grabbed my attention. I moved in for a closer look—it was our missing multi-purpose Gerber tool. *Shit... Same scuffed-up old black sheath.* I bit my tongue. *Don't need the confrontation now. It won't help matters here.*

Our portable generator, one of the alternators, and both starters were under varying stages of repair in Ronnie's shop. At that point, I still had hope that the engine could be started. I had found a place to buy a new battery, battery lugs to replace those destroyed in Hermit's overzealous clean-up, and a gallon of battery acid in hopes of revitalizing our sunken house batteries.

No charts were available for purchase in Lorengau, so I calculated a compass course from Hermit to Madang from Ronnie's chart of the area. A course of 167 degrees magnetic—south-southeast—would put us square into the channel between the high volcano of Karkar Island, just to the north of Madang, and mainland PNG.

Our salvaged Garmin 48 GPS had traveled with me for safekeeping, so I entered Madang's lat/long coordinates into its memory. This would give us a compass course to follow at sea no matter where the currents pushed us. I had obtained a fresh supply of AA batteries and was still amazed that the little GPS was communicating with all the satellites overhead. *Goin' to get us out of Hermit and into Madang,* I thought, every time I turned it on and pointed it skyward.

Almost a week and a half passed, and I felt it was time to put out a *Toksave* to the guys at Hermit. *Time to go "home" to Hermit with all my supplies, new-found info, and a plan—yes…a workable plan to get us off Hermit.*

The staff at Radio Manus was most accommodating and helpful as they explained their *Toksave* procedures. First, my message had to be translated into Pidgin, which they kindly offered to do, and then it would be broadcast on three consecutive evenings. They knew about us, for articles in one of the national newspapers had recently described our plight. One article concluded with saying that we had been "rescued." *"Rescued" indeed—what an interesting choice of words.* I read the article and let it go at that, having too many other things to concern me. Although, from time to time, people would stop me on the street and jokingly tell me that I was called "the wreck lady." *Yes, a lone, tall waitskin meri with her black umbrella for rain or shine, daily lugging heavy bags does stand out in the small town of Lorengau.*

Now to go home. Home to Banshee *and Leslie and Booby. Home to Hermit.*

A FUEL SAGA AND FINALLY COMING "HOME"

Joy

Lois called up to me from the bottom of the stairs, "Some men are here to see you; can they come up?"

Footsteps came up the stairs and Paul and Stanley bounded into the room. Even though I had put out the *Toksave*, I was quite surprised to see the two of them, the links to the rest of my life.

After hugs and greetings, I offered tea, PNG style, with loads of milk and sugar along with bread and butter. I had learned that commercial white bread with great globs of butter was considered a delicacy by villagers. At my urging, they devoured the whole loaf.

I was truly glad to see Paul and Stanley, as I had been feeling quite alone and cut-off. With my Internet source gone, I had no way of contacting friends and family or researching for parts and supplies. Phone calls were insanely expensive, but fortunately, I had warned my email contacts that I could be cut off at any time.

"When did you get in? Who came with you? Where did you sleep last night?" My questions tumbled out. It was as though they were part of my family.

"Me 'n Paul, we sleep *long* speedie so no *wan stilim* (steal) *kagos o* engines. *Mipela* PNG men. *Mipela* sleep anywhere," Stanley replied. *"Mipela* get to Ronnie's dock *tudak* (at dark), so *mipela* send *meries* and others down road *long wantok's* house (Roy Joseph, Okip's brother). *Gat* full load; *planti* people come."

So much for the fuel-conserving, light load of just two people that we agreed on. This is PNG way: all the family comes and it's better when it's free.

According to them, there had been no big dramas on Hermit, and Leslie, the boat and the *puskat* were all just fine. They had a sealed letter from Les, which they politely waited for me to read. I recognized that all the taping was her attempt at confidentiality and smiled inwardly. According to her, there had been many big dramas, but she was coping and finding it best to stay on the boat and keep out of harm's way.

Leslie's requests in her letter were many, and most were impossible in the small town of Lorengau. One item she asked for was a propane stove. Our sunken one was a total loss, but it could be used as a gimbaled base for a two-burner stove. Could I find one? Both men assured me that a cast iron Chinese one was commonly used in PNG and available in town for under K100, but I better be sure that the hose size and adapters would fit our system.

They, too, had heard about the gasoline shortage, but I told them that the people at Shell had reassured me that the tanker was under repair and would be underway "soon"—whatever that meant. I told them that I had paid in full for the two drums of gas the Hermit men required and I had the receipts. That gave them some reassurance. They told me that when gasoline shortages occur here, things can get nasty, with a lot of rock throwing.

I took the opportunity to thank both of the Hermit leaders for what the village had done for us. Now that my finances were in place, I wanted to provide a donation to the village for all that they had done. I pulled out K500 that I had set aside and used the opportunity of being alone with them to present my donation.

"Ah… *Sapos* you *laikim*… u-up to you," Paul stammered as I pushed the ten crisp K50 notes in his hand. That amount of money was a lot to villagers but what they had done was so much to Leslie and me.

"You must take it, Paul—for the village. The Hermit people gave us back our life."

"*Orait,*" he solemnly nodded. "I tell people *long* community meeting. *Em i hamamas long* (praise) you, true. But, I *mas* tell you, please, you no *ken givim* money to men *halpim* you. *Em i wok bilong village. Sapos* you do, *mekim bikpela heve*—people talk and men *paitim* (fight) *long* money. Church council decide what man *wok* and who *havim* pay."

As we had agreed back on Hermit, I also gave them some *kina* so they could buy food for themselves in town. Paul's wife, Hedis, had come along, and she and the other *meries* at Roy's house would take care of the cooking and housekeeping.

All we needed now was fuel.

The trek out the hot, dusty, dirt road to the fuel depot was long, but along the way I located a suitable propane stove and the vital adaptor. Still no sign of fuel, but the fuel depot office verified that my receipts entitled me to two drums "off the top," as they said, meaning I wouldn't have to stand in line behind all the other fuel-starved patrons. I was so glad I had paid in advance before all this fuel shortage panic set in.

By the first of the week, rumors were flying: Lorengau was dry. Speedies with empty fuel tanks were piling up along the shore. People couldn't get back to their villages and had to stay with *wantoks*. The shortage didn't affect most land vehicles as they ran on diesel. But the main village transport was outboard motors, and they were very dead. In the villages, power and lights from gasoline generators vanished and people returned to their kerosene lamps.

By mid-week, lines of people were beginning to form at the fuel service station in town. With their fuel jugs, they sat along the road in groups. Their place in the queue was guarded zealously by *wantoks* sitting in shifts.

Shell made an announcement: The tanker would not be arriving, but the *MV Manus* would unload a limited supply of gasoline in drums on Friday night. The drums would be delivered to the town service station on Saturday morning, but as the service station was SDA owned, pumping would not resume until sunset.

The SDA church had entered my life again.

The queues grew longer, and a fierce demeanor hung over the crowd as they clung to their jugs.

No way was I going to get involved in that melee at the pump; it was no place for a *waitskin meri*. Not even my Hermit guys would go near the place.

"Wantoks i gat planti rocks."

Val, that's who to talk to. Knight Shipping, the MV Manus. *Yeah, she'll know what to do.*

And, she did.

It was Thursday. Discretely, I was to go see the owner of the Shell service station.

"In the shop, at the back there's a stair; office upstairs. Ask fer the owner by name. Tell the shop girl I sent'ya. 'E's got private stock for 'is own use, like we all do. Show 'im yer receipts. E'll make a little on it, but y'want yer fuel, don't cha? 'E can replace 'is stock when the tanker gets 'ea. Just sign o'er those receipts you been hangin' onto. You'll be right. Lemme know."

Getting past the shop girl was my first hurdle—the usual protective stance—but dropping the name Valerie Knight eased things up. Soon I was in front of a very kind and patient national man who listened to my story. He knew Paul and Stanley and the Hermit community (the SDA brotherhood, of course). "Anything I can do to help?"

Mission accomplished.

Now to put the plan in motion. First to Roy Joseph's house. Actually, Roy and his wife, Doreen, a nurse, lived in Goroka in the Highlands. His house in Lorengau was for the use of the extended Hermit family when they had to stay in town getting supplies or traveling through to the mainland. During my stay in Lorengau I had met both of them and liked them instantly: educated, well-spoken charming people. He looked so much like his brother, Okip, it was startling, but the resemblance stopped there, fortunately.

Roy's house was very close to the guesthouse where I was staying. I hesitantly poked my way in, calling out for Paul or Stanley, and was quickly stopped by menacing, yapping dogs. A voice from within called them back and they retreated, cowering under the house as I approached. The building, with its veranda along the front, was a ramshackle old thing standing above the ground on the usual house poles. Broken sidings, holed doors and steps, peeling paint, and a muddy, tire-tracked yard with old planks over the worst of the potholes characterized its exterior. As I got closer, the smell and the flies told the rest of the story.

As I climbed up to the veranda, Paul and Stanley appeared, and then came Hedis and others. I met another brother, Alwin, who had a house on Hermit. We chatted while I swatted at the hordes of flies descending on my feet and legs.

I had a plan to get fuel.

While sitting amongst the extended family and SDA *wantoks,* I explained how things would work. Heads nodded knowingly at the mention of the owner of the shop and service station. They smiled eagerly at the plan—"one up" on the aggressive locals in the lengthy queue in town.

Stanley, along with Paul, would handle my precious receipts, now signed by the shop owner, and Job would drive Ronnie's truck. Quietly, they would arrive at the back of the shop (unbeknownst to the crowds out front) just after sunset on Saturday, before pumping began at the pump, and meet their *wantok,* the owner. My receipts and their empty drum would be exchanged for two drums of 50:1 outboard petrol. Then, they would quickly get the full drums down to Ronnie's compound where they could be hidden and guarded for the night. They loved the sense of drama and intrigue and assured me that it was *"wan gudpela plen."*

I was to be ready to depart at sunrise on Sunday when Job called for me and my *kagos.* If I didn't hear from them further, all was well. "Be ready, *mipela lusim moningtaim tru,*" they insisted.

Believe me; I was ready to go.

Long before daylight, I was packed with bags waiting at the door. I had been warned that the trip could be wet so cardboard boxes for *kagos* were not a good idea. Also, I had been asked to "cover-up" anything that I had bought, including the battery. An oblique reference to the communal culture—one sees, one likes, one asks for and it must be given. Particularly so in our case, as rumblings of *pebek* (payback) were beginning to be heard among some of the more disaffected on Hermit.

All over the Pacific, big zippered reinforced plastic carryall bags, called "rainbow bags" because of their bright striping, are the norm. Mine were colorfully arranged awaiting Job and his truck. *Ready to go to sea, but in a 26-foot open speedboat?*

Soon Job arrived and my *kagos* and I were whisked down to Ronnie's dock. The boat was loaded and ready to go. But no Ronnie. Where was all my repaired gear that he said would be ready? The shop was locked up. No way was I leaving my generator, alternator, tools, bucket and two starter motors sitting in there. Ronnie, I was told, was somewhere sleeping off a big Saturday night.

"Just stop, okay? I'm not going without my stuff and that's it. So let's find someone to open up."

More drama. I sat and waited.

Presently, a sleepy-eyed Francis, Ronnie's mechanic, appeared with a large pair of bolt cutters. One "whack" and I had my generator and engine parts.

"My tools—vise grips and screwdriver—and the good 5-gallon bucket; I need them too. Where are they?"

Francis looked uneasy. *"Aidono. Me tingktingk you go now, okay?"*

We left quickly. Ronnie would not be pleased. That chain was big and expensive; no one wanted to talk about my missing things and with lingering thoughts about our Gerber tool, I didn't either.

The speedie was heavily laden. *So little freeboard left and we're still in the harbor.* Twin Yamaha 40's were mounted on the transom. Two-by-four timbers and a wooden loading palette sat on the inside and supported the two drums of gasoline, securely lashed and sitting upright ready to provide fuel for our voyage. Numerous bags and boxes were secured under a heavy tarp on the palette.

Stanley and Paul were at the stern driving. Hedis sat next to me, also in the rear part of the boat. I knew from experience that aft, away from the pounding of the bow, was the more comfortable position. Men and women whom I didn't know very well made up the rest of the passengers. We were a crowded lot in a very small, over-loaded, open boat heading towards 140 miles of unsheltered ocean. I longed for the security of *Banshee's* comfortable cockpit and cabin.

I know Stanley has a GPS, but what about life jackets? That's a joke. A portable VHF radio? But who would one call? Never in my right mind would I ever consider doing this, but do I have a choice?

We headed over to the beach in front of town where the other speedies, flush with last night's fuel supply, loaded passengers and *kagos.* Passers-by stared at me. I'm sure I stood out: one lone *waitmeri* among a throng of village nationals. We sat in the hot sun and waited while Paul fetched yet another passenger and more *kagos.*

Be calm. Endure. They do this all the time. I just have to trust them.

The hot sun beat down on us as we slowly motored out through calm water inside the long northern barrier reef of Manus Island. The wind we created as we moved along was cooling, but I knew too well the burning, dehydrating effects of the tropical sun's rays. I made a place for myself under a tarp, shading my face and arms, but letting enough cool breezes in to keep the sweat down. The farther we got from land, the more the boat's pounding increased. I settled back for a long ride (about 12 hours, Stanley had said) and I was glad I had remembered my cushion.

Talking was next to impossible over the drone of the engines. We resorted to hand motions when we had to communicate, but mostly we were left to our own thoughts.

White puffy tradewind clouds set in a brilliant blue sky. Dark jungle green along the receding shoreline accented the white foamy spray of waves crashing on the reef.

Rolling swells announced the end of the reef as we headed out into the open sea. Apprehension nagged at me. I had done this so many times in a proper seagoing boat, but not in this…this "dinghy?"

No one seemed a bit concerned. *They've all done this a hundred times in their lifetimes.* I was reminded of the story I had been told of Stanley's wife, another "wreck-lady." Some years ago, she and their young daughter had gone as passengers on a speedie from Hermit. The driver didn't carry a GPS, their compass was off, and they missed Manus altogether. They were adrift at sea for weeks existing on coconuts, rainwater and fish they caught. All survived—these hardy people—and were eventually picked up by an Asian fishing boat somewhere near Tarawa, over a thousand miles away. When Stanley told me the story, his abject worry still showed through his words. He said he went *longlong* and used almost all of the village's gasoline in his futile searches. Unfortunately, this is a far too common story among the people of these tiny islands. So many have been lost this way; no wonder they so value the modern miracle of a portable GPS.

As the day slowly moved on, a flat calm enveloped us. The tropical sun and intense heat beat down mercilessly as we sought shade under the tarps. The steady drone of the engines sang an endless mantra to our thoughts. Sitting near Stanley, my job became that of "navigator." A small compass hung in front of the outboard's tiller, and helmsmen alternated, steering and staring at the compass's swinging numbers as fatigue and rest permitted. To conserve valuable batteries, their little Garmin GPS was only turned on intermittently at the call of the *stia* (helmsman). Under my steaming tarp, I called out the bearing and distance to Hermit. My GPS saw its satellites through my cover as I sat and sweated.

The call of *"Sel-O…Sel-O,"* jostled my thoughts, the Hermit cry for any sighted boat. Peering out, I saw a PNG fishing boat hanging on to an anchored "FAD" (Fish Aggregation Device). Leslie and I had learned from locals (and from personal experience) that these FADS, far out from land, were common in PNG waters. Anchored to the sea bottom by long cables, these large floating steel drums accumulated marine growth, attracting a population of fish, easy prey for commercial fishing boats. They were hazards to navigation, particularly when they became adrift and wandered out to sea.

At first, I wondered why the Hermiters were so elated by this discovery, diverting our course, laughing and calling out to the fishermen aboard. The attraction? Fish, of course! A frozen load of which soon arrived in the bow of our little boat. Wet burlap bags were thrown over the rapidly thawing, fishy-smelling bodies of whole yellowfin tuna, guts still intact. Occasionally, someone dowsed the lot with buckets of sea water as we continued on our way. Now the odor of going-off fish permeated our little sweaty company while a fishy, scaly, run-off washed over our feet.

Didn't bother them a bit. In fact I think they liked it, smell and all.

As we neared Hermit, eyes scanned the horizon. I didn't bother with my customary look-out when nearing land and instead concentrated on giving continual bearing and distance GPS read-outs to the *stia*. At least I felt useful and not like just a passenger. Guided by overhead satellites to the lat/long GPS waypoint at the entrance to the Eastern Pass, they would be led straight into the waters of their familiar lagoon.

Primitive people, traditional ways, modern technology—another PNG contrast.

The familiar green and red markers of the pass materialized and we were propelled inside to the lagoon's calm waters by a rush of small waves breaking on the sides of the pass.

Luf village with Banshee *right there, anchored out in front like nothing had ever happened. I'm coming home.*

As animated Pidgin conversations swirled around me, I sat passively awaiting their next move. Paul and Stanley seemed to be debating a plan of approach. As we neared *Banshee* and I saw Les come on deck, they switched to their English *patois* and addressed me.

"We bring boat *long sait Banshee* and put *kagos antap* so no problems, okay?" We no want people *lukluk kagos bilong* you." They both grinned and I understood when they said, *"Tumas toktok long beksait."*

They wanted me to continue with them on to the beach where the village landing party had gathered, now laughing and shouting at us. *Fine with me,* I thought, understanding their need for a good "face-showing" that they had done their job and brought me back alive and well.

The beach and the crowd came close, and soon we were all jumping out as the men pulled the boat ashore. Smiles, hugs and greetings all around; we were now part of Hermit, it seemed. Lynnah stood alone off from the crowd and caught my eye. *Of course; Lynnah's special—she's family, our family.* And I walked straight to her with outstretched arms.

As I started to make my way with Lynnah toward her house, Stanley pulled me over and quietly said, *"Sapos* you *laikim pis* (fish), you take now, *bipo mipela givim long* village." *Mmm…yellowfin, that's usually good.* But the smell of the fish lying all that time in the hot sun rather put me off. *No matter, I guess,* and soon I was walking down the beach arm in arm with Lynnah and carrying a quite dead fish by the tail.

Les found me on the beach and gave both me and the fish a big hug. She had so much to say, she was just bubbling over.

"Later, dear, we'll have plenty of time after we get back home," I said as I gestured toward *Banshee. That's all I want. Just to go home…away from all these people.*

But I knew that village formalities and the communal culture had to be appeased, so I put on a smiling face for "my family." Lynnah wanted to cook my smelly fish and was insisting that I stay in a proper house—hers, of course—not out on "that boat of Leslie's." Les defused everything by grabbing the fish, and proceeded to have a meal of sashimi right then and there. Lynnah reacted in disgust at the thought of "raw" fish and steered me up onto the veranda where we had a courteous chat, which included, of course, looking forward to the "gifts" I had brought her.

The culture's customs finally served, I grabbed Les and we made a getaway in the dinghy. My fish could end up in someone's pot, I didn't care. I was back from insanity and "home" was right out there in front of me, floating.

Whatever condition Banshee *is in, she's home and that's where I'm going.*

LIFE *BILONG* HERMIT

Joy

The early light of dawn awakened me from a deep sleep—haven't slept like that in a long, long time. A little damp, but it is my bunk, not someone else's. Yeah, guess I haven't been home for a long time. Quietly, I crawled out of bed so as not to wake Les. Coffee…and I'll just go up and watch the sunrise—been waiting for this.

Paint chips were everywhere. It was like white rain. One look in the mirror told me I was covered in white dandruff-like flecks. Les had mentioned something about it last night, but in the dim kerosene light I couldn't really see what she was talking about. Of course…the interior paint was very old enamel and when things dried out so did the paint. Even before the sinking some of it was peeling anyway. Oh well, part of the clean-up. But really, she's done a fantastic job—looks like no more diesel and sand in the cabin. It's actually almost livable. Amazing—she must have worked so hard.

The only cushions inside the boat were those we had slept on in the forepeak. All the bare seat benches were littered with neat little piles of fittings, hardware, and tools—looks like she's been busy sorting. While my coffee water heated on the outside barbeque, I found a spare cockpit cushion and plopped down inside to survey our very changed home. When Les cooked and made tea last night before we went to bed, she had explained that the barbecue was now our stove. She'll be happy that I've found a two-burner stove that we can put on top of the one that sank. The old stove no longer functions, but it will serve as a gimbaled platform for the new one.

With a steaming mug of coffee in hand, I moved outside to where I could watch the sunrise from the bow. When we came in yesterday, I noticed she'd turned Banshee around so we faced bow-out from the village. *Good idea—those incoming swells were getting bad.* Booby followed and sat with me, figuring that I belonged here after I found food for him. The dawn's purple haze gradually gave way to bright fingers of light on the high hills that slowly worked its way down their inclines. I loved this part of the day.

Les came out, made her tea, and sat with me. "I see you've figured out the stove arrangement."

"Not bad, Les. Not bad at all. It seems that damn slippery diesel stuff is gone—what a job you've done. You know, I really feel we're going to make it now."

Last evening when we had come aboard, the daylight was quickly fading. We fumbled around lighting the kero lamp in the dimming light, and we resolved to do this earlier next time. The bugs were bad at that hour. Even though we were anchored a fair distance from shore, the mosquitoes still found their way out to us. Rummaging in my bags, I found mosquito coils, a great prize. Les told me the mosquito problem was really bad, particularly on still nights, and was glad our Larium anti-malaria medication had survived. So many people were coming down with malaria in the village. We needed to find our hatch screens today.

Being together again in our private place, away from the constant communal society, helped both of us immensely. It was now late November—almost a month since the sinking. Not since our time before that awful day had we had any privacy, except for a few stolen moments in Lynnah's back room or on a brief beach walk. How different our two cultures: one demanding and expecting privacy and aloneness, the other abhorring it and needing the constant closeness and approval of the group.

We looked around and made a survey of our floating world. It was still dismal, dirty, broken, and smelly, but so much progress had been made. It gave us hope. Together we went over the changes and how they affected our daily lives.

We had no electric lights. A kerosene lamp provided dim flickering light at night, but its heat, added to the already hot tropical climate at one degree from the equator, made the cabin feel like an oven. And it had to be filled and lit before dark, otherwise there was much fumbling around with precious matches and our rapidly deteriorating flashlights.

I had brought back our Honda portable generator, which was now in a semblance of working order. Somehow our 110-volt Shop-Vac wet-dry vacuum cleaner still functioned perfectly—a great blessing for the clean-up work to come. It was incongruous to be in such primitive circumstances and turn on the generator, plug in the vacuum, and suck up all the grit and grime.

Les had organized a bathing and washing system using our huge blue plastic bin that we formerly used for storage in the quarter berth. It sat on the side deck, and we filled it with water by dinghying bucket loads of water from Lynnah's well. It was a time-consuming, laborious process. We needed so much washing water; the cleaning was endless. To fetch our supply, we paddled the dinghy to the reef, poled it over the shallows to the beach, and lugged buckets of well water back to the little beached boat. It was back-breaking work—twice daily, morning and night.

Left sitting for awhile, the well water would clear as the fine silt settled to the bottom. Reasonably clean wash water could then be scooped from the surface. Every few days, the accumulated silt would be washed overboard. Baths consisted of the standard PNG bucket bath—scoop up, wet down, soap down, and rinse off. Our nails turned brown with the silt, but we were clean. For drinking water we used our rain catchment system off our cockpit overheads.

Rainwater was also available for drinking and food preparation by siphoning from the barrel that collected the run-off from the community center's iron roof. Ben had directed Les to use his family's barrel, a plastic one, and she was admonished not to use anyone else's. She told me that Ben usually helped her carry our 5-gallon water jug, but we had to be very conservative with its use. If it didn't rain frequently fresh water could be scarce, and what they collected had to take care of the whole village. In a pinch, there were springs in the mountains and catchment tanks on the nearby islands, but fetching it was a laborious exercise.

Overshadowing all else was the continual and crucial labor of preserving the engine. We still had hopes of getting it running again. Who knows, perhaps a ship would arrive with a mechanic aboard. Two or three times a day, every day, the engine had to be rotated while a mixture of diesel fuel and oil was poured in the open injector orifices and the oil fill. Then when full, that mixture had to be pumped out and more oil poured in. We sorely missed our ½-inch drive ratchet handle for turning the engine over, and had to make do with our non-ratcheting breaker bar instead.

Spills were common and unavoidable, and wipe-ups took more water and more soap. We tried to soak up the worst of it with our remaining washed-out 3M oil-absorbent pads and emulsified the rest with laundry soap. Ben and others wanted the used oil-diesel flushing mixture to kill the *wait anis* (termites or white ants) around their house posts. Our environmental concerns about this common practice appeared to be lost on the villagers.

The toilet was simplicity itself: a plastic bucket half-filled with seawater and emptied over the side. Unglamorous, but it worked. Before the sinking, we had an electric flush toilet, and I kept a manual replacement in case it malfunctioned. The innards of the manual pump, along with its repair kit, had disappeared.

The fresh 12-volt battery that I brought back from Lorengau now resided on the cabin floor, and we installed a solar panel on the cockpit roof to charge it. A spare Caframo cabin fan had survived in a Ziploc, which we now moved to various brackets still on the ceiling. Each day the sun provided enough battery charging to run the fan day and night.

Leslie had retrieved the companionway ladder and all of the cabin floor boards except two of the smaller ones. The cabin's foam seat cushions were still ashore drying out under the roof of Lynnah's covered woodpile. Ben assured Les that it was his family's firewood stash and no one would ever go under there. Meanwhile, the bare benches inside became sorting tables for all the mixed little bits and pieces returned to us: outboard parts, stove parts, engine parts, fasteners, hardware, and much more. The lot was all stirred together with a liberal dose of sand, salt and silt.

Our main galley sink is a deep one for washing dishes at sea. However, due to *Banshee's* low freeboard, it had an electric pump-out for the wastewater, sending it out through the stern transom. So now we had a sink with no way to drain it, since the pump no longer worked. In our new way of living, it became an inside bucket of well water to be filled, used, and then bailed out and filled again. We washed dishes in the cockpit in buckets of seawater.

We were down to boating simplicity and rather primitive living, but it was living nonetheless, and each day brought progress.

The refrigeration system was a total loss. Its deep, top-loading cabinet first became another washing basin, and then later we turned it into a storage locker for equipment needing repair. Les had retrieved bags of our canned food—now mostly without labels—and had dumped them into what used to be our neatly-organized canned food locker under the starboard seat bench in the cabin. Opening cans became rather mysterious, as we could only guess at the contents. Whatever was opened we ate, as we had no way of preserving it.

For fresh vegetables, Les had been eating *aibica,* a nutritious leafy green of many shapes and sizes that grew prolifically in Lynnah's *haus gaden* (house garden). Nutritious, yes, but unpleasant to handle and eat. The sap of the cut leaves and stems is a white, sticky goo, and when cooked, it has a slimy texture. Occasionally someone would give us snake beans, which are fat, two-foot long things with large hard seeds in the hollow insides. The large sack of dry onions and garlic I had brought back improved the menus considerably.

The locals lived on *tapiok* (cassava) and *saksak* (sago), a prepared starch extracted from the pith of the sago palm. Various varieties of taro and tropical yams were grown plentifully in village gardens, but most of these we found to be too starchy to be easily digested. The PNG staple, the *kaukau* or sweet potato, wasn't grown on Hermit due to some local pest that devoured it. The large sack of rice I brought back sadly did not last for long.

We salvaged a large Ziploc bag of chili powder from the sinking, and it became our method of preserving foods overnight. After a cooked meal we'd sprinkle chili powder on the leftovers, heat them up with the pot lid on, and turn off the fire and let it sit. The combination of chili powder—a preservative—and the heat and trapped steam in the pan seemed to keep the food from going off for a while.

Early in our stay on Hermit, fish and crayfish had been plentiful from the men who came by to sell or trade a bit of their catch. Les told me that they rarely came anymore. We were not friendly tourists any longer. We were refugees and there was a growing unease about our continued presence. Gradually our salvaged supplies dwindled, and our food choices became fewer. We both lost weight and our civilized pudginess vanished.

People began to be concerned that we might be running short of food. Time was passing and it was a legitimate concern. Paul told me that this concern had reached the village council and they had made a decision: at a morning's general meeting, all villagers had been told to assist with seeing that we had food. In Pidgin he had announced the council's edict:

"*Sapos* you *havim dupela pis,* you *givim wan long waitmeries. Em* no *ken kisim pis, ol manmeri long Hermit givim, tasol.* (If you have two fish, you give one to the white women. They cannot catch fish so all men and women of Hermit must give to them, that's all.)"

And so began my morning trips to the beach to stand in line for my fish along with the other *meries*. Lynnah loved having me there and always selected the kind we especially enjoyed.

"The red fish, Lynnah," I told her, selecting a fresh tasty Red Emperor, my favorite.

"*Wan long* smoke, *wan long* cook now. *Gudpela.*" And off she went with my fish to smoke for tomorrow's breakfast. Once she understood that we liked ours done, as she called it, "*long* dry-smoke" (without the coconut milk soak), smoked fish became a great addition to our diet.

In an attempt to assuage community feelings and give something back to the village, I volunteered to be the village medic when Pauleo, the government medical officer, left on vacation to the mainland. I had first aid training and soon the presence of "*dokta meri*" was requested at various medical emergencies.

Infections were a constant problem. Bently was stabbed by a toothy "stick-fish"; the wound became septic and his whole leg swelled up dangerously. Others had similar injuries from bush knives and sports. If leaves, disinfecting bleach, and hot soaks didn't work, and the swelling looked menacing, I resorted to our replenished supply of Amox. Pauleo eventually returned, both he and Paul thanked me, Lynnah was grateful, and life went on.

Banshee now lacked the radio and music that had been so much a part of our lives. We had no books, either. Paperbacks (the sailing cruiser's standard entertainment), reference texts, and magazines had all vanished into pulpy papier-mâché or beachside fires. We had little idea of world news and events. Although many of the villagers listened to small shortwave radios for music and news, the broadcasts we heard were usually in rapid Pidgin and mostly concerned local goings-on in PNG. The passing weeks were marked by the heralding of the Sabbath gong on Friday evenings.

Then there was laundry. I discovered, much to Leslie's chagrin, that she had not gotten rid of all the salt in our salvaged clothes, towels, and bedding. The well-meaning *meries* had been washing it when I left and then Les took over, hanging it on the lines strung between palm trees on the edges of the soccer field. The communal problem again—"I see your shirt and I like it. You have many, so you give me." And the item was gone, later to be seen on someone else's back walking around the village. "Excuse me…ahh, I see you're wearing my shirt," didn't work very well. In fact, tempers became ruffled—a cultural clash. Lynnah explained that asking for the return of things was not done. Les solved the difficulty by simply gathering her belongings and stuffing them safely in *Banshee's* lockers, salty or not.

My daily chore from that point on was a long process of taking bags of the stuff ashore, soaking the clothes in baths of well water, and then keeping an eye on them while watching them dry from Lynnah's veranda.

Our missing possessions became an increasing concern as we sorted through piles of returned bits and pieces. We were grateful for the return of our boat, but a cruising sailboat requires an immense amount of specialized stuff and so much of it was just not there anymore. *What possible use could dwellers in a little island village of primitive thatched houses have for such things?* I'm sure my nagging at Paul frustrated him. Eventually, he and Stanley told me to provide them with a list of missing items after we had taken a careful inventory. *An inventory—how easy to say and how difficult to do with the scrambled mess of our possessions.* We barely had a scrap of paper to write it on. His instructions became even more onerous when he required us to draw pictures of the missing items.

"Many of my people no read. You *mas* draw *piksa* (picture) then they *save wanem kain propeti* (what kind property)."

Nonetheless, we produced the required document and presented it, after handwriting a copy for ourselves. *Once I was a product of the computer age, with terminals, telephones, faxes, and copiers; now I laboriously hand print and illustrate lists on scraps of paper with a broken pencil sharpened by a dull, rusty knife.*

For days nothing came of our list-making. I didn't have to ask Paul. One look at his face told me—he was frustrated. This was a village power struggle and he didn't want to be placed in the middle of it. More days passed, and I stopped looking at him.

Leslie reported that Paul had spread a large tarp near Lynnah's house and that at the regular morning community meeting he had requested that the people of Hermit bring back the *dupela meries'* possessions and deposit them on the tarp. "No *askim nating*" (no questions asked).

Nothing was deposited. The tarp lay bare until it became a point of jokes.

One morning the village gong sounded the emergency signal. All villagers must obey its strident call and report directly to the large, spreading banyan tree in the community's center near the *haus boi*. We watched from *Banshee's* cockpit as people dropped what they were doing and scurried to assemble at the tree. When all had assembled, Paul addressed them as their leader. Out of earshot, all we could do was watch and try to figure out the pantomime going on ashore. It appeared that Paul and several of his men, including August, the policeman, had "rainbow bags" and were gesturing with them. First there was silence and then a lot of loud verbal commotion as the entire village population sat rooted under the tree. "What is going on?" we wondered.

Paul and his chosen men then appeared to fan out to people's houses and enter them, but their owners didn't budge from their seated positions. It was apparent that they had been told not to move and they weren't going to disobey. Whatever was going on was well organized and went according to plan. Within an hour, the party of men with the bags returned to the group and dispersed the inhabitants back to their activities.

We watched as Paul strode down to the water's edge and stared at us in the cockpit. He didn't yell, but one assertive downward wave of his hand told us that we were summoned.

A solemn man amid a crisis faced us on the beach.

"For you I go *behain* backs *bilong* my people. I call *olgeta* and keep them out their houses so no one *ken haitim* (hide) things. I go *long insait* private houses. I open doors and search private things. I *lusim* trust.

"*Hia, painim nating!*" He disgustedly threw down the contents of his rainbow bag: a tee-shirt of ours, a tiny fishing reel minus the line it used to have, a few rusty tools, and a woman's bra (not ours) tumbled out on the sand.

A frustrated, defeated man turned on his heels and walked away, leaving us standing alone on the now deserted beach.

Responding to village pressure and their family's needs to get back to a normal routine, Lynnah and Ben became more insistent that we "*hariap*" and move our possessions out of their house and yard. What we didn't know at the time, and they didn't let on, was that their rather well-appointed house and compound really was not theirs at all but was the village guesthouse, and that was the main reason we had been placed there after the sinking. They had been living in it in comparative luxury for over a year since Lynnah's old family home had fallen down in a storm. Her husband, Ben, an outsider from Madang, knew he had to build a new one, but family and church duties intervened and he never got around to it. Now, a new government schoolteacher was on her way to Hermit, and the village council needed the guesthouse returned to the community. Ben had to build a new house.

The village was having a gathering—a "*bung*" it's called in PNG. Each family would prepare food, and later there would be sports games for all. It sounded like a nice midweek break to us, and we were invited to attend with Lynnah and Ben's family. I used the opportunity to stand up and thank the entire community for saving our boat and home. We both got quite tearful and choked-up during my speech, and afterward many came up and expressed their appreciation at our public show of gratitude. A first for Hermit—"no *waitskin oltaim mekim toktok olsem bipo.*" So much had happened, both good and bad, that I felt I had to say something to them as a community.

My finger had healed quite well and presented no problem to any activity. By now I had grown used to having a slightly shortened version of the original model. The Ninigo people told me I had a *"tamumu" pinga*, their *tok ples* word for a cut-off finger.

Leslie seemed to thrive on all the hard work that everything entailed. She had lost weight (but was happy to see it go), and she could eat anything with a good appetite. For me, our diet was limited and unappealing; I ate because I had to. From time to time, the digestive problems that had attacked me in Lorengau returned with a vengeance. Gradually, I was losing weight and energy due to poor diet and chronic diarrhea. I tried the few medications they had given me at the pharmacy in Lorengau, but nothing seemed to really stop it. Lynnah and her *meri* friends all had their own plant remedies, and I was regularly treated to various leaves and brewed teas. The most effective one was an unpleasant tea of Aloe leaves. It worked for a while, but sometimes I was very glad that the ocean water was within sprinting distance.

After the equalizing "boil-out" and refilling with fresh acid, four of our six heavy-duty Trojan batteries showed signs that they still could hold a charge—at least enough to run some lights and a fan. Namo was happy to have one very dead one for its lead, melting it down for fishing weights, and the remaining marginal one we saved for a spare.

Les had salvaged a few 12-volt electric lamp sockets, bulbs and switches, and with solar panel charging, we hoped to eliminate the unbearable heat and smoke of the dim kero lamp inside the cabin. The modern concept of throwing a switch to chase away the darkness was getting closer.

One of our great finds was a 100-foot spool of sunken but unused 10-gauge Ancor tinned electrical wire. Paul returned it to us, saying "boys *laikim tumas*, please *haitim*." Normally, I would have rejected it as too corroded due to the sinking, but now it was a treasure and just what we needed for wiring the solar panels.

We stacked the salvaged batteries on one of the cockpit seats, linked them to make 12-volts, and began to create our primitive household wiring system, using the solar panels on top of the cockpit roof for charging. The little analog multimeter I had bought in Lorengau told me I had in excess of 12-volts so the system was definitely charging. The old batteries certainly couldn't handle heavy loads, but we had enough for low wattage interior lights and our surviving fan. I worked out a wiring diagram for Les, and she went to work hacking out the old, broken and corroded wires in the battery compartment, salvaging any that looked promising. We loaded the batteries back into their compartment and rewired them to fit our new plan.

One evening I was ashore fetching well water and my dry laundry. I had left Les working on the wiring as the daylight faded at dusk. Someone called out from Lynnah's house.

"Lukluk, light *long selbot. Em i laitimap* (light up).*"*

People stopped along the shore and stared. I could hear their chatter. Electric light was a highly valued commodity. One small light shone from our cockpit. The modern miracle of electricity had returned to us.

Tonight would be different—it would be cool in the cabin.

As early December approached, the weather steadily deteriorated. The intensifying winds shifted from north of west to southwest and were laced with sharp, blinding squalls of intense rain and gusty wind. In our anchorage on the eastern side of Luf, we had protection from the worst of it as long as the wind didn't shift around the south headland of our bay.

Hermit was directly south of Chuuk Atoll in the Caroline Islands. Chuuk was at seven degrees north and Hermit sat at one degree south. That meant that we were only 480 miles away from one of the major typhoon breeding grounds of the Pacific, and, although late in the season, it was still possible for one to track north of us as it developed strength along its path of destruction. If one did form and pass to the north, we would surely feel the effects of its tail of spiraling winds.

In our "cut-off from the world" state at tiny Hermit, without weather broadcasts or even a simple barometer, we could only guess at the source of the nasty weather. But I had lived aboard *Banshee on* Guam, the typhoon capital of the world, enduring many of the worst storms the world has seen (i.e. Super Typhoon Paka in 1996), so my guess was a pretty educated one. Something was going on up north, and it probably was a typhoon.

In our bay, we were still firmly anchored bow and stern, but we were on rope rodes, not chain. This allowed for a lot more swinging and yawing than would happen with an all-chain rode at the bow. Our 300-foot rode of 5/16 inch BBB chain still lay in a pile under water. *Banshee* now faced out from the shore, lying basically head to wind—a sailboat's safest position—when the southerly squalls rolled in. However, when the wind came around the headland, the gusts would catch *Banshee* on the starboard bow, heeling her over on her stretched-tight mooring lines.

So far we had had only a few of these occasions, but they were quite stressful. I had been meaning to talk with Paul about assisting us with reattaching our normal bow chain rode in place of the rope one and moving its anchor away from the reef. The weight of the heavy chain would keep the bow down and provide a much more secure anchor, and one that wouldn't chafe through on the coral.

One afternoon I was ashore on Lynnah's veranda when I saw a dark squall approaching Luf.

Leslie

Inside the boat, I heard shouts from the shore. The mooring lines creaked and groaned and *Banshee* heeled sharply over. Looking out I saw the heavy squall. A wind line with big swells behind it was coming directly for our side. The visibility completely "whited out." I raced on deck, grabbing the laundry and anything else loose on deck. I could see Joy on shore watching in horror. *But what can she do over there? I know where our anchors are, I checked them and they're not going to move.*

Joy

Lynnah insisted that I come up on the veranda to stay dry as she dispatched her kids to carry my dinghy onto higher ground, but I couldn't move. Rollers began crashing on the normally placid sand beach. *Things have to hold—things just have to hold. Les can handle it.* I was transfixed for what seemed to be an hour until it finally blew over. *I've got to find Paul—put our chain out, that's what we need to do—as soon as it's calm again.*

Paul, of course, was not particularly pleased with more problems from his uninvited "guests." He was dubious, but drawing my usual pictures in the sand, I showed him why it was necessary and how to do it. With a speedie, a few strong men, and Leslie diving, we could resurrect the sunken chain, reattach its anchor, and set it in the mud of the deep lagoon, away from the dangerous reef. "When you go *long* Lorengau, we *putim* chain down *long wara*, now you no *laik?* Why you change *tumas,* Joy?" he asked resignedly.

More pictures. More explanations.

"Chain is heavy, Paul. It holds the boat down. We must get away from that reef, it's too close."

"How you *holim* chain *long* boat? No *ken pasim* (tie-up) chain."

"We have a chain-stopper, Paul." I drew a picture of it in the sand.

He seemed fascinated at the idea of such a device. "Yeah? You *gat?*"

I nodded as he smiled…*He'd help now.*

In the calm of early morning, it all went perfectly to plan. Les and I had worked it out beforehand and when the men arrived, we were ready with our instructions.

Without an engine to hold us in mid-water while we exchanged anchors and rodes, we had to carefully change them one at a time. The men reluctantly bent to their task, grumbling that they had just put all that chain down underwater and now we wanted it back up and re-set far out in the deep of the lagoon. The foul mess of shell, coral and little sea critters from the retrieved line littered the deck, and the stench was overpowering. Paul powered out the anchor and chain in his speedie, and Les followed the anchor down to the bottom to set it in the 100-foot depth far ahead of us. Many hands on the "just in case" winch pulled us out and away from the troubling reef to starboard. When the chain appeared on the stem head, I quickly secured it under the heavy bronze chain stopper and ran it home into its locker below. Seeing what we had done, the men finally understood and were impressed. We thanked them as they returned home, and Les, exhausted from her heavy work underwater in those depths, retreated below for a rest while I scrubbed and bucketed off the filthy mess on the decks.

When the winds rose again, we were ready for them. Our re-anchoring maneuver was none too soon. A few days later, we were both aboard when another terrible blast hit us. We stood in the cockpit, watching our lines while *Banshee* yawed and pitched in the violent squall. This time the bow stayed down.

We watched as our home slid back and forth between the reefs that surrounded us. If we had hit one of them and sank again, it was a 50-foot vertical drop to the bottom this time—no way would we be able to raise her again. Without a means of propulsion we were powerless against the storm's fury.

Later Paul told me he had run to his speedie and was preparing to go and assist us when the squall hit. He had his boat partly in the water when the full brunt of the storm appeared to let up. Seeing that we were managing okay and the winds were calming, he pulled his boat back up onshore but continued to stand-by for a while just in case a boat with an engine was needed to keep us off the reef. *How reassuring*, I thought. *He really does care and wants us safe. All his authoritarian demeanor is probably just for show.*

Now that *Banshee* was reasonably habitable, we had to make a decision about the hull. It was our greatest area of concern. The remains of our depth sounder transducer was still trapped in place by the emergency hull repair. The cabinet in which it lay continually seeped seawater. The repair was holding and the bilge pump could easily keep up with the present leakage, but nothing more could be done. The hull was compromised and the solution was yet to be found. It was a constant worry and we discussed so many options: patching from the inside; using the large tides to block up the boat to get at the hull; careening her; collision mats. None were viable choices. We were spinning our wheels. We knew the answer. We had to have new underwater epoxy along with something to give it structural strength to handle the stresses of the rigging and the open ocean.

Who would go this time? Again, I was the obvious choice. The only way we could locate the special epoxy was through the Internet, and that was my area of expertise, not Leslie's. And it had to be Port Moresby this time. In Moresby, I could guarantee phone and Internet connections, research information on epoxy products, get the supplies, and make arrangements for shipping it. Since Moresby is the capital of PNG and the hub of Air Niugini, I could easily catch a flight to Moresby from Lorengau.

"Okay, now we have a plan—how can we make it happen?"

"Sel-O"
Of Boats and Planning

Joy

It was December now, and the ambience had changed. We could feel it. There was a definite chill in the air, and it wasn't the weather. We were stranded refugees dependent on the good will of the villagers, not tourists. The unspoken question was: When will the *dupela meries* go?

We still attended Sabbath services—by village edict, of course—politely nodding at the fixed smiles of the village power structure, shaking hands as we left the church, and mouthing "Happy Sabbath" to those who came near enough. Emerging from the dreary service, we moved as quickly as possible to our dinghy, shedding the hot laplaps that covered our shorts. Back to our little "spaceship" where we were allowed to hide until the gong at sundown. We had long since given up wearing shoes; our feet were now toughened against small rocks and coarse coral sand. Bare feet washed off easier and kept the sand out of Banshee and the dinghy. In church we could bury our bare feet in the sand to keep off the flies.

We still had loads of stuff in Lynnah's back storeroom. Lynnah finally put a small padlock on the door and gave us the key, telling us, "Tumas toktok long beksait. Tumas stilim. No laikim people long my house. You kisim key. You laikim go insait, you go. No wan come now." I could see she was frustrated and we gratefully took the key.

The "thieves" had become so brazen that they just walked inside the house and into the storeroom in broad daylight and grabbed what they pleased. The Kago Kult had finally opened its doors to all, I told Les. She had only heard scattered reference to the fabled story and had trouble understanding some of the villager's behavior and ideas. I tried to fill in the missing gaps of the myth by explaining that its roots went back to World War II, when the primitive peoples of PNG, the Solomons, and Vanuatu were caught up in a conflict on their lands that they had nothing to do with nor knew anything about. The wartime materiel and manufactured goods they saw offloaded from ships and literally dropping from the skies, called "cargos" by the soldiers, were overwhelming to them. With no knowledge of the world's factories beyond their shore-line, or past the borders of their isolated mountain valleys, they reasoned that it all came from a "god" somewhere. The mythical belief flourished for long after the war and its cargos had vanished, covered over by jungle. In its wake, cults came and went. The memory of the cargo remains.

Of course, present day PNG and its neighbors have long since officially debunked such outrageous beliefs, but the Cargo Cult mentality still exists. *Waitskins* have the "Secret." Villagers see it every time a yacht or trading ship rolls in and every time they go to a city and see expats and tourists. But the villagers don't have it. Something doesn't fit, and so the myths still remain. We heard it on Hermit—*"Sapos mipela kisim samting, moa kago bai i* come (If we take some, more cargo will come)."

When *Banshee's* possessions were secured aboard a functioning yacht, that was one thing. But when all that "stuff" was offloaded onto their village beach, well, perhaps "The *Kago*" and its "Secret" had arrived.

Village communal custom prevented Lynnah from accosting the intruders; a lock solved the problem without confrontations. We knew it was bad when Ben put another padlock on the front door whenever they both went to the garden.

It's sad that it's come to this with this kind family.

Our continued presence had become a strain on the tiny village.

The weather cleared, our hull leak worsened, and I wanted to leave. I had to find some better epoxy to secure the hull, and my health wasn't getting any better. As usual, my first line of approach was meeting with the power duo, Paul and Stanley.

"You *laikim* go out again? *Tumas.* No *gat* petrol. You *longlong meri.* Why you no *plen gud bipo?* Why you no *kisim* right epoxy when you go out *long Manus?* Petrol cost *planti money.*"

I was submissive. I was apologetic, and a few days later they spoke to me.

Now the obstacle was Namo. He owned the outboard engines needed for travel, but Stanley controlled the gasoline. I could overcome the fuel problem with money, they knew that, but Namo wanted his speedie repaired and money didn't buy that. However, it was almost beyond fiberglassing. Before our sinking, he had been absent when Leslie had fixed so many of their boats, and had missed out on the repair scene. Now, he felt left out.

Negotiations began again, and he wouldn't budge.

To me, the situation was ludicrous.

"Let me get this straight, Paul. Are you seriously telling me that I can't pay him for the rental of his engines, pay for a driver and expenses, buy the gasoline, and get off this island to save my boat from sinking again?"

Grim-faced and sheepish, Paul nodded.

"So, basically we are prisoners here until Leslie fixes his boat using our fiberglass, our epoxy, and days of Leslie's time. Instead of working on our boat so we can get off this island, she must now go work on his."

Silence. Paul just continued staring at the ground.

"Right," I said, and I got up and walked off. I was fuming, and knew I had to get out of there. *Now I've got to tell Leslie. Good grief.*

For several days we went ashore only for necessary water runs. The turn of events had left us both with uncomfortable feelings. We stewed over our options, analyzing our approaches.

Fiberglass work is very toxic. Under normal conditions Leslie uses a protective vapor mask, goggles, a washable coverall, and disposable gloves. Those sunken supplies weren't very functional any more. Particularly bad were the haz-mat filters for her mask, and she didn't feel comfortable about using them.

"Okay, okay. I know I've got to do it, but I am not doing the grinding or the lay-up. I don't want to breathe the chemicals or handle any more of the stuff than I have to, and my shoulder can't take the strain of grinding—it's just starting to heal from the sinking. I'll do the mixing, because they'll mess it up, but there are lots of strong young men just sitting around here. Get them to help. I'll tell them how and supervise what they do. Try that on them and see if they'll agree."

Back to negotiating.

Our standoff was interrupted by the village warning system—the *pikinini*.

"*Sel-O! Sel-O!*" came the cries. Children scampered about, jumped in their little dugouts and paddled to the headland, or climbed up to their lookouts on the hillsides.

"*Bot—we? Wanem kain?*" I yelled as *pikinini* raced past.

"*Selbot, selbot. Long Maron. Em stap.*"

"I'd better see if I can get over there, I've got to talk to them," I told Les as I got ready to go. *Maybe they'll be able to help us. A sailboat, from the outside! But damn, what's it doing over at* Maron? *Crocs live there.*

My reception ashore, if not frosty, was decidedly cool. Stanley was emptying his speedie from fishing and told me that a small sailboat had anchored at Maron Island last night.

"*Wanpela* man, *tasol. Mipela* no *laikim bot* anchor *long hap* (over there). *Bilong hia long* Luf. *Em* sleep now."

"I want to go over and talk to him. Please, maybe he can help us. People in sailboats usually help each other."

There was a pause, a stare and a grumble. *Not a good sign.*

"You *gat* petrol?"

"Yeah, sure. Me *gat.*"

Hurriedly I paddled back to *Banshee* to fetch a jug of gasoline while Stanley cleared the short trip with Paul.

My spirits were racing as we sped across the blue lagoon to the anchorage. Stanley drove and Bento and a young teen-age boy came along for the ride. Maron, like Luf, was connected to its neighboring island, Akib, by a long, flat isthmus. It once had a village inhabited by another clan in *pastaim,* but it was now the location of several crocodile "fens"—burrows under ledges—homes of the dreaded beasts.

As we sped along, a small sailboat came into view. It felt so strange to see one of our own community anchored peacefully in the bay. *Maybe, just maybe he'll help, or get a message out—anything. I am so tired of this place.*

We yelled, we knocked on the hull, and finally a sleepy head appeared in the companionway. He was a singlehander, an older man from Sweden. It soon became obvious that the fellow wouldn't offer any assistance and wasn't even interested in our plight. *How un-yachtie like.* I remembered my days of helping other boats as we migrated on the "coconut-milk run" across the Pacific. *Have times changed so much that we don't help each other anymore?*

He didn't even seem interested in Stanley's proffering of the Hermit "Boat Book" in which yachtie visitors post squibs and photos of themselves and their boats. Finally, he turned down Stanley's invitation to come over to the village at Luf.

Deflated, we left. They were as puzzled and disappointed as I was. Familiar with friendly people on yachts visiting their island, they couldn't understand why the guy was so reticent. This, plus the fact that he sailed alone, made him even more of an enigma. *"Em i longlong* man, *tasol."*

As I thought more and more about my plan to get off Hermit and find the hull-patching epoxy, I was frustrated by my lack of information. I figured I would have to go to Port Moresby, but I knew nothing about flight connections, accommodations, services, and safety in a place I had never been and had only heard dreadful scare stories about. All I heard from the villagers was, "No *gud* place *bilong waitskin meri."*

Les provided the contact, someone who had been there quietly in the background all along. Daniel, who had been in Leslie's diving skills class, was an older man, more of an academic type than a diver, but obviously educated and well-spoken in English. I had noticed him giving sermons in church and holding Bible study groups along with his wife, Mary.

I really needed someone to talk with, someone from PNG. Les encouraged me and told me that his wife was away visiting family in Moresby.

"She goes there alone?"

"Yeah, sure, so does their daughter. Seems to be no problem for them."

Why hadn't I talked to this guy before? I'm on my way.

Daniel was a quiet-spoken fellow who felt he should stay out of all the politics and controversies surrounding us. He and his wife were the former SDA teaching missionaries on Luf. They were retiring and moving back to their home island of Liot, ten miles off the coast of Ninigo. He was happy to talk with me, but he asked that we keep it private. He told me that all the men on Luf had been his students, and with several of them, their behaviors hadn't changed since they were *pikinini* in his primary school. *Thanks for the insight, dear Daniel.* Talking to him was like conversing with an academic colleague, which he was, except that he was Papua New Guinean.

I often stopped by his large, well-appointed house to chat when I was ashore. Daniel provided me with an outlet and a knowledgeable source of information. He would repeat his favorite advice as we planned things out together: "Remember, your disaster isn't over yet, and won't be for quite a while. You have a long way to go, but you can do it if you keep at it."

Daniel helped me plan my trip from Lorengau to Port Moresby. He described the Air Niugini flight schedules, what I would need to do in Moresby, and how to keep safe in that hostile environment. Where to go, who to see, how to accomplish my tasks, and how to get my *kagos* back to Hermit became our topics of conversation. My managerial abilities were returning and the crisis mentality that had plagued me was diminishing. I was in charge of my own life again.

Les and I went over to Namo's compound to try to end the stand-off concerning his outboards. Much of his area was dominated by his *haus tul* (tool shed), the outside of which was adorned by his two prized 40 hp Yamaha outboard motors and other engines in varying states of repair. Les and I were never allowed inside the shed, and we were admonished if we even got close. *What was in there,* we wondered. Old loading palettes were scattered everywhere and used for working surfaces. There was no *haus kuk*, just a collection of stones near the shore where his wife and girls arranged cooking pots over an open fire. Next to this unkempt area was an immense water tank with iron roofing for rain catchment, complete with a bronze faucet for filling containers. Whether it was his or not we never knew, but he certainly was in charge of it.

Resigned to our task, we explained to him that our supplies were getting short and our fiberglass cloth was salty, but it could be washed out with fresh water. We were so careful with our drinking water supply we hesitated to ask.

"No worries. Me *gat planti.* You *bringim* fiberglass, *meries wasim gud."*

Great, we save every drop and this guy's got water to spare—never offered us any.

Les said that she would mix the resin but wouldn't do the grinding or lay-up. She would supervise and train anyone he designated. And as long as we were negotiating, I made a plea for drinking water. We reached a compromise and shook hands.

Leslie's boat repair project at Namo's place turned into many days of long hard work. She accumulated students and many on-lookers. The highly prized fiberglass speedies have one fatal flaw: when damaged the owners can't repair them. Whether due to overloading with fuel drums or cargo, hitting reefs, or beaching and dragging over a rocky shore, they are not repairable by untrained villagers without professional supplies. The supplies are impossibly expensive and terribly toxic even to trained professionals with protective gear. Old, holed, and damaged boats litter the landscape of small coastal villages.

When they had seen what Leslie could do to bring a dead boat back to life with fiberglass and resin, their appetite was insatiable—there was always one more boat to be repaired.

And there was *pebek* involved. That deeply imbedded custom in PNG culture that demands and requires one to "pay-back" for all gifts, services, improprieties, damages, and slights. Whether it's in cash, in kind, or in services, *pebek* is required and violence is the alternative. As many long-time PNG expats phrase it, "It is never enough, and it never ends."

Leslie was doing our *pebek*.

Yells came from ashore and a boat roared past *Banshee*—*much too close.* I stuck my head out and saw the police jet-boat pulling up on shore. *Ronnie must be here.* I braced myself for another encounter. *Would he help with our engine? Do I still trust him? He says he's a mechanic. Maybe all this daily turning of the damn thing will pay off. Could he get it going?*

I just had to go ashore and talk with him. Every visitor brought some shred of hope, *but how to approach him?*

Noticing that the Lorengau Police chief was with him, I stuffed our list of missing items in my pocket—*in case he asks. Who knows what they're here for?*

The police jet boat was pulled up on the sand next to a ramshackle old house, the home of Lynnah's father, the traditional chief of the village. At high tide the water lapped halfway under the house. When it was built many years ago, the back house posts were on dry land. "Now *wara i* come high up." As coastal people living on a flat low-lying isthmus, they were very concerned with our planet's rising sea level. Underneath, at the still dry front end of the house were all manner of ropes, buoys, and anchors, With sitting headroom only, it was one of several "place *bilong* man" that *meries* did not tread.

I pulled up next to them in my dinghy, smelling the strong odor of diesel as I peered into the familiar government jet-boat. *Hell, there's our 5-gallon bucket, just sitting there plain as day. The same one I took to Lorengau. Sure looks like they're making good use of it.*

On a large log under the old house, Ronnie Knight was holding court. At least twenty of the village men surrounded him, all hanging on every word of his rapid-fire native Pidgin, punctuated by laughter and nods of assent. Teen-aged boys perched within earshot, eagerly listening to the macho goings-on.

As the conversations died down and the men drifted away, I caught Ronnie's eye, and he came out from under the house to talk. *I know better than to go in there.*

I was direct and to the point.

"We've got to have a mechanic, Ronnie. Can you help us get out of here? Or take me to Lorengau so I can fly to Morseby to get some decent epoxy?"

He wouldn't give a direct answer. They were in transit to Vanimo, on the north coast of PNG, looking for "pirates" that had stolen a boat. He didn't know when he would return to Manus. Seeing this was going nowhere, I changed the subject to our missing possessions. *At least that's a police matter.* I produced our annotated list. Surprised by something definite in writing, he motioned to the police chief, the short betel-browed Highlander.

More back and forth in Pidgin ensued between the two men. Then turning, they abruptly terminated my conversation with a gruff. "We talk *long* Paul," dismissing me as Ronnie loped off. *Wait a sec, not so fast there, guy.*

"Hey, what about my bucket in your boat?" I said to the Chief.

A look of surprise colored his scowling features. Women do not address men like that, and to a police chief, my manner was unthinkable. He stammered as I pointed to what was obviously mine in his government boat.

"Ah….*b-baket bilong* you? You…you *ken* prove?"

"Yeah, sure. See that writing on it, in that foreign language? Well, that's Spanish and those are warning labels. In my country, we are required to write warning labels in both English and Spanish, because we have lots of Spanish-speaking people who can't read English. Well, I bought that in my country and I want it back."

As I started fluently reading the Spanish, he stopped sputtering and just stared at me.

"Yeah, there's no Spanish on your stuff that comes from Australia. So please just get your tools out of it, clean it up, and one of us will be back for it later, okay?"

A call came from the beach and I went in to pick up Leslie and our bucket. Of course, the bucket wasn't clean. A young guard sat on the police boat gossiping with Okip, who had arrived to place his large bulk in the center of anything interesting.

Leslie immediately got into a tussle with the young guard, who knew nothing about my exchange with the Chief. Commandeering the long lost bucket, she went to dump the waste diesel in some crab holes—the acceptable "environmental" practice on Hermit as everyone hated coconut crabs.

A crowd gathered as Okip started to make loud accusations that we were drug addicts who were high when we crashed into their reef. Syringes full of *"bikpela* drugs" had been found in our strewn possessions. *Someone had opened our prescription box and pawed through it, taking anything they pleased, and syringes were always very "interesting" to the young males.* The police were here, according to Okip, to look into the matter. Namo had seen the syringes, so I better *tok stret* with him or have one *bikpela heve.* I firmly explained the necessity of carrying prescription drugs, including injectable pain killers, on yachts making ocean passages, which silenced most of the gossip.

"You *gat skrip* (prescription) *long* drug? *We?*"

"Where everything else I had made of paper went. *Pinis.* We sank, remember?"

Like a deflated balloon, Okip and his inflammatory gossip ran out of gas.

Still no closer to finding a way off Hermit, we trudged back to our home before the sand flies came out.

OF SHIPS AND HOPE

Joy

December wore on. The waiting was getting to us. It was obvious that no one from Hermit was going to help me to get off the island. Leslie had finished repairing Namo's boat, but no plans were forthcoming about my trip. *Had all her labors been just a ploy?*

We heard talk about an annual SDA conference being held on Wuvulu, about 130 miles due west of Hermit. A *bikpela* ship was expected from Kavieng, in New Ireland, to take the faithful. They would be stopping at Manus and the surrounding islands with SDA villages to pick up all interested parishioners for the island-style convention. Was the ship coming to Hermit? Answers to my questions were vague and non-committal. My mind was spinning. Daniel told me he would go to the conference if the ship called at Hermit.

"But don't hope too much. Many times big ships like that bypass Hermit because there are more paying passengers on the bigger islands. You had better get aboard if they do stop, because it might be the only ship for a long time."

Okay with me. I'll even endure a weeklong SDA conference in a pandanus hut to get off this tiny strip of land. They've got to return to a port with air links eventually.

I was ready to go at a moment's notice. But *"Sel-O"* never happened. Some days later my friend Bento, the devout SDA from Wuvulu, told me sadly that the *"bikpela white sip"* had been sighted passing to the south of Hermit.

Ronnie had left, to "chase local pirates at Vanimo." *I suppose any reason's as good as another to have a boat trip and a little adventure at government expense.* We were both happy to see him go along with his ineffective sidekick, the Police Chief of Lorengau. Before he left, I inquired of the chief what he was going to do about the list of our missing possessions I had given him.

"Ah…hmm…You *lukim hia. Mipela* no *ken givim proteksan* (protection) *long* you *hia, olsem* no *ken kisim propeti bilong* you. Sorry *tumas. Em pinis.*"

Joen, the temporary schoolteacher, provided a little insight. We'd been chatting under the trees near Daniel's one day while I was doing the laundry. Her English was pretty good and she was easy to talk with, although I did have to be careful, as Okip was her father.

"Joen, please *tok stret* with me. Where are all our things?"

"Oh *hia,* they're all *hia.*"

"Really?"

"Oh yes, you just haven't given *inap* money. You *ken* have your things back, but you *mas pebek.* You *save,* Joy, the custom."

I reminded her of the K500 donation I had made to the village through Paul back in Lorengau. I knew that he had announced our donation at a village meeting and everyone seemed to be suitably impressed. That was a big sum to villagers who could barely hope to earn a *kina* a day, if that.

"No, Joy you no *save* these boys. That money was for village. They want money for themselves. Money they can buy things with."

"Yeah, right. Money for smoke and things that come in on ships."

She nodded, silently.

Our begging Paul or Stanley to get me off Hermit was also futile. They did agree that I was getting rather thin and weak-looking. I told them I needed to see a *Dokta.* They joked with me about it and told me to see a certain *meri.* "*Ol* people *hia* go *long dispela meri.*"

Been there, done the leaves. Nothing.

Once more, the cries of *"Sel-O, Sel-O"* came from the *pikinini* as they paddled around us in their little child-size dugouts. Over by Paul's landing place near Natalee's, an overloaded speedie was pulling up to shore. I joined the crowd on the beach.

It was from Ninigo: a good-sized speedie with one 40 hp on the stern and a spare one tarped down amidships. They had just done the 50-mile crossing and would sleep here tonight, then leave tomorrow afternoon for Lorengau.

"*Mipela gat* place *long wan moa.* You pay?" they replied when I asked if they could take me.

"But it's the Sabbath tomorrow, and…" Big betel nut-stained mouths opened to interrupt me and laugh. "*Mipela* no SDA, *mipela Katolik* (Catholic). No worries, Mama (PNG term of respect)."

The speedie's owner, Daniel Kapis, the President of the Ninigo-Herm Community

Association, approached. I had met him before, definitely a *bikman* in these parts. The noise quieted as he addressed me. Yes, he could take me, but the final decision was up to Paul as there was only one more seat.

However, if I could provide him with a complete list of all the supplies and equipment needed to repair speedies, along with instructions, he would be more inclined to take me. It appeared that Leslie's fame at fiberglass boat repair had spread beyond Hermit.

I rushed back to retrieve Leslie before the Sabbath's gong.

"You've got to drop what you're doing and go over right now. Give him what he wants, and then maybe he'll take me."

Leslie dutifully complied, spending over an hour with him and his buddies sitting on the beach, enduring their smelly chewing and spitting as she explained the intricacies of fiberglass work. As it was, she barely made it back home before the dreaded clanging signaled work's cessation for the week.

"Well, we'll see," we both agreed.

My packed bag, jacket and cushion stood at the ready in *Banshee's* cockpit all day. I had approached Paul after church but he was non-committal, and he wasn't allowed to talk about work on the Sabbath. The standard "you wait," was all I could get out of him.

Towards the end of the afternoon, we saw the speedie pull out. Joen sat amongst the tarps, self-consciously turning her head away from us as they motored past and waved good-bye.

"Wan place *tasol,"* and it wasn't for me.

It was nearly *Krismas* (Christmas), usually a *bikpela,* long-awaited celebration of singing, feasting, and festival in PNG. We wondered what our Hermiters would be doing for the holidays. Their answer took us by surprise.

"Samting nating."

Krismas, they replied, was an event of no consequence. Further questions seemed to make them more defensive. In the austere, fundamentalist view of SDA dogma, the joyous celebration of the Christmas holiday was almost pagan and therefore something to be disdained and avoided. *What manner of religious tyrants did this to a primitive people whose lives revolved around natural beauty, adornment, gaiety, and celebration?*

"Sel-O. Sel-O," the announcing cries came once again. This time it wasn't from the *pikinini* but from adults on the west-facing side of the isthmus village, near Daniel's.

"Bikpela sip. Bikpela white *wan. Wan* go *long Wuvulu.* I come. *I* come *bia* now."

Music to my ears.

My ship has arrived, and this time I am waiting at the dock.

The *Elfride,* out of Kavieng, was indeed a *bikpela* ship. We waved happily and laughed from *Banshee's* deck as we watched her pull close to the beach and anchor nearby.

Pikinini swarmed over her as the village men pushed speedies into the water to take her lines.

Her size dwarfed the small anchorage.

"Guess I've got my ticket, Les."

As the numerous passengers disembarked and were ushered ashore to awaiting friends and families, we heard the story.

The *Elfride* was nearly out of fuel.

They had made it to Hermit from the SDA conference on Wuvulu but could go no further. A supply ship with drums of fuel was being dispatched from Kavieng. In the meantime, the passengers would find lodging among the various houses in the village. The SDA community was like extended family and all were warmly welcomed.

We knew there would also be supplies for sale aboard: packets of delicious dry whole milk from New Zealand, laundry soap, kerosene, and if we were lucky, onions, potatoes and rice. These cargo ships circulate throughout the small coastal towns and islands of PNG, carrying passengers, cargo, bringing goods for sale, and functioning as trading ships for local produce.

The main money crops of Hermit were trochus shell and *beche du mer*, the dried sea cucumber so favored by Chinese palates. The locals could already feel the coins jiggling in their pockets from the sale of each family's stash of the smelly, smoked, and dried slug that brought cash to an almost cashless economy.

Trochus, a relative of the conch so popular in Caribbean dishes, was not eaten here, at least not by SDAs, but was taken for its shell to be used for buttons in the Asian garment trade.

The *beche du mer* business was more of a cottage industry. The *meries* of every family were continually engaged in preparing the shoe-leather-tough commercial product. The unappealing creatures were boiled, sun-dried, and then smoked in each family's *haus kuk*. A foul-smelling crate of the dried creatures resided near my bed on Lynnah's veranda, ready to sell when the next trading ship appeared.

Visitors and ships were welcomed on Hermit. They brought news, gossip, friends, family, supplies, and indispensable cash. Hermit village was happy that night as groups of men chatted around fires on the beach and women congregated on verandas or in the many kerosene-lit *haus kuk* of the village.

On *Banshee,* we joined in their happiness with bowls of hot rice to go along with our standard fare of grilled fish for dinner.

Leslie

Becoming more and more frustrated with the state of our engine, I was still hopeful that someone could get it started. *There'd be a mechanic on that ship. They gotta have one to keep that big engine going.*

With no fuel for the generator and her passengers and crew ashore, the *Elfride* fell silent, sitting like a ghost-ship in the lagoon. All we could see were a few men lounging on deck in the shade of a tarp.

As I walked down the beach, a short national man who looked vaguely familiar came up to me, grabbed my hand, and acted as if I was a long-lost friend.

"You got any more of that homebrew you had? Sure would taste good right now."

I still wasn't connecting with him, so he continued, "Mack—Bob Bedford's friend—in Kavieng three years ago? You gave us all that homebrew beer when we were there. Remember?"

"Wow! Yeah. I remember you with Bob, Joy's friend from Australia. Couldn't forget you or Bob, for that matter. You with that ship?"

"With it? Hell, I'm the *Keptan.*"

"You are? Fantastic!" *Definitely the person I want to talk with.*

As I started blurting out my story to my friend from the outside world, he propelled me along the beach, still holding my hand firmly. Then, at his urging, we walked blatantly through the village swinging our arms, proclaiming our friendship bond in true PNG fashion. He must have heard some disgruntled rumblings from the *bekslaiders* and figured I needed a bit of "showing face" solidarity with an outside national. And a cargo ship *Keptan* has plenty of clout among the coastal villagers, who depend on his choice of favored anchorages on his cargo run.

His grinning face at the staring onlookers gave the message. *"Prens bilong* me, you *save!"*

I returned to *Banshee* with his instructions, spoken loudly for all to hear, to "bring the starters over and meet my engineer, Peter" still ringing in my ears. I could feel my status rise among the bullying guys who enjoyed keeping me in "place *bilong meri,"* as they put it.

Peter was as helpful and charming as Mack, and while the ship and visitors were in, the "boys" from the village turned into respectful young men. *Amazing how a little social pressure among their own can improve life so quickly.*

Sitting on the top outside deck of *Elfride,* purposely for all to see, Peter instructed his crew in the overhauling of our starters. Scavenged parts from the worst one were used to repair the other, creating one usable starter and solenoid. I gave the rebuilt starter a final coat of salvaged galvanizing paint and took our finished work home to dry. Peter promised to be over in the morning to do the installation.

Instead of just waiting, we had accomplished something. It felt good.

Peter arrived as scheduled and gasped at the mess that Bill had made of the brass fuel lines leading to the injectors.

"It take time to *stretim* these up so I can seat injectors properly. What *kain* nut case got his hands in *hia*—it *olsem* what you call sabotage, yeah?"

Most of the morning, Peter sat in the cramped engine space, scrunched up and straddling our engine, patiently re-bending the tiny tubes. He took our three injectors back to his workshop to test them, telling me to come over in a couple of hours to see his results.

Our injectors checked out perfectly and Peter returned with ideas of getting the engine running. But first, he wanted to use the starter to spin the engine rapidly without the injectors in place to be sure there wasn't more water inside. Water could damage the injectors and we didn't need that.

We both held our breath.

"Hit it!" he yelled. Joy touched wire to wire for ignition. Spray went everywhere.

"Water or fuel, Peter?"

"Mostly water."

"Taste it. Is it salty?"

"Yeah, sorry." His voice showed his disappointment as he climbed out of the engine room, wiping his face. Poor guy, he was a mess and the engine space was once again an oily hole. However, more saltwater had been spit out of the engine block and that was good, *if* it wasn't coming from somewhere else.

"*Tumas* water come out injectors. Maybe you *gat* blown head gasket or cracked cylinder, or maybe jus' *moa* water still *insait. Aidono. Planti* sorry. But no time now *long wokim moa. Keptan* Mack *i tokim me* fuel ship come now—*autsait* reef." He pointed to the east entrance.

We looked at each other without saying a word. The decision had been made for us. There would be no engine for *Banshee's* next voyage. We would have to use sail alone to reach Madang.

Joy

Soon there would be two ships in the harbor—either of which could take me off this rock. In anticipation of this, I had been talking with Paul about my leaving. His major concern was that *Banshee* might sink right in front of his village during my absence. With no *Keptan* aboard, in his culture, he was responsible. It didn't matter that Les was half owner of *Banshee*, to him I was *Keptan* and that was the way it was. If *Banshee* sank, it would be a loss of face he could not endure. His leadership tenure might well come to an abrupt end, and, in his view, he would be disgraced.

"*Wan bikpela heve,*" he said.

We were concerned too, but had more knowledge and experience to have a better-informed opinion. My job was to ease his fears and to give him something that he could hang onto emotionally, if things got worse or community pressure built up. He seemed grateful.

I told him that, yes, the leak was getting worse, but we had pumps, a manual and an electric one hooked up to solar charged batteries. We felt the pumps could keep up with it. The patch wouldn't just let go in a massive failure. Paul still wanted something more definite, something physical. He suggested planks nailed over the crack.

Not reacting to his naïveté, I patiently explained that that was impossible with fiberglass and would damage things further. However, he started me thinking—could we use something else?

My idea came from Mack, when I asked him what he would do if his boat was holed or cracked by coral or an errant floating log, buoy or cast-off shipping container, all real hazards in PNG waters.

"A collision mat, ropes, and lotsa men. Got 'em all."

A collision mat. I've read about such things and always figured I could fashion one in an emergency. Looking around, I focused on our cockpit lee cloths. *There's two mini-collision mats hanging right here—strong Sunbrella cloth strung between the lifelines and toe rails with lots of grommet holes along the sides. If we were to smear one side with that gooey 3M 5200 adhesive that sets up in water, and hold it in place with lines through the grommets, those cloths would make an impervious barrier.*

I described my idea to Leslie. She looked at me strangely.

"Well, yeah, but think of getting all that dried shit off the hull. Your new underwater epoxy that you're gonna find would never bond to that mess."

"C'mon, you and I know it's not going to come to that," I said bravely, not wanting to bog her down in worry when she would be alone. "I've got to give Paul something to hang onto. Let's see, what can we call it? Aha, I've got it—a 'boat *nappy*.'"

My humor was lost on Leslie, who wasn't familiar with the Australian or English idiom for a baby's diaper. After I explained, she roared in laughter.

"That's what they call them? Really?"

"And when I tell Paul that a ship like the *Elfride* carries such a collision mat, it'll make it seem even more like I know what I'm talking about."

My plan went over perfectly. He caught on immediately as I laid out the diagram of my "boat nappy" showing how it would work. Of course, he knew the term and kept laughing at my use of it. Although non-existent on Hermit, nappies were a greatly desired item among the young mother set.

"You *gat dispela* glue stuff? Sinking no *bagarap*?"

"Nah, it's sealed and we have the caulking gun to apply it, too."

Smiles. He had what he wanted—a way out.

"You *ken* leave now. *Emi i orait.*"

Michele, a small, rusty, steel cargo ship, steamed in at dusk the day that Peter could do no more on *Banshee*. She was heavily laden with fuel drums for *Elfride*. The *Keptan*, Mikah, was a devout SDA.

The fuel transfer from *Michele* took most of one day, and we heard that both ships would be leaving the next day, a Thursday, the week before Christmas. The guys told me that *Elfride* was a very slow ship, steaming at only 4 knots, and would stop at every little village along the south side of Manus before reaching Lorengau. It might take two weeks or more. Due to the many reefs and small islands, they would anchor for the night and most would find lodging ashore. *Oh no, not more pandanus huts and villages. I wanted to get to civilized Moresby, and quickly.*

Paul and several other churchmen noticed my urgency and inquired of Mikah if he could take me and make a stop in Lorengau. His route was to Kavieng direct, but due to my circumstances and the approaching Sabbath, he would seek permission by radio from his boss, the vessel's owner. The devout Mikah did not travel on the Sabbath.

All Wednesday afternoon and night, I wondered which ship would give me passage. *Michele* was fast and could easily make Lorengau overnight, as she steamed along at a respectable 7 knots. I tried to be patient, not wanting to appear pushy, or I might lose my golden opportunity. *Good grief, what if I am stuck on the slow one for two weeks?*

It was late morning before the answer came. Mikah could take me to Lorengau and was leaving at noon—in two hours. My bag was already packed, but Les kept tossing cans of food inside.

"Joy, you're too skinny. They're not going to feed you on that rustbucket. It's a cargo boat. You'll have to eat—take something. Lynnah told you everyone brings their own food on local ships."

"Right." *Along with the pillow, the sheet, the bug cream, the packet of coffee, and the soda bottle full of rum: life's little essentials.*

A horn resounded throughout the bay—*Michele's* departure warning. A hug good-bye and I was in the dinghy, Les paddling on the bow. Mikah had the engine running and people were untying her lines. Someone grabbed my bag and backpack and I was aboard.

I watched as Les in our tiny teacup of a dinghy got smaller and smaller and then *Banshee* too receded from sight. I couldn't look any more—*bad luck to look back.* I climbed up on the foredeck and focused ahead on the open sea beyond the reef.

Where Banshee *would be soon, if all went right.*

LESLIE ON HER OWN AGAIN

Leslie

Please, Joy, stay until you find the epoxy, however long it takes. It's our last chance to save Banshee. I stood in the dinghy until I could no longer see *Michele* on the horizon. Then I crumpled down and sobbed. *She's got to find the stuff. She just has to.*

The little dinghy drifted down by Namo's beach, and *pikinini* came out in their child-sized dugouts.

"You *orait misis?* You *tingktingk?* Pray?"

I smiled. *Little children, they care.* "Yes, boys, me *tingktingk*, now."

Shaking myself back to reality, I paddled back to *Banshee* and climbed aboard. Booby greeted me with a small cat noise. We talked to each other, carrying on one of our long conversations. Boo-boo was a good listener.

Time to go ashore, get water, pick aibica for dinner, grab some things in the storeroom. Maybe Lynnah's got a piece of fish for me, and I've got rice too.

Lynnah found me in her back room.

"*Tumora*, Leslie, come, *havim* tea. *Mipela* talk. Pray Joy be *orait.*"

It was dark when I returned to *Banshee*, but at least I could switch on a light now. The usual jobs of turning the engine, lighting the outside kero lamp, feeding Booby, and washing up kept me busy until late. My mind wouldn't turn off. A capful of Joy's rum solved that, and I was fast asleep.

I woke up long before daylight—so many plans for the day. As much as I missed Joy, I worked harder when alone. No distractions and I ate only when hunger drove me to it. Joy had worked out several plans with Paul before she left, so I wouldn't have to do the political walk-around.

As soon as I went ashore, I heard that a message had come through *Elfride's* radio that Joy had arrived in Lorengau and had gone *"stret long* Moresby" on the airplane. I was glad for that, but had lots of reservations about that city. Just hope she stays safe. *Elfride* and my friend, Mack, left soon afterwards on their slow roundabout path to Manus.

I needed a worker, someone to do the back-bending drudgery of loading and lifting, paint scraping and sanding. We had agreed to offer the going local wage of K10/day—a big deal in a village where there are few opportunities to earn cash. Because everyone in their communal society had village responsibilities, the person to work for me had to be assigned by the village council. It had to be a church member and a man without a family to provide for. One of my former guards, Peter, fit the bill. Unmarried and from Madang, he had been adopted into a Hermit family and had come to Luf to live. He and Ben, also from Madang, were *wantoks*. This established a communal, almost family-like, bond between the two. The *"wantok* system" is one of the main driving forces in PNG society.

Ben's *wantok,* Peter, was hard at work helping to build Ben's new house. The time for the family to vacate their present house had long since passed, and they had to have a place to live immediately. As the house neared completion, Ben gave Peter permission to assist me (after the council had first passed their approval). No one in the communal village acts independently. "Small scale communism that works," Joy called it.

I went off to find Peter, avoiding any confrontations from any of the roaming males—Okip, Bill, and Namo, to name a few.

Peter had no difficulties obtaining the wheelbarrow for carting out the remainder of our stored possessions. His reasoning was simple.

"I am a man and a church member, and you are a guest and a woman."

How understandable from the PNG male's point of view, particularly the way he looked when he said "a woman," as though one of our gender couldn't be trusted to take care of anything.

Peter was easy to work with, particularly because his English was good and he had grown up in the city and was used to outsiders. He admitted to being a former *raskel* who had done his share of robbery and mayhem, but he had now "found God" and was leading a moral life. He featured himself as my prospective "husband" even though I said I wasn't in the market. Also, he was about my height, so we literally saw "eye to eye," and there wasn't any of the usual male size domination stuff that I hated.

It was Friday and I wanted to get all the stuff moved out to the boat by the evening gong, so I could spend my secluded Sabbath inside putting stuff away. *What they can't see from the beach, they don't care about.*

Poor Peter had to endure some harassment from the *haus boi* loungers, but he seemed to carry it off well. Their Pidgin was so rapid that I had no idea what they were saying and tried to ignore it. All day we worked hard, and by dusk, few things were left in the storeroom. Such a pleasure having someone else do the lugging, lifting and carrying.

I hoped to be relieved of the Sabbath's church attendance duty, but Lynnah insisted I appear at evening service and again in the morning.

"Paul *tokim* me, *mipela* pray *long* Joy. You *sanapim* (stand up), *mekim toktok. Givim tenkyu long ol people hia long halpim* you *tumas.*"

I groaned inwardly. *Public speeches are not me, and especially in a church.*

Protesting had no effect, so I just had to clean-up and get ready. Lynnah promised me that she and *"olgeta pikinini long me"* would be sitting right by when my time came.

"Then I go home, right?"

She nodded, pleased with her accomplishment, saying, "Yes. You come *bek tumora long* 9 o'clock."

So much for seclusion on the Sabbath.

Sunday was Games Day, and I was still at work cleaning, stowing, and sorting through our possessions, saddened by what was missing and surprised by what had made its way back home.

In the afternoon, I wandered around watching the hotly contested sports and the antics of the unapproved but barely hidden betting going on among the spectators.

I found another willing hand in David, a young Catholic man who had married into Okip's family. Although he had his family obligations to deal with first, Paul again approved of my using him for some work. We had already become friends, bringing me fresh fish when I let him use one of our remaining sets of mask and snorkel for night fishing from his canoe.

Work went along peacefully for the remainder of the week. The beastly job of rotating the engine twice daily was passed on to my two young helpers. The big job was the peeling paint on the walls and ceilings. The guys spread gooey, strong-smelling toxic paint remover from our salvaged cans over the mess, then scraped it down and sanded with wet-dry sandpaper. Not accustomed to using protective haz-mat gear, they scoffed at goggles and masks. The fumes had to have made them light-headed, or perhaps worse, but these macho guys wouldn't tell me even when I asked. However, they were amazed at the *vakem* (vacuum) that still ran off the generator; they instantly liked it for sucking up all the muck and paint chips. A great improvement over the coconut broom.

They would leave for lunch break, sometimes returning and sometimes not. Peter seemed the more industrious and reliable from my point of view, but village concerns kept interrupting David's working time. But then, David was a married man with wife and *pikinini* and had to leave early to go fishing for their daily meal; Peter ate with relatives, as men did not cook. Overall, though, things were going along quite peacefully during the week and so much was being accomplished with the two workers that my concerns about being alone without Joy were fading away.

Until things started to unravel...

Sparks, crackling, and then flames and smoke. I looked down at the strung-out wires lying on the cabin floor. Tongues of flames licked along as the fire streaked towards the battery, burning off the varnish as it went.

"Paia!"

Yells came out of the forepeak where David and Peter were working. They tumbled out, pushing me aside.

"What happened?"

"Joy bot boinim (burn) down, *bot boinim* down," they kept repeating.

"The fan! Go back and turn it off!" I yelled, as I pulled the wires off the battery. *Damn, the cans of chemicals—sparks. They'll catch fire.*

"Wanem? Switch *we?"*

I grabbed David, yelling at him. Then turned him around and marched behind him as he shut off the hot and smoking fan switch. Peter had taken refuge outside, coughing from the smoke. Booby was perched as high as he could climb, nervously meowing as though another sinking might take place. The cabin filled with smoke and long burn-trails marked the already scuffed and roughened floor.

Sitting in the cockpit, we let the smoke and smell filter out. Unaccustomed to working around items using live electrical current, David had leaned against my twisted-together wires and they had shorted out. He felt very discouraged that he had destroyed our one fan, and he'd had enough. I tried to console him, but he was now out of the mood for work and took off in his canoe. I suppose fishing was easier than earning cash around *waitmeri's* unfamiliar electrical gadgets.

Peter and I returned to work. The *vakem* made short work of the mess and somehow I was able to coax the little fan into a few more days of service.

"Good morning, Merry Christmas," was Peter's greeting on the 25th, one of the few holiday greetings I received on that tight little SDA island. *A place where Christmas isn't even celebrated? And they're Christian?* I was having a lot of trouble with their avoidance of the holiday. *People all over the world enjoy the gift giving and the spirit of the season. What is their problem?*

We talked about it for a while over tea. Having lived in Madang and other places, he knew first-hand the festive, religious nature of the holiday as it's colorfully celebrated in PNG—"but not with Adventists," he consoled. I tried to understand, but I was saddened. I had too many memories of Hanukkahs and Christmases; *all that food!* I didn't feel like working and so we went our separate ways, with me taking Booby for a walk on the beach in front of Lynnah's. *I miss Joy, my family, and I'm so far away.*

David approached me and told me he couldn't help me anymore: *"tumas pamili* (family) pressure," he said. I was dumfounded as he seemed to like to work and I enjoyed him being around.

"What are you talking about?"

"They say you don't finish your obligations and you *mas* do this if I work for you."

"Huh? What obligations? David, what's going on? I finished Namo's boat and I've done at least six other boats around here. What now?"

I listened as I received a lesson in the communal *pebekim* (payback) system.

"It's your obligation here. Women send their *pikinini* to you asking for baking powder and sugar for their breads, and you say "*nogat.*" Collen wants fins for the repairs he did—you don't give any to him. We saw you loading *planti* food when Joy come *bek*. You don't give. You must always give things when they ask. You can never say no, it is not done. So now, you go *painim* things to give because you owe *dispela* village. And Namo say he no *laikim* you working on your boat; he *laikim* you working on his boats. I cannot help you any more. People talk. Then, they see the smoke and hear yelling and think you are *longlong meri* and cannot do your work."

Good grief. I was frustrated and my anger smoldered, but I didn't show it. *Hell, I can play PNG runaround all day long and never get anything done. And what is this shit about more boats of Namo's? First I've heard about it.*

I tried to find projects to occupy the weekend—the Sabbath and Games Day—so that I could stay secluded on *Banshee*. I hated the church going and wanted a break from the Hermiters, as I'm sure they needed a break from their over-staying guest.

Every day, Booby would go fishing for his meals in the dinghy. Little sardines lived in a great cloud-like school under the boat, sustaining themselves on the food chain that had grown along our hull. Small fish attract bigger fish, and the feeding activities going on below would erupt in streams of leaping silvery bodies landing in the dinghy and on deck. Booby loved it—live food landing between his paws.

He loved to play cat games with the quivering, jumping fish, dragging them all over the boat. However, their heads were not on his menu, so they were left to dry out in hidden spots among the buckets and lines. The rains came and the deck runoff funneled down into the tank.

What are fish parts and eyes doing in my sink?

Aha! As I glanced outside and saw scaly pieces littering the rim of the open fill tube—*mystery solved.*

After this unpleasant discovery, my weekend project was to extricate the fouled water tank from its moorings under the floor and clean it out. And I knew that if Joy found the epoxy I hoped for, the tank would have to come out for access to the damaged area inside the hull. *If I get the tank clean, then we can use it for water storage again.*

The thought of enduring the church stuff again was grating at me too. *If I don't stop going, they'll just assume that I'll always be there—they'll own me like they do the rest of those poor downtrodden women who sit there every Sabbath without their men.* As a start, I begged off this time with Paul, saying I had a big project to do. He relented as long as I was out of sight.

"No talking *long wok,* no thinking *long wok* and no seeing *wok long* Sabbath, village rules, *tasol."*

With this in mind, I devised a plan to keep me and my work discretely out of everyone's sight, creeping out only when necessary, checking to see if anyone was on the beach and slinking around on deck as low as possible.

The foul-smelling tank was almost full and much too heavy to move. I found an electric pump under the sink that we used to pump seawater into the galley—a very tiny Shur-flo Nautilus. Hooked up to a 12-volt battery, it still worked. Stripping down the tank, I peered inside at all the fish parts and scaly residue. *Booby, you've surely had your fun—I had no idea.*

The little pump did its job and soon the mess was pumped out into buckets. Fresh water for cleaning was so scarce that I let the *dreck* settle out and then scooped relatively clean water off the top. Nothing even resembling fresh water was ever thrown away.

I worked below removing the two cabin sole boards and their crossbeams. Then I rigged up lines around the tank and led them up through the cabin hatch to a block and tackle above. Slipping discretely outside, I sat down low and slowly pulled the bulky tank out from its position in the bottom of the bilge and out into the cockpit. Many fresh water rinses later, plus a lot of shaking and maneuvering, and my tank was clean enough to use. However, on examination, I found so many cracks and gouges in the thing that I figured some fiberglass repair was needed too.

The next evening, *Supamanus* rolled in, a one-off open fiberglass boat built in Lorengau. *Supamanus* seemed to have gotten its design inspiration from the old paddle-driven Manus canoes built entirely out of one giant log, which used to haul cargo and passengers all over the Admiralty Islands. Roughly built with a decked-over enclosed cabin in the bow, she belonged to Roy Joseph and was the local carrier from Wuvulu and Aua to Ninigo and Hermit and back to the supply town of Lorengau. In between fairly regular runs, she beached at Hermit, the home of the Joseph clan. She had brought *kagos* for the impromptu "Joseph Stoa," which would spring up on tables whenever she came in.

Passengers also came on *Supamanus,* familiar faces to Hermiters, but unknown to me. Teen-aged kids coming home for vacation and relatives visiting for the holidays—not Christmas, in this SDA stronghold, but New Year's.

When I paddled ashore to Lynnah's, a woman swam next to me in the shallows.

"Hello, I've just come in on the boat and wanted to meet you. I was just cooling off," she said in perfect Australian-accented English.

English? She's speaking English to me! After months of Pidgin and broken English, it was a shock. And from a *meri?* Except for Natalee, it was hard to converse with any of the women. Girls weren't usually educated beyond the village school—"*tromwe* (throw away) *kina*," the men said.

"I'm Mary, Daniel's wife. He told me about you. I've just come from Moresby with our daughter; she's a teacher, like us."

I was delighted with my instant new friend. In the days to come, she became my companion, my counselor, and my source of village survival information, along with the food that her whole family provided. I felt lighter. Some of the heavy weight of loneliness and oppression seemed to lift from my shoulders.

On Monday, Peter was still with me and hadn't yet succumbed to communal pressure. We carted the bulky tank, generator, and tools to shore. Lynnah gave me a place to work so that the grinding dust wouldn't be a bother. I covered up and started to grind out the cracks in the tank in preparation for the fiberglassing job.

Onlookers gathered, as always happened whenever I tried to do anything ashore, and soon Namo arrived with his usual sidekick, Okip.

"Why you fix tank, Leslie? You no need. *Dispela* tank *em i bagarap.* No *gud.* You no need tank *long wara,* you *usim* coconuts, *mipela gat planti* coconuts *long dringkim* (drink) *long* trip."

The heckling began to get heated as others chimed in, with Okip agitating among the fray.

"You no *usim* resin, resin *bilong* me now. Joy *tokim* me. You *stap—ol* resin *bilong* me. Now you fix *ol bot long* me."

"What? What are you saying, Namo? I fixed your boat and this is my resin, not yours."

I stopped and stared directly at him. *This is totally insane.*

Small-sized Peter backed off, sensing this was no place for an outsider like him. By now, I was outnumbered and completely surrounded by a chorus of men acting like dogs in a pack.

Reason was useless. I was flat up against their payback logic.

"Me *gat planti bot. Ol bot long* me come *hia.* You fix *ol.* You owe. You promise—Joy promise."

He's nuts…and I'm outta here.

Hastily I dowsed the grinding dust off the tank with a bucket of well water, grabbed my generator, tools, and the half-finished tank, and tossed them to safety in the dinghy.

"I'll come over to talk tomorrow," I yelled to Namo as I pulled the little boat out. *Enough! I'm never going near that guy again.*

Joy and I talked about repairing only one boat—his. The one that was always leaking. What the hell is going on? I've got to talk with Paul.

"Forget Namo—don't go down there. *Lusim,* neva' mind. *Tumas toktok ol* time. Why they *mekim* my job hard? I *laikim* things to go right *long* you. I take care of it."

Reassuring Paul—great. I'll just act like it doesn't bother me..
However, it wasn't okay with Peter.

"They give me hard time, Leslie," he whined. "They tell me I shouldn't work with you, cause you owe *planti*. Leslie, I have to eat and they won't feed me if I keep working with you. I am outsider—I have no *meri*, no *gaden*, and soon I have no house *long sleep*."

Another one gone…back on my own again.

Tomorrow would be New Year's and there would be a community feast and singing. The rationale, I was told, is that Jesus would return in the New Year and this was a cause for celebration. He was supposed to have returned on January 1, 2000, but there was a "delay," for which the reasons weren't clear. However, we had to be ready to greet him and be swept up, and I, as a Jew, which is close enough to being an Adventist, would be carried along with them.

But first, Ben told me that people were running a bit short of drinking water and there would be a water run to the catchment tanks around the other end of Luf. At least three speedies were going and I better *hariap* and get in on it.

"Bringim ol kantaina (container): bottle, *baket, samting. Fulimap* (fill-up).

Mipela come *klostu* (close-by), you *kalapim."*

The ride over was fun, racing through the stark blue water streaked with white foam from the big engine. Carolyn sat close to me and looked down at my feet, still sore with slow-healing coral cuts and continual sand fly bites. Having so many other concerns and working so hard, I simply tended to ignore the bites and sores until someone pointed them out to me.

"You *putim lek* (leg) down *insait solwater. Wara hia* clean. *Em mekim gud gen* (again). No fly *long hia. Lukim* Leslie, foot *bilong* you *gat soa,* you come."

Tentatively at first, I dangled one and then another. It stung, but I knew the lagoon's cool rushing waters would soon clean out the red, swollen sores.

For now, they're really being kind. Even the men: "You small. *Mipela lukim* foot *long* you. You *gat soa.* Sorry true, Leslie. *Mipela karim* (carry) *ol kantaina long* you."

The catchment tank location was a leftover from German plantation times. Toppled and broken cement walls and foundations littered the thick stands of coconut palms. Up from the beach there was a "PNG permanent house"—wooden frame with veranda and tin roof. Someone had the key so we went inside. "House *bilong* Alwin Joseph," they told me. That would be Okip's brother, and also the brother of Roy Joseph, the *bikman* who lived in Mt. Hagen, a businessman and a large benefactor of Hermit.

The only furnishings were wooden beds with foam mattresses. It appeared that everything else, except for a large solar panel array with its wires leading into the hut, was locked up in a secure corrugated steel hut. Numerous padlocks and locking hasps of many different kinds adorned the one door. I stared at their strange arrangement.

Looks like my old Manhattan apartment.

"Bilong Alwin," I was told.

A few Sepik men lived there as guards for the property. Drying crocodile skins displayed their way of earning cash money. *At least these guys have no problem with crocs.* For the Sepik people, they provide meat for the table and skins with a high market value.

The coconut groves were overgrown with low jungle growth and the ground was covered in coconuts, some newly fallen, some sprouting and others rotting in the undergrowth. An abundance of papaya gave everyone plenty to pick. *And my favorite, fresh chili peppers.*

Every conceivable type of *kantaina* had been brought to haul water: jugs, buckets, plastic soda bottles, glass bottles, and large washing pans. We filled up, gathered coconuts, and picked fruit until the speedies were full. On the return trip with our bounty, as we neared *Banshee,* I heard, "You *gat* petrol?" and knew it was my time to chip in.

The next day would be New Year's—*a day off, a celebration, and all that food.*

OFF TO PORT MORESBY

Joy

Low ocean swells bit into *Michele's* bow. Unlimited horizon again, bounded only by trade wind clouds and rolling waves. I stood on the leeward deck, sheltering from the spray. *Sure a different motion than a sailboat's. Doesn't matter much where the wind is, they just aim and go.*

I surveyed my new surroundings. My duffel and backpack had been placed in the corner of the dinette seat inside the small cabin.

"That'll be your area over there. You, your gear—all safe *hia*. The rest of them will be outside. Stay with us, okay?" Mikah said.

How protective. He'll look after me.

Mikah, the captain, was around my age, grey-haired, spare and strong. He'd spent a lifetime in the PNG merchant marine on ships of all kinds, traveling to far-off Pacific ports. A well-spoken, complete gentleman, devoutly religious in his SDA faith. The other two crew were his engineer and the young *tekboi* (deck boy), who doubled as cook and cleaner.

Michele was built of steel for the PNG coastal cargo trade. She was about forty feet in length, with a simple cabin housing the nav seat and wheel, some lockers, and a dinette and table—my "home" for the trip. Her rusty steel exterior with its chips and dents spoke of her workboat life. Aft and outside of the cabin was a covered cargo and passenger area with a high box structure housing the prized English Gardner engine. *Nothing stops a Gardner, workhorse of the world—25-30 years and they just keep on going.*

The other passengers, several men and one woman who had jumped ship from *Elfride,* traveled in the open aft area, some of them lounging on top on the engine box for warmth from the cool sea winds. They had brought snacks of cold *tapiok* and taro and plenty of *buai* for chewing on the long trip. The only seats to be had were a few hard wooden benches or on the cargo bags of dried copra, rotting boiled trochus, and *beche-d'mer* stashed along the deck. The smell was gagging.

I stood at the aft rail watching Hermit fade into the distance. The roar of the big Gardner made conversation impossible. The seas were calm with light winds—*powerboat weather.* Mikah had the engine revved up to take full advantage of the easy conditions; *he told me it'd take 17 hours to reach Lorengau, if the seas remain calm. That'll be early morning.*

The exhaust stack above us spewed smelly, grey smoke tainting the fresh sea air. *These boats are good for a purpose, but I certainly prefer my sea-kindly, quiet sailboat.*

I spent the hours napping, thinking, planning, and staring out to sea. The mental "combat-fatigue" that had plagued me lifted. The passage of time, Leslie's unending work on *Banshee,* pledges of support from her family, the "home base" provided by Lynnah and Ben, and long conversations with my PNG mentor, Daniel, had repaired my shattered soul. I was not the same person who straggled into Lorengau on the police boat in October. I had energy. I had a plan.

The constant drone of the engine numbed me, and I dozed in my corner. Dusk settled in and I was awakened by the sounds of cooking. The menu consisted of large bowls of rice covered by packaged ramen noodle soup full of fats and salt, something I stayed away from. I opted for plain rice. The young man serving the food looked at me strangely. This concoction is a PNG favorite whenever they had *kina* to buy it. *I know,* waitmeries *are strange creatures.*

Rummaging in my bag, I pulled out a prized salvaged tin of Argentinean roast beef and gravy. *I've been saving this for the right time. Yum, over rice, too.* Of course there was no can opener, but in PNG the bush knife works well. With a little help from the *kukboi,* I soon had beef and gravy over rice and a table to eat it on. I requested a cup of water and surreptitiously flavored it with a shot of rum from my traveling soda bottle. I kept my evening's cocktail hidden under my pillow during dinner, thinking my teetotaling SDA captain wouldn't approve, to say nothing of the effect it would have on my fellow passengers.

The night wore on. I slept. I dozed, and then the engine slowed and stopped altogether. The sudden change woke me up. Bright lights came on aft, and I heard Mikah speaking to his engineer and the passengers. We drifted and rolled in the swell. I heard something about "*hatpela* (hot) *tumas.*" I figured it was the engine they were talking about and stayed put. Eventually it came on again and we continued, but at a much lower speed. Yes, a problem "*bilong* overheating" had developed, but, "No worries, ma'am. *Em i olrait.*"

Occasionally I ventured out and sat on the foredeck under a starry sky and flat calm sea. Mikah and the engineer had their chart spread out and were plotting GPS fixes. This was reassuring, but when I watched them measure the minutes of lat/long off the longitude scale instead of the latitude scale along the side of the Mercator chart, I was a bit concerned at their technique. *Is this what they teach at their marine college? At one degree from the equator the error is minuscule, so I guess it doesn't really matter.*

Soon it was morning and I smelled coffee. That, and some sliced-up pineapples and bananas from Hermit made up breakfast. Lorengau came into sight and we docked at the public jetty at 7 a.m.

I hit the dock running. Bag in hand, backpack on my back, I thanked Mikah and was on my way. Lorengau had no surprises for me—I knew the place too well. By the time the Air Niugini employees arrived for work that Friday morning, I was sitting on their front steps.

"A flight to Moresby, please. How much?"

When I heard the price, I was surprised. "Is that all? For a round trip?"

"You want to come back to Lorengau?" Looks of incredulity spread over their faces.

"Yes, of course. My boat's at Hermit."

"Ma'am, all airfares in PNG are one way. We don't have return fares. You need to buy another one-way fare to get back here. You do want to come back?"

"Certainly."

"Good. You can pay for it now, but we can't book you a seat coming back because there are none—*Krismas,* you know. Keep ringing our office in Moresby and you'll get a seat eventually."

My flight to Moresby would leave at 2 p.m. and I had one of the few remaining seats.

"Is there a bus to the airport? I understand it's rather far away."

"Yes, the Harbourside Hotel will provide a shuttle bus to the airport, that is, if you are a guest. Are you a guest there, ma'am?

"Not exactly, but I will be very soon."

I felt in need of a hot shower and some normal accommodations, at least for a few hours.

"Are you a tourist to PNG, ma'am?"

I wanted to say, "No, I'm a refugee off a sunken boat," but restrained myself and gave a polite rendition of my circumstances.

The little office grew quiet. Heads turned.

I smiled, thanked them, and proceeded to my next stop, the Harbourside Hotel.

Someone at the reception desk remembered me from my previous visit and the newspaper article in the National. "You're the 'wreck lady.' We remember, you were *hia* in town before. Sorry true. You *olrait* now?"

"It's getting better. Now I'd like a half-day room and a bus to the airport for this afternoon's flight. Can that be arranged?"

Soon I was ensconced in what felt like incredible luxury. In actuality, it was simply a clean room with basic accommodations. It appeared that half the hotel was closed up and not even operating. *Hardly any guests here, but then who comes to Lorengau?*

After a long self-indulgent shower in unending hot water, a change of clothes, and a bit of a nap, I was ready to take on the world. Phone calls to Sue in the U.S. and to our ambassador's office in Moresby were on my agenda. It was wonderful to hear Sue's voice and, although concerned about Leslie being alone again, she filled me in on the missing gaps during our isolation on Hermit.

On my last trip, we had only communicated by email, which lacks the personal and emotional touch of a phone call. I had no idea of what had been going on with family members and how involved they had been, particularly Sue, who had been on the phone daily. Then I tried the U.S. Embassy.

"Oh yes, we've heard of you, and I'd like you to know that we've certainly done more than enough for you two ladies," was the opener.

Okay. What do I say now? What did Mark Prokop tell these people?

Trying to be polite but completely unaware of all the conversations and decisions that had taken place on our behalf since October, I was unprepared for what felt like an officious rebuff. *Use some tact, Joy, these are government employees who exist in a city office world and have no idea of how we have lived for the past two months.*

Eventually, I was connected with Heather Guimond. Heather had been Sue's main contact and she now became mine. The U.S. Foreign Service can be proud of her. Whenever I had a bureaucratic problem, Heather took care of it.

I told her I was hesitant about arriving alone at the airport in Moresby. Could she recommend a safe but inexpensive hotel? Was there a possibility of someone meeting me? Port Moresby has quite a scary reputation, and I was nervous about getting into a taxi alone. She was understanding, and kindly said she would look into it; either she or Susan Jacobs, the ambassador, would call me back before my flight.

The hotel's buffet lunch started serving at 11 o'clock, and I was ravenous. I locked my backpack inside my room and went off to lunch. The dining room was empty; not even Valerie Knight had showed up yet for her daily "lunch bunch."

After a leisurely meal (including my first cold beer in two months), I returned to my room and planned to have a little nap in air-conditioned comfort.

My rum—where is it? What the hell? No, not in my backpack. C'mon now, I put it in there to be safe just before I left. Damn, it's just gone—a whole quart—someone's been in here, that's all there is to it.

The front desk directed me to the manager's office—a small building across from the entrance foyer. I knocked and entered. A heavily overweight national man sat behind a desk stacked high with papers. I sat down. He said nothing, he didn't even look up.

"Ahem..."

"Yes? Do you need something? See the girls at the desk for any problems. Can't you see I'm very busy?

His imperious tone as he waved me off set the stage for the rest of the exchange. "Something is missing from my room while I was at lunch. I did lock the room."

He cut me off. "Are you making accusations? What's missing?"

"A bottle of rum."

"Rum? You had spirits in your room?" he thundered.

"Yes, my Philippine rum. Brought it with me for my trip. You know spirits are quite expensive in this country."

"Yes, yes, I've heard all about you and your problems."

Charming…What's with this guy?

After barking at me for a while, he finally relented and agreed to check with the housekeeper assigned to my room. She was at lunch but he would let me know before I left for the airport.

I knew how that would turn out. *Accept it. I'm out of stock. Rumless.*

Amidst this, Valerie Knight bustled out of the dining room. I was surprised at her strained greetings, but I went ahead and told her of my run-in with the manager. She quickly brushed me off and hurried outside. *How come she doesn't want to talk with me either—what's going on?*

The time for my bus to leave was fast approaching, but still no phone call from the embassy. I called back. After being passed around a bit, a male voice with an American accent came on the line.

"Look, there's no one here, and it is the week before Christmas. They're all gone. You're safe there so just stay put and don't go anywhere. Call in on Monday, okay?"

I started to object and explained that I was flying to Moresby, but didn't get very far. His voice became even more officious.

"I've been instructed to tell you that if you call here again I am to discontinue the conversation. Goodbye, Ms. Smith."

I stared at the dead receiver in my hand. *My U.S. Embassy?*

I was shaking. *Where do I go from here?* Part of my plan assumed that the embassy would surely help me. I called Sue back. She was shocked and offered to call them herself.

The bus was at the door—time to go. I paid my bill, grabbed my bags and left. *Truly on my own now.*

The view from the *balus* was beautiful, with tiny islands and coral reefs studding a brilliant blue ocean. White surf crashing on the coast. Then a green carpet of jungle— the mainland. Small cleared areas showed remote villages unconnected by roads. Then it all disappeared into the mist as we crossed the high mountain ranges. *You have to fly above this country to appreciate how vast and remote it really is.*

As I settled back for the ride, I contemplated my arrival in Moresby. *It will be evening in a large bustling airport, unfamiliar to me, no reservations for the night and no idea of where to go in a city known for its violence.* I watched as the well-groomed attendants distributed refreshments and cared for passengers. *Of course, customer service—most airlines assist "tourists." I'll try to stay away from the term "refugee," it might frighten her off.*

One of the flight attendants was happy to sit down with me during a lull in her duties, and as I described my plight and story, her eyes widened.

"Your embassy, of course they are meeting you?"

I tried to make that unfortunate story as brief as possible, but she shook her head in disbelief.

"But they should help after what you've been through. I mean, if that had happened to me, I'd like to think that even my poor embassy would be there. Well, Air Niugini can help you. We do have a customer service department."

She insisted that I wait for her at the baggage claim.

"Don't go any further. Things happen to people here. Talk to no one unless he or she is wearing an official ID badge and, please, keep your hands on your bags at all times. Air Niugini feels very responsible for its passengers, especially in your case." Her concern told me my fears were not unfounded. *What a lovely person.* I was touched by her concern and care.

Bump and we were down. Bright lights and tarmac greeted me as we scurried off to the baggage claim. Crowds of unruly people pushed and shoved—politeness was an unknown concept.

I felt relieved when I saw my caring attendant wave at me. She rapidly ushered me to the Air Niugini service desk.

"They'll find you a hotel. I've spoken to them. Remember, keep your hands on your bags and stay near a security guard. Good luck."

The crowd jostled me; people shoved and cut in to get to the counter. Walled-in by bulletproof Lexan panels, the employees beyond communicated with the masses through a little area of drilled out holes in the thick, protective shield. The crowd noise was deafening, making communication through the barrier even more difficult. Each time I thought I was going to get assistance, someone pushed me aside. Uniformed, tough-looking security guards with long wooden batons on their belts were everywhere.

Eventually the crowd thinned; even the airline's people were going home.

"Wait, please help me. I have no place to go."

A drained, tired-looking woman in a rumpled uniform eventually heard me and listened. I kept my eyes on her, clutching my bags close. She made some calls and passed a note through the slot.

"The Grantham," she said. "Bus will be along. You wait *autsait.* Stay near security."

I obeyed.

I had my choice of guards. They were everywhere. Explaining my situation, my chosen protector looked surprised.

"No *wan* come *long kisim* you?"

I shook my head. Amazement on his face.

As directed, I found a piece of pavement near the *buai* sellers, sat down, and camped on top of my bags. My growing knowledge of Pidgin helped, bringing a smile from my guard.

I waited.

He promised to call me when the appropriate bus arrived. People stared at me, especially the expats. No one spoke to me. After a startled stare, they looked away. *Guess I am what I look like—a refugee. Endure, it'll be over soon.*

An hour passed. Cold and tired, I sat and watched the street with one eye and my guard-friend with the other.

"Bus *bilong* Grantham, *misis*. You go *long hap* now."

"*Tenkyu*, true. You *gudpela* man," as I pressed an unexpected tip into his hand.

We hurtled through the streets, lit up by blazing mercury security lamps overhead. Graffiti, barred windows, cement walls, rolls of razor wire, and huge gates topped with spikes told the story. *A city under siege.*

Arrival at the Grantham was no different. We pulled up to a massive steel plate security gate set on rollers. The driver punched a code into the remote terminal, the gate noisily rolled back, and we were inside. It clanged shut again.

The hotel's rooms were in a maze of one-story buildings arranged around a large central patio. The set-up was designed for housing and feeding large numbers of people in the cheapest way possible. It was totally encircled by high cement walls covered in rolls of razor wire. The front desk, offices, a cafeteria-style restaurant and a bar all opened onto the cemented-in central area. A few scraggly plants stuffed in planter boxes were a feeble attempt at aesthetics.

I checked in and was led to the tiniest hotel room that I had ever seen. Stuffed into this windowless unit were a single bed, a desk and chair, a TV, and a bathroom with stall shower and toilet. *If that air-con unit ever stops, asphyxiation would be next.*

My eyes fell on the phone sitting on top of a directory. I smiled. I was itching to start my search.

First a meal. *I sure hope the place is still open, it looks pretty deserted at this late hour.* I bought a beer at the bar and wandered in. "Meal service, *misis, em i pinis*," said the server as she pointed at the clock. I must have looked as bad as I felt. I gave her a pleading look. Soon a plate of something with gravy, potatoes and canned vegetables appeared out of the kitchen. I wasn't particular, just grateful; I thanked the kind woman.

I've come a long way from Hermit—thirty hours and another century.

THE SEARCH FOR THE MAGIC EPOXY

Joy

Little flickering beams of sunlight made their way around the humming air conditioner and into my windowless concrete cubicle. *Morning?* Slowly awakening, I had to remember where I was. *Port Moresby—I've come so far. Now I've got to find that damned epoxy.*

My first day of the search had begun. *I've got a telephone and the phone book. It's eight on a Saturday morning—local businesses are all open till noon. Can't wait around till Monday, I've got so many questions.* I turned to the index. "Fiberglass, Fiberglassing, Marine Equipment, Marine Repairs," and "Salvage, Marine" were all headings that jumped out at me. By the end of three hours, I had talked with almost every nautical expert in Port Moresby. Notes and jottings covered my desktop. Most of my contacts were Australian, along with a few nationals. Most of them were caring, astonished, amazed, and helpful. A few weren't—I ignored them, not allowing them to slow my momentum. I knew one good contact would eventually lead to another.

United Salvage of Port Moresby sounded promising.

"How do you patch sunken ships in the water?"

"We use bog, mate. Like what you call 'car bondo.' Mix 'er up, plop it in a baggie, throw it down to yer diver 'n he plasters it all over the crack. It works. It stops leaks. Then we can pump 'em out 'n raise 'em."

"Is it strong enough for the open ocean?" *I had my doubts, but I'll ask anyway.*

"Well, actually no, but the harbor's calm and we ken tow her right quick to a dock 'n keep the pumps goin."

Right, I'll keep on looking.

My product search was discouraging. Z-Spar Splash Zone, which we had used to patch *Banshee*, wasn't available in PNG. Apparently the only thing obtainable locally was a small amount of Poly-Poxy. *I know that stuff, it's not strong enough to withstand the hull flexing and pounding that we'd get in the open ocean. It'll crack. Fiberglass gets its strength from being woven and flexible.*

If I couldn't find something locally, then it would have to be shipped in, and that brought me up against another problem—two-part underwater epoxy is considered hazardous material and can't be shipped as air freight to PNG. *How about shipping something up from Australia by sea? There was no problem with hazardous materials as ocean freight, and a steady stream of supply ships steamed from Townsville to Port Moresby every week.*

It was noon already, and businesses were closing for the weekend. I took my newly-found knowledge along with my discouragement to the cafeteria for lunch. As it turned out, that was one of the best decisions I made.

"May we join you for lunch?"

The educated English voice with a German accent surprised me. I looked up at two well-dressed men in comfortable sports clothes. They looked to be in their mid-thirties.

Happy to have company, I encouraged them to sit down.

They weren't German, it turned out, but Austrian. We exchanged the usual "What are you doing here?" tourist conversation, until they zeroed in on my saga. They were fascinated and wouldn't let the subject drop. When I mentioned getting off Hermit due to my damaged finger, one of them grabbed my hand and started to examine it.

They exchanged *"Ja's"* and nodding heads as they conferred over my roughly-healed finger. My puzzled expression made them laugh.

"We are surgeons and hands are my specialty."

They were charming. The hand surgeon deemed the healed fingertip satisfactory. "However, I could have improved on the job, the technique is rather rough."

"Technique!," I laughed. "They wanted to chop it off at the next joint, but I stopped them."

When I told them that our goal was to sail the boat to Madang for repairs, they gave me the most valuable information I could ask for.

"We just came from Madang. You must go see Glenn Ritchie and Greg Mitchell at Bush Development. They have a fiberglass boat-building factory right next to the government marine railway. Ring them this afternoon, they'll certainly help you. They build boats there."

I was ecstatic to have this information. Gobbling lunch as politely as possible, I couldn't wait to run back to my room and get on the telephone.

As PNG has only one phone directory for the entire country, Bush Development, Ltd., in Madang was easy to find. One ring and I was talking to the affable Glenn Ritchie himself.

"You can bring your boat in right behind me when me yacht's off the slip. No worries, just get yourselves here." He answered all my questions about the situation in Madang for repairing *Banshee*, and how to get in there with an engineless sailboat.

"Don't worry, darlin', we'll come out 'n fetch ya. Can't sail yer bloody boat in here, there's no wind, so you'll need a tow. Just call us on Channel 82 when you get close."

Wonderful news, but still we had to get there.

Glenn then gave me crucial sailing directions for our trip to Madang. He had sailed his own boat throughout the northern islands of PNG for many years and knew it well. He told me we must pass outside the two large islands, Karkar and Bagabag, that lie to the north of Madang in Astrolabe Bay. "Do not," he cautioned, "attempt to go through any of the narrow straits between the islands or the mainland." He said they all have very strong currents, and at dusk, the wind may die due to the high mountains and large land mass of the mainland. "Without an engine yer'd be in serious trouble."

Remembering Ronnie's chart, I knew this would make a much longer trip than a direct passage through the strait between the mainland and Karkar. But his was the voice of experience, and I listened.

"Underwater epoxy, though, that's another story. We don't have it here, I can tell yer that. You ought'a try down south. Bring some up on a ship. That's how I get all me hazardous in."

This was all great to know, but I still need to find the epoxy. It's time for an Internet search.

The Grantham had no Internet service, but it was available at the Gateway Hotel. Standing at the front desk, I looked up at the imposing gates of my current "fortress" accommodation and asked for transportation.

"When would you like to go, ma'am?"

"Now, please." *There was no time to waste.*

Soon my driver-guard and I were driving through the streets of the fortified city and into another gated fortress. As he dropped me off and I entered the foyer, I realized just how upscale the Gateway was. *Definitely five-star.* I felt conspicuous in my shabby, tattered clothes and unkempt, raggedy hair.

I inquired at reception about Internet services and was waved to the Business Center "ova thea." *Sort of an improvement on "long hap."* My dialect understanding was improving. *Wonder what they think of mine, in this completely Australian-influenced place?* I felt stares following me; I was sure that I looked much too disreputable to be taken as a tourist.

The Business Center was behind glass doors and manned by an efficient national woman in hotel uniform.

"You are a guest *hia?*" she asked dubiously, giving me the once-over.

When I shook my head, she explained the per/half-hour charges for non-guests. *Ouch. Better hurry—it could add up quickly.* Seated, with an Internet computer terminal in front of me, I was in a world I understood. *The planet's information in front of me.*

I sent the search engines whirling, tracking down what we needed. An hour sped past—nothing encouraging yet. I got up for a stretch. *Damn, all this stuff is hazardous. It will have to come by ship. And then I have to get it to Lorengau—that's a plane ride for sure.*

A well-groomed man occupied the next door office in the Business Center complex. The sign on the door said, "Paul Burke, Manager." *Hmm, Australian.* I asked him a question. Soon I was sitting in his well-appointed office chatting away to an avid listener. He was intrigued, and my "refugee" appearance underscored my tale.

"What are they charging you at the Grantham? Rather a dodgy place, isn't it?"

His accent said Educated and City, not Working-Class or Outback. I had lived in Australia long enough to know the difference.

"A hundred ten kina a night."

He groaned and rolled his eyes.

"Look, for a third less, I can put you up here. This is a slow time and we've got lots of rooms."

"You can?" I stammered, amazed at his offer.

"Sure, no worries. When can you get over here?"

Almost at a loss for words, I managed to say that I had paid for two nights with the proviso stamped on my receipt—"no cancellations, no refunds."

He laughed. "Yeah, I know, that's the Grantham. I'll send the bus to pick you up, let's say 9 a.m. tomorrow?"

As I stumbled out of his office in a daze at my good fortune, he called after me: "Tomorrow you'll be a guest and the Internet's free. Use it all you want, it's on 24 hours. Perhaps you'll find what you're looking for."

I was speechless, as he quietly told the attendant that Ms. Smith would be a guest and all present charges would be waived.

All I could do was smile as I dialed the Grantham for pickup. Words could not express my gratitude. I tried. He waved me off, saying, "It's a pleasure. Enjoy yourself while you are here with us."

It was as though the Grantham staff knew that I had been stolen away by the Gateway. Their resigned looks said, "We just can't compete." Another dreary evening ensued, featuring cafeteria-style gravy-soaked food and then back to my jail cell. By nine the next morning, I was eager to depart.

The check-in at the Gateway was an incredible contrast.

"Oh yes, Mr. Burke told us to expect you. Just a moment while I ring him."

Shortly, Paul, in impeccable hotel manager attire, came striding across the foyer, greeting guests and directing staff, and headed straight for me.

"Good-day and welcome to the Gateway."

"Please have Ms. Smith's bags taken to her room, and Joy, we're serving Sunday brunch at the pool. Please join us. It's right this way," he said guiding me to the terrace.

"By the way, we've put you in one of our Premier rooms. Hope you enjoy it. Just ask the staff for anything you may need."

The poolside brunch was lovely, the setting out of a glossy tourist magazine, and I felt sinfully guilty as I sat down to a full plate of goodies that I hadn't tasted in ages. The sheer luxury overwhelmed me. I felt rooted in my soft chair as I surveyed the tourist public happily taking in Sunday brunch, with the kiddies splashing in the pool and running back and forth to indulging parents.

My room was lovely—much too much for me. *I've never been in a "Premier" room before. Not exactly Motel 6.* The amenities that most people would take for granted in an upscale hotel room came as a shock. I took a long hot shower and napped on one of the giant beds. *My god, the bunk on* Banshee *is a quarter this size.*

Soon I was back on the Internet, searching for epoxy. The unlimited computer access also gave me an opportunity to communicate with family and friends, and to catch up on world news. One of the first stories I read was of the destruction on Guam from Super Typhoon Pongsona, in early December. *We were right. That was when all that heavy weather hit Hermit, just before the typhoon hit Guam.*

I started e-mail conversations with Sue and Larry, Leslie's mother and father, and with Tammi, Leslie's sister. I also contacted my brother, David, and learned that my mother was still okay at 90—they were taking her out to dinner for her birthday. She knew I was all right and that *Banshee* was saved. I was coming out of isolation. *I'll have a lot to share with Les.*

I learned that after Sue had received the call from the U.S. Coast Guard when the water-activated *ACR 406 MHz EPIRB* went off, she called Tammi on her cell phone as she was driving home from work. A shocked Tammi quickly notified her father, Larry Brown, a maritime attorney in Connecticut. My brother, Dave, also received a similar call at 4 a.m., as both he and Sue were listed as dual contacts. Unknown to us at the time, Sue, Larry, and Tammi went to work sending emails and telephoning contacts on our behalf, since the Coast Guard told them that we were out of U.S. jurisdiction.

Tammi recalled that she had received a brief satmail communication from Leslie while we were anchored at Hermit, sent via the *Magellan GSC 100*, just three days prior to the EPIRB beacon going off. Larry, through his shipping contacts, notified ships in the vicinity to search for and report any news of the missing yacht. All three worked with the Australian Search and Rescue office in Canberra, Australia to coordinate efforts with PNG officials. Sue, through her travel connections, contacted Sir Peter Barter, owner of the Madang Resort, and also a prominent Member of Parliament in PNG. Both Sir Peter and his son Andrew Barter provided invaluable assistance in getting through the PNG bureaucracy.

Tammi sent out numerous e-mails, finally ending up with a contact in Wendy Johnson, at the U.S. Bureau of Consular Affairs-American Citizen's Services. She put

Tammi in touch with our American ambassador in PNG, Susan Jacobs. Sue began a daily routine of telephone contacts with either her or Heather Guimond at the embassy in PNG. The ambassador told Sue that the Hermits were a series of small islands with no communications available. However, she made Sue one promise.

"If they are alive somewhere, we will find them no matter how long it takes. I will send an officer with an Iridium satellite phone and a digital camera, so that when he finds them, you'll hear your daughter's voice."

A police patrol boat was located in Lorengau, but funding was not available to dispatch the 22-foot high-speed diesel boat to Hermit. A U.S. Foreign Service officer, Mark Prokop, was detailed to make the trip to Manus. He arrived on the island on Saturday, October 26. On Sunday, he reported to the embassy.

"I have learned from local residents that both women were sighted alive and well on Wednesday, the 23rd, at Hermit Atoll on the small island of Luf in the Admiralty Chain west of Manus."

Sue immediately provided funding for the boat trip to and from Hermit, and Mark left on his mission to find us. Then, in the middle of the night of October 28, she said her phone rang and she heard Leslie's voice.

"Mom, I knew you'd find me. I knew you'd never give up."

The story unfolded. We were not alone anymore.

The next day Paul Burke took me along as he had some shopping to do. He was having an old local motor boat restored, so knew all the marine stores.

"Maybe they can give you some information or leads."

He dropped me off at a fiberglass materials shop and I had a long discussion with the very knowledgeable owners. It was the same old story, though—the only stuff available in PNG was polyester car filler—everything else was hazardous cargo and could only come in by ship. *And then how would I get it to Lorengau from Moresby? The MV Manus? I couldn't leave Les on Hermit that long.*

I was becoming rather discouraged at our prospects and at the depressing conditions in Port Moresby. I felt trapped having to exist behind gates and razor wire. I wanted to walk to relieve some of my stress, but all I could safely do was pace inside my gated fortress. On the four-lane highway leading back to the hotel, we passed huge movable spiked gates on massive poles at the side of the road.

"What are those?" I asked Paul.

"When the locals riot, the troops can swing the gates closed across the highway. If we need to, they can block off the city from all vehicles coming in. We've got them installed on all the highways leading into the city."

My god, it was a war zone. How does anyone live here?

Finally, I realized that I needed to change my Internet search criteria. I typed in "Epoxy non-hazmat, epoxy air-shippable" Bingo! The words leapt out at me. "Epoxy air shipping, non-hazardous." I clicked on www.epoxyproducts.com, and read the words I'd been hoping to find: "Air-shippable two-part underwater epoxy. We ship worldwide." I just sat there and stared, scrolling down the page. I felt like crying, and probably did. It didn't matter—I was all alone in that little room on the day before Christmas.

We'd get Banshee out of Hermit, now. We were going to make it.

I quickly dispatched an e-mail to the contact person—Paul Oman, the owner of Progressive Epoxy Polymers—and calculated the time difference. Paul was on the other side of the world—fifteen time zones away in New Hampshire. I thought about how cold and wintry it must be where he was as I padded through the tropical lobby in my faded shorts and worn-through shirt. *Maybe he checks his e-mail at home?*

Which is exactly what happened—I got a reply within hours.

"Yes, we can help you. Our products are exactly what you need. Here's another email address you can use, it's at my house. And don't worry about Christmas, I'll be home all day. I'm happy to write and answer all your questions. We've saved boats before."

What followed was an intense back and forth communication between the east coast of the U.S. and PNG. I needed to know the technical details of their products and exactly how to use the stuff, so I could pass the information on to Leslie. *Imagine me telling Leslie, the fiberglass expert, how to use it. What a laugh.*

I soon had pages of notes detailing the use of the high-tech products. My final shopping list included their *Wet/Dry 700*, an underwater *Kevlar* reinforced epoxy paste; *CorroCoat FC 2100*, a brushable version; and the aptly named *911*, a quick-setting emergency repair now called *Quick Fix 2300*, made to stop leaks fast. I took the gallon sizes of the first two and quart size of the 911. What amazed me was that *CorroCoat* was used to saturate fiberglass cloth tape, which was then applied over a base of the *Wet Dry*. I had never heard of using fiberglass cloth underwater. *There's the strength we need for the hull. It'll handle the flexing that we're going to get at sea. Now we can do it!*

Paul said he could ship everything directly through to Lorengau by DHL via Air Niugini. All it would take was my sunken credit card. I was ecstatic—absolutely floating on air.

The rest of my stay in Port Moresby was definitely anticlimactic. Getting a return flight to Manus was next to impossible during the holidays. I placed myself on every standby list and called Air Niugini twice daily.

I spent the time web surfing and writing long e-mails. I remembered to order a Caframo fan for the ghastly equatorial heat and a handheld VHF radio from West Marine, thinking of all the ships we would pass in the night during our engineless, unlit passage to Madang. Sue wanted us to have another Magellan GSC 100 to communicate via satmail. *Fine. The sunken Garmin 48 GPS is still working, so the Magellan's GPS will give me a backup.*

The posh trappings of the tourist hotel were lost on me. There were two choices for eating: the hotel dining room and the Italian bistro on a lower floor of the complex. I felt guilty about residing in such unaccustomed luxury and was terribly concerned about the expense. The streets were hazardous to my health, so it wasn't as though I could nip out for a quick bite at MacDonald's.

I limited myself to one purchased meal a day and kept fruit and snacks in my room's refrigerator. The hotel kindly arranged an escorted visit to a local supermarket—*Boroko Food World*, where I saw normal, everyday citizens going about their shopping chores seemingly inured to their violent surroundings. My stash of rum was gone, so I paid too much for a bottle of heavy, dark PNG rum. I consoled myself with an evening drink in private with the TV for company. Christmas was lonely, but the dinner was sumptuous. I thought about Les and talked with her in my imagination.

My position on the Air Niugini standby list was improving. I was told to show up and wait at the counter at flight time, and I'd have a good chance of getting out of there on Sunday, between Christmas and New Year's.

And it actually worked, although my baggage was a problem. Air Niugini only allows 18 kg/ person, about 40 lbs. With all my goodies bought in the Big City, I was over the limit—my baggage might have to go on a later flight. While standing in line, I hurriedly repacked everything, putting essentials in my backpack. I scurried out on the tarmac at the last minute and was relieved to make it aboard. From the little plane's window, I watched the baggage cart as it wheeled close to the plane for loading. There was my familiar bag and box of "must haves" piled on top. *Yes! I did it, mission accomplished. Now get me out of here.*

JOY IN LORENGAU TOWN AGAIN

Joy

Back on the *balus*. The plane soared high above coral-fringed islands and reefs set on an azure sea. The view this time was made even more spectacular by a low-altitude flight leg into Manus after a stop at Kavieng.

Before leaving Moresby, I had arranged with the Harbourside Hotel in Lorengau for a two-night stay so I could take care of shopping in town first, and later move to the much cheaper Akau guesthouse. Then, I'd await the arrival of the epoxy and my other stateside purchases and find passage out to Hermit. I remembered all too well my previous stay in Lorengau and all the hard work of lugging heavy supplies on my back out to Akau's. I didn't want to repeat that and had quite a list of supplies to buy for our voyage to Madang. Confident in my plans, I enjoyed the aerial interlude.

The little plane touched down on the runway's rough surface. Momote Airport and the long, two-lane road connecting it to Lorengau were built by the Seabees in WWII to service Lobrum naval base, home of the American fleet. Now only a cleared field in endless jungle with ramshackle buildings lining an old runway remained of the once vital airport. Open and staffed solely during scheduled flights, it appeared lonely and desolate so far away from the civilization of town.

Bags collected, I watched and waited for the Harbourside's bus. Cars and trucks left with friends and relatives and the crowd thinned out. The Air Niugini attendant inquired, "You have transport?"

I explained that I had made arrangements with the hotel. He gave me a guarded look.

"Harbourside Hotel bus *em* neva' late."

The last trucks left carrying newly arrived missionaries. *White women with long skirts, they're easy to spot.* I became concerned and asked the attendant to phone the hotel.

"Yes, *Misis*. We told the manager that you want to stay and about your flight when you ring from Moresby. *Misis*, sorry, true."

Something's not right.

The airport staff began to lock up, loading the cargo bags and boxes onto the big Air Niugini truck.

I stood by the gate, watching and waiting. It was very lonely.

"*Misis*, you cannot stay *hia*. It is dangerous place for you to be alone. Whatever happen, you come with us, okay?"

I climbed up into the back of the truck, holding onto the roof's supports to keep my balance on the narrow slat benches, and shared space with the cargo guys and their various boxes and bags. It was a rough, back-jarring, half-hour ride into town, but I was grateful for their kindness. *What had happened with my reservation? Why no bus? I could have been in a lot of trouble out there alone in that deserted place—thank you, Air Niugini.*

Trundling my baggage in my rusty cart through the potholes in the dirt road over to the hotel, I was confused and upset. It was late afternoon now. *Why didn't they come and get me? Where am I going to sleep?*

The receptionist looked very embarrassed. "*Misis*, you go see the manager. We told him you were coming. Sorry."

I knocked on the manager's door and a gruff voice said, "Enter."

Same desk, same man, same attitude. He wouldn't look at me. I stood there and stared.

"I made reservations. I rang from Moresby. What happened? There was no bus. Air Niugini brought me in."

Silence. He kept shuffling his papers.

"Go somewhere else, you're not welcome here. You cause trouble, tell stories."

"What are you talking about? What stories? Please, I just want a room for two nights. What's this all about?"

"You tell stories. You lied to me to cause trouble and upset people. You didn't have any spirits with you; you just made that up to cause problems here."

I felt my legs getting weak and sat down. Tears welled up in my eyes. I felt alone and unjustly accused. *I've tried so hard to say and do everything right. Where am I going to stay? It's getting late...*

"Please sir, what's this all about? Honestly, I did have a bottle of rum in my room. I brought it with me from Hermit, from my boat."

He loudly cut me off.

"You're lying!" he shouted. "You didn't have any spirits. You couldn't have. Your boat sank on Hermit and you lost everything. There's no liquor on Hermit, yours or anyone else's, and you know it. If you had it, it was sunk when your boat went down.

Stop lying to me. You made up that whole story just to cause trouble here. We know all about you."

I was in shock. *This guy is nuts.*

"Who told you all this?"

"Valerie Knight."

I was incredulous. *Why, Val's my friend.* I tried to reason with him. I asked for a phone, thinking I could call Akau's guesthouse. His cruel, cutting laugh rang in my ears. Nothing worked. He just kept yelling, "Get out! Valerie Knight told me and she knows everything, her son was there on Hermit."

I left. I needed air.

I wandered out the hotel's gates. I was shaking. *Got to find a place to stay… need a phone… going to get dark soon. I'll find Val and ask her.* I dragged my bags over to Val's nearby office.

V. AND R. KNIGHT SHIPPING read the chipped and peeling sign above the dilapidated roadside office. I went in and walked through the mess back to the ticket counter. I called out Valerie's name.

No answer.

Angie, Ronnie's kind, hardworking wife, came out to me.

"Shh… she's not here. Joy, I can't say anything, but I know what is going on. Please understand, I want to help. Go wait in front of Air Niugini and I'll ring Akau's. They come down and get you. They like you over there. Go now, before someone comes. Don't say anything about me, please."

I sat on the cement curb in front of the closed Air Niugini office, my bags and cart in front of me. *Like some homeless person again.* It was dark now and the security light of the office illuminated my patch of cement. Several people stopped, stared, and then continued on their way. A couple of drunken men tried to sit next to me, but somehow I got rid of them. *I must be a strange sight to them—white women do not camp out on street corners in this country.* I nervously planned my next step. *Okay, if they don't come, I'll just start walking up the main road to Akau's. Dangerous, yeah, but what are my choices?*

I held my breath at each pair of headlights coming down the road. They all went on by. *No, wait… One's stopping. C'mon, is it the Akau truck? Is that Lois?*

"Joy, get in quickly. Throw your bags in back. We can't stop *hia.*"

"Lois, thank goodness. What's going on?"

"Please, Joy, I can't say anything. You stay with us, okay? You eat yet?"

I shook my head, totally confused by all this drama, but very thankful I still had some friends in this crazy place.

I settled into the familiar routine at the guesthouse, even got my old room back. I soon got over my unpleasant arrival in Lorengau, chalking it up to a small-minded attempt to derail my boat rescue progress. It didn't take much thought to figure out the motivations involved—I knew the main players too well.

This time I did all my own cooking. I didn't have too many options: I had gotten sick at one hotel and was banned from the other, which left only the *kai bars*. One look at those on my last visit told me to stay clear. But now, I actually wanted to cook and eat my own food. Perhaps this and my resilience about the arrival incident was an indication of my return to a normal mental state.

The lugging of my purchased supplies was the same pain it was before, and I had a lot of purchases on my list. This time, however, I discovered a shortcut along the beachfront by the Knight compound. I never saw Ronnie; I heard he was off somewhere and hoped it wasn't Hermit. Val ducked inside if she happened to see me along the beach path. *What strange people— I had thought they were friends and wanted to help us.*

I had no idea of exactly how I was going to get back to Hermit, but as my stateside purchases hadn't arrived yet (due to the holiday postal jam) I couldn't leave anyway, nor make any commitments. In the back of my mind I knew that Joen was here and staying at Roy Joseph's house, and at some point she would want to return to Hermit. School would resume soon, and she was still the teacher.

New Year's Eve was never one of my favorite holidays. Too much noise and I never could stay awake until midnight. As I was the only guest, the Akau family invited me to watch TV and "party" with them. I politely declined and went to bed early, only to listen to the sound of too many people banging around below, a blaring TV, and rats scurrying over my head in the attic.

The New Year brought a wonderful new friend to my little "home" at the guesthouse. Betty was thirtyish, university educated, and charming. She was from Rabaul, and had come to give a three-week training seminar for the Manus employees of Telecom, the national phone company. Through her, I gained a new insight into the educated upper class of PNG nationals and the culture of her industrious ethnic group, the *Tolai*. A considerable contrast to the laid-back Hermit islanders.

Betty and I became fast friends, and shared shopping and cooking duties. One night it would be "American" style cuisine from me, and the next would be one of Betty's *Tolai* favorites. I remember coming home and finding this well-dressed woman in the kitchen, her skirt hiked up to her knees, straddling a coconut grater bench grinding away preparing coconut milk, which is so often used in PNG dishes. I teased her about *meri* city turning into *meri bilong bus* (bush). My Pidgin improved rapidly, as she insisted—"for your benefit"—that we generally speak nothing else.

I started making regular stops at Roy Joseph's house to see Joen on my daily town forays. Conversation didn't flow as easily between us as it did with Betty, but I had to make the effort—Joen was my Hermit link, and would know whenever there was a boat returning to Hermit. I had to lather myself in Rid cream to deflect the hoards of flies and mosquitoes that infested their house and yard. I hated to go over there, and Betty teased me about it, telling me she wouldn't go near the place. I learned that there is quite a bit of class consciousness among various groups in PNG. "Some places one doesn't go," Betty said.

Joen told me she would be returning to Hermit "soon." Eventually I determined that she was talking about going on *Supamanus. Good, now how do I get aboard, too? Going to take a bit of delicate politicking. To get to Hermit, you can't just buy a ticket unless a cargo ship happens along.*

On one of my visits, Joen handed me a duct tape-wrapped letter from Leslie. She spoke of harassment from the men, particularly as they wanted more and more repairs done to their fiberglass speedies. Most of the items she requested were fortunately unavailable in Lorengau. I had no interest in purchasing more fiberglass supplies for Hermit, not after the quarts and quarts of expensive resin that we had already "donated." I concentrated on the women's cooking needs—baking powder, yeast and flour, and on our own provisions. I'd had enough of the men's demands. Her letter made me sad that I couldn't be there to deflect the men's authoritarian insistence. A young-looking single woman in PNG has a rough road.

Two of my three packages arrived at Air Niugini cargo. I had to beg Lois to collect the heavy gallon cans of epoxy in her father's truck. The missing package was the replacement Magellan GSC 100 GPS unit. I had no Internet connection to track the missing package, just the phone line to Port Moresby. I called daily for the entire week after New Year's.

Nothing.

Friday morning I saw a large white ship at the jetty—the *Elfride*. Racing over, I found my old friend, Mikah, the captain. Yes, they were going to Hermit, departing on Sunday.

"Would you like a ride?"

Would I ever! But I had to decline, as the Magellan hadn't arrived yet. *Damn.* However, I took the opportunity to quickly put together a large rainbow bag of goodies and provisions for Leslie, and included a hastily scribbled note. Mikah smiled at my proffered fifty-kina note and promised that the message would be personally delivered.

Betty and I had a guest over for dinner, a *Tolai* friend of hers whose husband was from Manus. Somehow, Betty had acquired some delicious mangrove crabs for our meal, and we sat there, the three of us, picking through the shells. The woman was a public health nurse employed by the Manus government. The conversation that night was, for me, a revelation into PNG society. These two intelligent women easily carried on in three languages: their vernacular *Tolai tok ples*, Pidgin, and fluent English (presumably for me).

After dinner, Betty's friend pulled out a smuggled pint flask of scotch. Betty and I smiled. Over-the-counter sales of spirits were prohibited in Lorengau, a sad fact I had discovered after my bottle from Moresby poured its last drop. *Perhaps another reason my "stolen" bottle of rum had caused such a stir.* The conversation warmed and I learned a lot.

"In PNG, health problems are so rampant—in remote villages there's no health care at all, unless there is a missionary presence. Simple infections are often fatal. There's also TB, and now the AIDS crisis is becoming uncontrollable—the population is already weakened by endemic malaria, and it's rapidly turning into an African-style pandemic of AIDS. The men, the prostitution, the cultural taboos and superstitions, and the practice of multiple wives are all making this an insurmountable problem. What can we do when even the governor of our province has two wives? Both the UN and WHO have been here and warned us. It's only a matter of time. You can't change PNG men and the culture."

They both nodded. One was married and the other single by choice.

"I don't want a PNG man ordering me around," Betty said. "I've done very well by myself with a management career and a house that I share on my land with my mother. I would like to have children someday, though, but what can I do?"

One morning as I was pushing my shopping cart through "Papindo's" narrow aisles, a familiar face stopped me. Roy Joseph.

"I hear you need a ride back to Hermit."

I nodded and smiled. *My plan was working.*

"Good, I have *Supamanus* leaving Sunday night. Can you be on it?"

"Of course." *Surely, that Magellan will arrive sometime this week or I'll really be stuck.*

We talked about my numerous *kagos* and the cost of shipping them along with me.

"No worries, I won't charge you extra, plenty of room in the covered bow section. You talk with Joen and she'll set it all up. My boys will come pick you up. You stay at Akau's, right?"

Mission accomplished, Hermit-style.

The Magellan arrived later in the week. I couldn't get the damned thing to work; it simply wouldn't pick up a satellite. Complaining about it to Lois, I told her that if I could just find an Internet connection, I could contact the distributor and maybe find out what was wrong.

"Oh, I have Internet."

"You do? I had no idea. Can I pay you to use it?"

All this time I could have been getting on-line! Damn, wish she would have told me.

We made arrangements and I was connected to the outside world once again. Sue was delighted to hear from me and so were Larry, Barbara, and Tammi, but the Magellan was a dead issue. Nothing could be done from my end; perhaps the unit was a dud.

Once I left Lorengau, I knew that we would be out of communication until we reached Madang on *Banshee*. I used the Internet opportunity to give family contacts an idea of when we might be arriving in Madang. I also corresponded with Mitch at Bush Development in Madang, and provided a rough timetable for our repairs and voyage. He agreed to be our contact person in PNG for officials and family.

I told everyone that I wasn't sure if our life raft would work, so we would make the passage to Madang with our Avon hard-floor dinghy inflated on deck. If we had to ditch because the epoxy patch wouldn't hold, we would get in the Avon and activate the EPIRB.

I wasn't being dramatic. I didn't want to scare anyone, I was just being factual. The voyage will be risky and dangerous, but if we were going to save our floating home we had to do it.

LESLIE'S "*PEBEKIM* TIME"

New Year's Day 2003

Leslie

The loud squawking of chickens and children's high-pitched screams of laughter punctuated the dawn as the gong tolled out the new day.

I made my tea and climbed out into the cockpit to check out the raucous scene on the beach. *Kids torturing chickens? No, killing them for the feast today.* I jumped in the dinghy, rowed ashore, and walked past the carnage. *It was revolting.*

"*Em* i *kakaruk* (chicken) *bilong* me, Leslie?" Lynnah asked.

"Beats me, I don't know one from the other."

"You come *bek long* noon when *kai* ready. *Bringim plet* (plate)."

When I returned to the house, Lynnah introduced me to Ben's brother from Lae, a large, articulate man who looked like he belonged in a city. She informed me that he would stay with me during the celebration. *They seem so very protective; I wonder why?*

We gathered near the ongoing volleyball game and watched for a while. I moved away from our little group and another large man approached me, Alwin, Okip's brother. He grabbed my hand as if to shake it, and while laughing at me, tightened his grip until I fell to my knees.

"Let me go, get him off me!" I yelled.

Ben rushed over and told him to get away. Alwin slapped me on the shoulder and stomped off to join some laughing women.

"What was that all about?" I asked Lynnah.

"He *soim* you he is *bikman*—*moabeta* (better) than you. You know, like… you not so strong, even *afta* you get your boat up. *Maski* him. Leslie, why you no stay right *hia* with us? Joy not *hia long lukautim* (watch out)."

My friend Mary broke the tension, presenting me with a big plate of barbequed chicken.

"Please eat now, I know you are hungry."

I gladly dug in, trying to forget the nonsense around me.

For the rest of the day we watched Stanley lead a chorus of *pikinini* in singing and screeching, as they tried to reach the higher notes. Finally, long tables were brought out and the *meries* started setting out pots of food. Stanley proudly informed me that they had slaughtered the only cow. I'm sure I offended them all when I told them I didn't eat red meat, especially from a freshly-killed cow.

As we had seen at community meals before, no buffet was laid out and no dish was shared. Each family ate separately. I tried to move around a bit to see what dishes other people had brought, and was motioned by Paul to stay with "my" family. *What a strange way of having a feast.* I wasn't pleased with being so restricted. I wanted to move around and visit, see what others were eating— "*schmooze,*" my mother would call it.

I heard that my "escort" was leaving that night on *Supamanus* to Lorengau—*I've got to get a letter to Joy.* I scurried off to *Banshee* for writing supplies. By the time I got back, he had gone to Peter's house. At first, he was very reluctant to take the note.

"I don't want problems. I'll be on a boat with those men all night. Maybe they think you tell Joy stories. I hear things, you know."

Eventually I persuaded him and he slipped my sealed and taped note into his pocket. Happy to get a message off to Joy, I returned to the peace and sanity of my boat, well fed and with my pockets bulging with leftover sweet bananas.

However, the evening was not over yet. Peter came out in his canoe.

"Paul wants something from you. He and Stanley want to do fireworks."

"Fireworks? Oh, you mean flares. I'd do almost anything for Paul, but not shooting off my flares. My boat's very close to shore, right where they'd shoot them off, and I don't need a fire right now. We're going to need them for our trip. We may have to signal someone."

"But you owe Paul."

Peter was disappointed and I could see that he didn't want to return empty-handed to his leader, but I wouldn't budge.

"Good-night, Peter."

So ended New Year's Day on Hermit.

I'd had enough maddening confrontations on shore and decided to stay on *Banshee* with my repair projects. The first was to fill the six-inch diameter hole in the cabin top where the "Charley Noble" of the cabin heater had been located. Made of cast iron, the cabin heater had been an antique made in the early 1900s in New Zealand, and acquired by Joy and her husband one cold winter down south. The immersion in saltwater had finally finished it off. A bucket was currently covering the hole to keep the rain out of the cabin.

I fired up the noisy generator and started using the grinder and jigsaw, knowing that I had to finish with such "machinery things" before the Sabbath arrived again. Namo's voice interrupted me.

"*Wanem kain wok* (kind of work) you do, Leslie? *Ol* village *harim* you. You *putim* fiberglass *long hul* (hole)?"

Surprised to see him, I started to explain what I was doing. He cut me off abruptly.

"You wait, Leslie. You wait till Joy come. You no *usim moa* fiberglass *long bot, ol* fiberglass *hia bilong* me now. You wait and *usim* fiberglass Joy *bringim*."

"What? Namo, this is my fiberglass resin and I will use it to repair my boat. The cabin has a hole in it which I'm filling with wood, but I have to use resin and fiberglass to seal it."

"You *lusim wok long bot* now. You owe me. *Dispela* fiberglass *bilong* me."

"Namo, this is ridiculous! Joy isn't bringing back fiberglass resin, she's bringing underwater epoxy for the hull so we can sail out of here."

"You fix my boat now. *Dispela* fiberglass *bilong* me. How much you *gat? Mipela* come *lukim* how much you *gat* later."

He stood up in his speedie, holding on to steady himself, and became so enraged that he was shaking and waving at me. I told him to get away and jumped below, closing the hatch behind me. I was shaking too.

My adrenalin was pumping. I tried to calm down and waited until I heard his speedie motor off. *What in hell does he think he's doing? I've got a job to do and I'm going to do it. This is my boat and my resin. He's got no business coming out here. Gotta go see Paul again.*

I furiously paddled ashore and made directly to Paul's on the other side of the island. The wind fit my mood—it was howling. No one was home. *Damn, no Paul, no Natalee and not even Lynnah to help calm me down.* Everyone was in the gardens gathering food for Sabbath. I stomped around to Lynnah's house. The only person I could find was Bill's docile little wife, Babra. Seeing my angry mood, she cut down a coconut and motioned that I should sit and drink it. I smiled and nodded, remembering that she didn't speak a word of English.

I stared at the house and spotted my outboard motor hanging on a rack above the veranda. *Shit, I've repeatedly asked them to return it and nothing happens. Soon, they'll figure it's theirs.* I loosened the clamps on the motor and gently lowered it onto my shoulders—all sixty pounds of it, more than half my weight. Carefully, I walked down the veranda's steps, into the yard, and across the beach to my dinghy, sliding its heavy weight to rest in the bottom of the little boat. Bill's wife just stared at me as I paddled away. With our valuable 8 hp Johnson hoisted and securely fastened to *Banshee's* stern pulpit, I felt calmer, going over in my mind what I would tell Paul. *Without Joy here to handle the politics, I have to do it myself, and I've got to be calm.*

Soon I could see people coming back from the gardens, so I paddled back ashore and found Paul, who was his usual gracious self.

"It's good you come to me. I want to know what goes on. You *havim* trouble. Me *save*. *Aidono* if I can help, but I try. Namo has a hard head. After Sabbath, when it time to talk about village problems, I talk about this to the church elders. We work out a plan. You must be with me when I talk to Namo so we know the truth."

I nodded solemnly and thanked him, promising to stay on the boat during the Sabbath. *Thank you, dear Paul. Without you we wouldn't have made it this far.*

The promised meeting between Paul, Namo, and me was scheduled for Sunday morning before Games. I was up early and consulted with Daniel and Mary, my two "counselors." They called Namo by his given name, Namoles, from the days when he was their student in Hermit primary school. They knew him well. Their grown daughter, a teacher herself, offered to accompany me as my Pidgin interpreter. "Namo and his friends know me and my parents, and they'll be more inclined to watch what they say with me there." I was happy to have her along.

When we arrived at his area, Namo was demanding and adamant, claiming that I had to repair three more newly arrived and badly damaged speedies. This, he said, was part of my required *pebek* for the use of his outboards in the boat rescue and in fetching Joy back from Manus.

"Namo, Joy never promised that, she only agreed for me to fix your personal speedie and I've already done that. I repaired six of them before we sank, using liters and liters of our expensive resin. Besides, Joy paid for all the gasoline for the trip, donated a full fuel drum to the village, made a big cash donation, and…"

My words were lost in the rising jeers and yells from his buddies—Collen, Okip, Dougie and others. Their contempt was obvious. My attempts at explanation made it even worse. In their culture, women did not stand up to men. And as their encrusted, dripping red mouths attested, they were all high as kites on *buai*.

Paul then squared off with Namo. He tried to get Namo to be reasonable, but Namo's buddies kept whipping up tempers and pointing fingers. There were yells and threats, and through it all I could hear Namo shouting, "Joy promise! You owe, you fix or else!"

The two of us women stood by on the sidelines, holding hands in solidarity. *What am I doing here? I'm an American, not a Hermit woman. They act as if I'm a slave.*

Nothing was resolved—Namo wouldn't budge. Paul ended the confrontation by telling Namo to stay away from *Banshee*, and I gladly agreed to stay far away from Namo.

I had a few days of peace, and then one of Namo's sons came by in his dugout.

"*Misis*, me *gat leta* (letter) *long* Papa. You *rit* (read)."

The rumpled scrap of paper said, "You come, Leslie. We talk. You come get water *long* my tank. We talk *long* fiberglass."

Okay, that's a reasonable offer. I can't keep taking water from Ben's supply all the time, now that the water supply is getting tight. I decided to go see what Namo had in mind.

Jugs in hand, I arrived at his beach and filled them up first, not knowing how long this "truce" would last. Then our discussion began. I tried to be reasonable, agreeing to give him a little more resin, but putting further negotiations off until Joy's return. More demands from Namo, and then threats.

I left.

The following evening another canoe came to *Banshee*; this time it was Noly, Namo's oldest daughter—our little friend. I read her folded up note: "I *laik* go my place *long* Jalun. This *bot* no good. One hour *liklik wok, tasol.*"

Disgusted, I tore it up and threw the scraps in the canoe. The little girl gave me a look of confusion and paddled back to Papa.

The following day I paddled ashore. Lynnah had made a delicious cinnamon cake— our salvaged cinnamon, of course—and our whole "family" was happily sitting down in the *haus kuk* to eat our treat. Dougie burst in, shoving the door aside and throwing another note in front of me. Ben was outraged.

"Dispela haus bilong me! You *longlong* man. *Hausat* (Why) you *hia?* You go."

I read the note aloud: "Leslie. You, Joy break promise. When your boat in trouble, Joy give her word, you fix all my boats. Now you liars. You come my house by sundown tonight, or else."

I wrote my reply on the back and he stomped off. Considering that my temper was reaching ignition point, my simple phrase of "No, I am not coming to your house" was an act of diplomacy.

Now the coercion began in earnest. I went ashore in the evening to fetch wellwater and pick *aibica,* my only green, for dinner. I heard yells from the *pikinini* and I spotted Nolyn, Mrs. Namo herself, poling my dinghy along the shallow waters back to her overseer. *Dinghy stealing now?*

Dropping everything, I raced into the water and confronted her, grabbing the pole out of her hands and commandeering my little shore boat. *Like stealing my bike back when I was a messenger in New York City.*

The craziness continued the next day. This time she got away from me and out into deeper water. I had to run down the beach and face her off when she landed at home. Stanley intervened and shooed the crowd away from me, avoiding a nasty confrontation.

For the first time I was glad when the Sabbath arrived. Nolyn obediently went to church and no one, not even Namo, disrupted Paul's Sabbath.

Elfride dropped anchor, and I was delighted to receive a big rainbow bag of food and supplies from Joy. Her note was reassuring, telling me about her success with the underwater epoxy, but sad because she was still delayed; one package, the Magellan, had yet to arrive.

To add to the air of confrontation, Ronnie and the police boat returned from "fighting renegades on the border." Now notes started arriving from Ronnie. At first, I complied with his requests because I still held out hope of retrieving some of our missing items. He wanted my generator, soldering iron and wiring tools for yet another attempt at repairing the village radio.

I wasted a day hanging around the health office, where the radio was housed, while Ronnie and his Hermit buddies sat gossiping and joking while he tinkered with the radio, and then I endured the usual aggravation and demeaning comments when I went to retrieve my precious tools and lug them back to *Banshee*.

His next message requested diving equipment, and I balked. Then he wanted flares and my flare gun. Then he asked for diesel fuel. I placated him with the fuel, as our engine was now a lost cause. After that, he left me alone and spent his time fishing and joy riding on the police boat.

Poor, browbeaten Nolyn continued to steal the dinghy whenever she could. I was afraid to go ashore for fear of her pinching it. I tried to keep my eyes on the little boat, but eventually she succeeded and I found it high and dry behind Namo's house. Ronnie was camped next to it, grinning at me.

By the time I found Paul, I was almost in tears. Night was falling, *Banshee* was dark and unguarded, and I couldn't get home without swimming. I sensed that Paul was fed up too as he walked with me through the village back to Namo's place. All the *buai*-chewing boys were there waiting for us, lounging around the shipwrecked speedies.

I didn't see Paul angry very often, but this was one of those times. He didn't request that they move my dinghy to the water—he *ordered* them, as the government-sanctioned leader of the community. They complied, reluctantly, but we had to agree to some concessions. Repairs to some of the damaged boats would begin tomorrow with a limited amount of our materials, but Paul insisted that he himself would do the grinding; all I had to do was supervise, they said.

Paul took me aside and said, "I *no ken* control them. We *mas* go along with it."

I went home, shaking with anger. *I am a free American. I am not a slave in this foreign country.* Crying, I found our U.S. flag and draped it over my fishing pole in the ceiling rack. Each day, it gave me connectedness: *I'm still an American, I have my family's support and Joy will be successful.*

For the rest of the week, I worked as an unpaid laborer. Thankfully, Ronnie and Bill disappeared off to Manus. Paul tried grinding for about two hours, but then quit and found a replacement in Stuart, who spoke no English. Namo translated, and I used a few Pidgin words and hand motions to guide him as he ground down the damaged fiberglass. None of the boys did a thing except stare, chew, and yell at me with commands and directions as he and I worked. Often, I had to do the finish grinding myself. Eventually, I stopped being such a perfectionist.

Our resurrected generator gave up and slowed to a stop. Namo's repair efforts were to no avail and my dejection deepened. We knew it was marginal after the sinking, and agreed to use it only for our projects. Now we would have nothing to power our salvaged power tools. Another generator was commandeered from Steven, a friend of Stuart's. But of course, my power tools wouldn't run on its 240v power. More tools were "borrowed."

Namo was having his way. I worked my way down the line of speedies in a one-woman assembly line. It didn't help that they took crowbars and demolished loosened structures that could have been easily faired and strengthened. They just laughed, yelling at me: "You *save,* you *wokim gud."* *I know Joy will stop this insanity when she gets back here. And, if I placate them now, hopefully they will let us out of here without harm.* Those thoughts kept me going. *"Pebekim* time" was very real and very painful.

Finally, Joy's *Toksave* came through on the shortwave. She was leaving Manus on the *Supamanus* this coming Sunday night. *The insanity would be over.*

Sunday night the weather deteriorated. The wind rose, and thunder and lightning blasted us in a succession of rainsqualls on Hermit. *I know* Banshee *and I will be okay, but Joy is out there in that strange little speedie in this god-awful weather.* I was so worried.

The foul weather kept raging all day. People stayed in their houses and I stayed aboard *Banshee* until afternoon.

There was no sign of *Supamanus.*

I was nervous and walked the beach in the gale to ease my tension. The wind-whipped surf crashed on the sand. Paul joined me. We stood on the beach looking out past *Banshee* at the crashing waves on the outer reef.

"Is *Banshee* safe? Your anchors *gud?"*

"*Banshee* is okay, but I'm worried that Joy's not going to make it. Last night was bad, I couldn't sleep."

"I am up *long* night too, Leslie. Hedis, me, we pray. Now I worry. *Supamanus* makes the trip many times. The *draiva, em i save* what to do. We pray *long* church tonight. You pray, Leslie, you pray, *tasol."*

AN ILL-FATED VOYAGE

Joy

Sunday afternoon and there was a town power blackout. My thirteen boxes and bags of *kago* lay waiting at the guesthouse doorway. The departure day had arrived for my ride on *Supamanus* back to Hermit. I'd been ready since noon.

The two big fans in the guesthouse common room were down, so we all sought the cooler shade and breezes outside. Eventually, I gave up waiting for my ride, ate something, and took a nap as darkness fell. I knew that the *Supamanus* crew wanted to travel at night, hoping for lighter winds. It was still the northwesterly season, which meant we would be heading straight into the waves going back to Hermit.

It wasn't until well after dark that the power came back on. Soon afterwards loud shouts and the noise of men clumping up the stairs to my room roused me from my comfortable bed. They had been delayed at the service station, unable to pump fuel until the electricity was restored. By the time we loaded up the truck and drove down to the beach, it was nearly 8 pm.

The truck stopped on a deserted beach lined with wind-whipped palm trees, washed-up logs, and other debris. Waves crashed on the sand. I'd never been there before and really had no idea of where we were. I was a bit apprehensive—it was a dark and lonely place. *I'm sure taking a lot on faith with people I hardly know.*

The only illumination came from flashlights as local people carried bags and boxes out to an old, broken-down stone and cement jetty. One white-skin *meri* among a crowd of Pidgin-chattering locals to whom this was a way of life. I found Joen and instantly felt more secure. I could talk with her in my own language, and she was a veteran of these trips.

I peered over the side of the jetty. It was low tide—*Supamanus* was a long way down. She was about thirty feet in length and narrow in breadth. She rolled and thumped into the old war-era jetty as each swell passed under her. As the guys brought out my *kagos*, I counted to be sure there were still thirteen. It was reassuring that they also counted, asking me to confirm that all were present and loaded.

The passengers boarded after the cargo was stowed away. *Gosh, this boat looks too small and tippy to carry so many people. And that heavy northwest swell coming in is a bit unnerving.*

I followed the women as we were assisted into the boat and directed to sit on a wooden loading pallet in the middle of the boat. A 40 h.p. Yamaha outboard hung on the boat's transom, and a spare one was secured and covered with tarps behind our pallet. I still had my resilient deck cushion and was very glad for it as I made a place for myself among the *meries*. One woman's husband was aboard—Douglas, from Lou Island, south of Manus, another SDA village. The rest of the *meries* were traveling on their own.

The spare engine lay athwartship, and the two upright 55-gallon fuel drums behind it formed a divider across the boat. One drum had a thin plastic hose stuffed into its opening, a no-nonsense fuel line. Plastic bags taped around it kept the spray and rain out. It took a lot of fuel for this run—at least one drum and perhaps more depending on the sea conditions.

The men stayed together behind this barrier. John, the regular driver, sat next to the *stia* motor on the transom, ready to start it up. *Typical PNG—men one place, women another, even on ocean-going speedies.*

One man sat alone on the bow's cabin roof with a heavy dive light in one hand and a long pole in the other. He was our guide through the shallow reefs off the jetty.

Sitting down next to Joen, between the *meries*, there was barely enough room to extend our legs. We were packed in like sardines. The women pulled tarps around us, and I got the idea that we were in for a wet and cold trip. *If it's this tippy now, what's it going to be like in the open sea?*

There was a noisy commotion at the stern when somebody, unbelievably, dropped the handheld GPS overboard. Edwin, the alternate driver, quickly stripped to his briefs and dived over the side. Surfacing in one breath, he held the GPS above his head, clasped tightly in his hand. It was very dead. *Do they have another one?*

Lots of loud male bragging ensued, claiming how they didn't need any GPS to find their way. Joen whispered to me in the darkness, "Shh, just let them talk. They're men. Don't say anything." The *meries* sat in stoic silence as the men carried on. *"Mipela go long PNG way. Compass, stars, tasol. Ol man hia bilong solwara. Painim Hermit,* no problem." I had my own GPS in my backpack, but decided to say nothing about it unless asked.

The moon peeked out from behind dark, low-lying clouds as we headed into the partially-sheltered lagoon along Manus' north coast. A few stars appeared overhead, but the weather seemed heavy and ominous as the boat pushed through the increasing northwest swell. *A major contrast to the calm daylight passage I had last time with people I trusted. Except for Joen, everyone aboard were strangers to me.*

We stayed behind the offshore reefs until they gave way to open ocean. The swell and waves increased. *Supamanus'* long pointed bow began to plunge into the on-rushing waves. Spray began to blast onboard. To keep warm, we pulled the tarp around us and huddled together on the pallet.

I rummaged in the covered bow cabin and found my ancient hooded rain jacket and pants in my bag. *It won't keep me dry, but it'll help with retaining body heat.* I also pulled out my quart bottle of drinking water. I recalled my basic survival skills: *don't get dehydrated, avoid wind chill, keep the neck and head area covered and don't unnecessarily exert yourself. It is going to be a very long night.* Feeling around in the dark under the tarp, I found a battered life jacket. *Only one on the boat, I imagine.* I adopted it for the trip and kept it very close to me—*who knows what will happen at this point?* I had very bad vibes about this whole voyage. The farther we got from land, the worse my feelings of dread became.

The *meries* were a meek and stoic lot, saying very little, just enduring the passage. The men silently bent to their task back at the helm, their macho joking ceasing as the weather continued to deteriorate. The night became very dark and very cold. The phosphorescence from the crashing waves and spray was our only illumination.

Hours passed, the waves grew larger, and the hull's pounding increased. I could imagine that it was taking a lot of concentration on John's part to keep us from being broadsided by the waves. I could just see his upper body crouched at the outboard's *stia* as I peeked out from under my tarp. Occasionally one of the men shone a light on the compass to keep him on track.

The clouds lowered and closed in on us. Lightning flared on the horizon ahead. The thunder's shock waves reverberated along the surface of the waves and into our little speedboat. The sky opened up and pelted cold rain down upon us, sizzling on the ocean as the squall hit.

"Go *insait!*" the *meries* yelled to each other. We pulled the heavy tarp overhead and tucked it around us. Streams of water poured off it into the boat.

I heard the wave coming with a long roar. *Crash!* The little boat shuddered as it hit. Saltwater cascaded over us. Under our slatted pallet, a river sloshed back to the men at the rear. I sneaked a look back. They were drenched under their rag-tag rain jackets. John pressed on, gripping the engine's handle as he steered into the oncoming seas.

More waves broke over us. Blasts of cold seawater engulfed our tarp. We were all drenched to the skin. Each breaking wave left heavy pools standing in the tarp's folds. If we moved under the tarp, cold water ran down on our bodies—it wasn't draining off.

I quickly figured out a technique. By now we *meries* were all lying on our backs under the tarp, our legs curled up to allow others room. When I heard the growl of an approaching wave, I lifted my leg straight up under the tarp. The wave would break on us but the tarp wouldn't fill with water. It drained off quickly, running under the pallet. Others saw what I was doing and took turns, stretching our cramped legs in the process. Much better than lying under heavy pools of cold saltwater that poured on you every time you moved.

My little watch said 3 a.m. *We've been going for six hours now and dawn is still hours away. I'm freezing cold and wet and so are the others.* I nudged Joen: "We've got to keep warm. I'm shaking. Let's all move next to each other and share our body heat. It'll help." She put it in Pidgin and soon we were all body to body, enduring the waves crashing over us while pushing the cold water off the tarp with our feet. The closeness helped. Joen's ample body on one side and someone else's on the other sent warmth through my thin frame.

The storm raged on, never slacking off for a minute. The waves pounded us. Squalls and rain lashed us. The wind howled. And *Supamanus* kept powering on.

Dawn found us tired, wet and sore. Bodies stirred and some of the *meries* tried sitting up outside of our tarp tent, only to be drenched by the waves. They returned to our protection shaking with the cold. One by one, we pulled our bodies up on the boat's rail and sat facing inwards, hanging over the side to relieve ourselves. The men, as always, had it easy. For us, it was an unwelcome cold saltwater douche.

The two drivers alternated during the long night, and between shifts slumped in exhausted sleep on their seats. Two younger guys were bailing. The drenching from the breaking waves was more than the scuppers could handle. If they stopped for very long, the water in the hull would build up to dangerous levels and overwhelm the little open speedboat.

More hours passed. The engine droned on, occasionally sputtering in the crashing waves. Low, dark clouds covered the sky, but the rain stopped. Large waves, breaking seas, and howling winds remained from the passing weather front. A weak sun above the cloud cover warmed us from the night's cold. Under the tarp, we were a soggy, humid mess. *Saltwater sores are next.* Our rough pallet bed and the pounding hull chafed against our sides and backs. *Got to try and dry out a bit.* I pulled my dripping weather suit off. Any waterproofing on it had long since vanished.

I managed to crawl over, get behind the cabin door, and find my bag. Reaching in, I found some small pull-top cans of spaghetti and pork and beans along with some hard candies. I offered them around to my companions under the tarp. Looks of disgust greeted me. I had heard several of them retching over the side during the night from seasickness; now they didn't seem to have the strength even to do that. The smell was getting thick under the tarp.

I opened my little cans and shoved the starchy stuff down. No spoons available, only fingers. Seasickness had never affected me, not even in the worst of my times on the ocean. I knew I had to get some food in me. *I have to keep going.*

Did we have more drinking water? I had finished my water bottle during the night, knowing that dehydration could be dangerous in these circumstances. *More important than food, actually.* None of the *meries* had been drinking any water—*not good.*

Just as I thought of this, I looked out and saw one of the young bailers grab our only five-gallon jug of fresh water, strip off his salty shirt, and douse himself over the head. *Shit, that's drinking water he's using!* "Hey, what're you doing—are you crazy? That's for drinking. Stop him!" I yelled.

The half-asleep men came instantly awake. Women in PNG do not yell at men, even half-grown ones. The startled guy just stood there, water jug suspended in his hand, as if paralyzed in shock. Silence—both men and *meries* stared at me. Mercifully, John broke the tension, berating the kid for his stupidity. Almost half our drinking water had splashed away. We had three gallons left.

From the stern, I heard a lot of Pidgin conversation from the men. Then they called for Joen to come back. When she returned, staggering to get under the tarp's protection, she motioned to me. "They ask if you have your GPS. They say you have one. Do you, Joy?" Her pleading look told me the story. I nodded towards the enclosed cabin. "It's in my bag." *They never would have accepted it until now. I had to wait. Women wait to be asked in PNG—you learn.*

A young guy crawled forward and carefully opened the cabin door between waves. My bag was in his hands. He didn't speak. The *meries* stared at me. Under the tarp, I turned on the GPS unit. Hermit's eastern pass waypoint was stored in the memory from my first speedie trip back to Hermit with Stanley and Paul. Bingo—course, speed, distance, and ETA (estimated time of arrival) all in one little handful. I poked my head through a fold in the tarp and called out the course and distance. *Supamanus* changed course—Hermit was on our bow again.

Joen hugged me. One *meri* touched me and said, *"Tenkyu,* true." They knew the importance of carrying a GPS as well as I did. There were too many stories of villagers lost at sea without one, and I would certainly never venture offshore in a speedie without my GPS. From that moment on, I regularly answered the helmsman's call of "navigator," a term of respect among these coastal villagers.

By afternoon, the engine's sputtering grew worse, and it suddenly died. All was quiet. The pounding motion ceased, only to be replaced by violent rocking as we turned broadside to the breaking seas. The relative calmness brought the *meries* out of their prostration from under the tarp. It was actually a welcome respite. Time for a "ladies pee break."

I heard more male Pidgin from the rear—something about tools. And then, the frustrating sound of an engine's starter rope being pulled and pulled and not catching—nothing. I looked back and saw them crouched over the coverless engine and heard the clatter of metal tools. One of the young guys held a tarp to shield the open engine from the spray and waves. They worked in silence.

Then more pulls and the beast sputtered and sprang to life amidst masculine cheers and cries of *"gudpela… gud* man. *"* My stoic companions huddled back down under the tarp and the pounding began again. The scene repeated itself several more times, with increasingly longer intervals between stopping and starting. *This is not looking good ...*

During one of our breakdowns, Douglas, the husband of one of the silent *meries*, came over to our little tarp tent and started conversing with his wife. Suddenly, we *meries* had a very domineering man among us under our tent! I was about to object, but Joen shushed me and shook her head. We stuck our heads out together and she whispered, "His wife *hia*, and it's his right. Say nothing." Outrage filled me. The oaf was pushing us out of the way and snuggling up to his wife. *Good grief.* The other men said nothing, giving their tacit approval. *A wife's job is to keep her husband warm, I suppose, even if he's hogging too much of our tarp.* I had no intention of getting my body any closer to him than I had to. The meek *meries* said nothing, just giving him valuable space on our little tented pallet.

The sun set and the wind still howled. Drinking water was passed around, but had few takers. Hermit was still over fifty miles away, which meant that we had another long night to endure. The drivers were exhausted, falling asleep at the *stia*. We plowed on until the engine quit again, this time for good. Try as they might, nothing was going to get that water-soaked engine started again.

Fortunately we have a spare. Getting the heavy engines exchanged on the pitching boat was in itself an act of courage. *One misstep and it goes over the side in thousands of fathoms of ocean.*

We drifted until after midnight. The spare engine wouldn't start; it had been drenched, too. More tools, more clanging, more pulling. I checked the GPS: twenty-seven miles to Hermit. So close, and now we were drifting back towards Manus. I fell into a restless sleep and woke when the boat's movement changed.

It was flat calm. Stars appeared between the clouds. Water lapped gently at the hull. The swell flattened out. *The storm is over as suddenly as it began.* A big oil tanker, lit up like a Christmas tree, passed by. I thought of the new Uniden handheld VHF radio in my bag. I had tested it in Lorengau, only to find that it wouldn't work on the cheap non-alkaline batteries available in PNG. It needed a 12 volt hook-up to charge its fancy nickel-hydride battery. That charge was available from *Banshee's* solar panels, but not at Akau's guesthouse nor on *Supamanus*. *Yes, we may know where we are, but without propulsion or communication, what good is it?*

Cough. Bang. Sputter. It was running! This time we all cheered. Hermit, our home, was a little more than thirty miles on our bow, and the sea was flat. The GPS gave our speed as nine knots and climbing. The *meries* hugged each other with me in the middle. Joen led them in thankful prayer. "Papa God"—they always began—*"Mipela tenkyu."* Though not religious, I joined them—I was thankful too.

Yells came from the bow. The high mountain tops of Hermit were in sight in the dim light of the stars. Soon, I saw the phosphorescence of waves breaking on the pass. The men knew the way in from years of experience. We shook off our tarp and sat staring ahead. Each thinking of home, a bath to rid ourselves of the filth, a warm bed, and loved ones. We were no different whether we lived in a pandanus bush house or a boat, it was home.

Supamanus pulled alongside *Banshee* sometime after three o'clock in the morning. It had taken us almost thirty-two hours for a voyage that normally takes twelve. "Leslie, it's me—Joy. Help me up. Oh, Leslie, I'm so cold."

HOPE, FEAR, AND A VISITOR

Leslie

Darkness. The wind howled through the rigging outside. Occasional squalls of rain blasted through the bay as *Banshee* jerked and rolled between her anchors. *It's awful here, but poor Joy's out there in that open boat. What if they get swamped? What if...* I couldn't stop my thoughts. I tried to sleep, and tossed and turned instead. Cold fear gripped me and wouldn't let go.

Gradually the boat's motion eased, the squalls dissipated, and I drifted off.

Sleep—hours of peace...

A low hum of an engine brought me half-awake. *Hmm... Getting closer now. Who'd be out on a night like this?* My sleep-fogged brain didn't focus. *The noise, yeah, it's stronger now—louder and coming straight for us. An outboard?*

Clunk, clunk... thump. Yells. Lights flashed on the deck. *They're coming alongside. Who is it?*

"Leslie, Leslie, help me."

Oh god, it's Joy! I grabbed a shirt and raced into the cockpit.

Supamanus was alongside. The scene was chaotic. Exhausted men staggered to stand up and hold on to our deck rail, their bodies shaking. Some of them were shining lights over the bedraggled passengers and soggy cargo that sat sloshing in pools of filthy water. The stench was nauseating. Dazed women huddled wet and motionless on a rough pallet in the center. I recognized Joen as she tried to help Joy to stand. Guys clutched at them as she started to fall. Her soaked red foul weather suit clung to her, dripping seawater and filth as she struggled to stand up.

"Help me… Please help me up. My bag, I need my bag."

"*Halpim* Joy. *Upim*—you hold, Leslie."

They pushed, I pulled, and Joy crawled, unable to stand, into the cockpit. I was shocked at her condition. Weak, wet, filthy, and only able to mumble simple words in a whisper, she slumped on the seat. There was some concern about her *kagos,* particularly the epoxy, but Edwin and Joen assured me that they would be safe and locked up in the bow cabin until morning.

"*Mipela halpim* people now. *Kagos tumora.* People sick. *Putim bot long* Namo. You come *long moning.*"

With that, they shoved off and I quickly returned to Joy.

"So cold… So cold. Heat water. Need to wash, warm up… Hot tea, rice? Got to have food… Haven't eaten, so long," she mumbled. *Got to help her fast—god, she's a mess and stinks too. What happened out there? It must have been awful.*

Her clothes and foul weather suit smelled so bad, I just peeled them off of her and threw them in a pile at the back of the boat. As I washed her down and poured warm water over her, she didn't move. Gradually the hot tea and warmth brought her around. I bundled her in blankets on the settee while she picked at the hot rice. The story spilled out of her—a ghastly experience. *Everyone on that boat is almost thirty years younger than Joy—she's lucky to have survived as well as she did.*

Joy

Morning. Sunlight streamed in through ports and hatches—a beautiful day. Les greeted me with coffee and a reminder that we'd better get over to Namo's beach quickly and retrieve our stuff.

"I see lots of people there already. We gotta go—you know what'll happen."

"Yeah, right," I said as I struggled out of the forepeak bunk. *Ohh… Everything hurts.* Les was already in the dinghy focused on getting over to Namo's. My head spun as she helped me to climb in. I knew I was bad off—the shaking wouldn't stop—but I too realized how important it was to get over there before the villagers got going on another *kago* bounty from their uninvited guests.

As we approached, we could see the crowd swarming around *Supamanus.* A young *meri* scurried off, her long blouse stuffed full with scavenged pickings. My shout of "Hey, get outta there!" made them scatter and summoned the guys into action. Seeing us, Edwin and Douglas (the pushy husband from the trip) assumed control of the *kago* distribution. Ours was only part of the boat's *kago*-run—much of it was either for personal orders or stock for "Joseph Stoa." In my stuff, I had included two cases of cheap PNG beer, disguised inside of other boxes to keep it out of sight. Our idea was to ration it to last us until we got to the PNG mainland. The island men, however, had other ideas. Either the boxes broke open in the rough seas or were ransacked, we never knew, but much of our food provisions and most of our beer had gone off to the village before we arrived on the scene. Paul hadn't shown up, and his calming influence was missing. However, Namo, his regular hangers-on, and most of the guys from the trip were in full swing and most of them smelled of our beer. It appeared that the party began when *Supamanus* landed and was still going on. John, our main driver on the boat, had disappeared, no doubt due to the combination of beer and total exhaustion. Edwin appeared to be the sober one, telling me that he had gone home to his wife and caught a few hours sleep as we did.

Supamanus was half-pulled up on the beach as we tied up alongside. Les scrambled aboard, and I stood ankle deep in the water next to her bow cabin and peered in. *Kagos* spilled out of the little doorway like a cornucopia's bounty—the offerings of the *Kago Kult* had returned. The tension among the crowd surrounding us was palpable—their party had been interrupted. We started loading our stuff into our little dinghy: two jugs of gasoline, cartons, rainbow bags, and the loose spilled stuff—canned food, boxes of epoxy, and what was left of the beer. The dinghy's waterline sank as Les handed things down to me one by one. She tried to hurry, as the beer-drinking guys continually harassed her as she worked. Things must not have been going the way Douglas wanted it: as she bent down to pick up the loose beer bottles, he grabbed her from behind with one hand and the back of her neck with the other, shoving her head down to the hull. His loud voice commanded, *"Bia* (beer) *bilong mipela* now, you *rausim."*

"Let 'er go now, Douglas. Get your hands off her. Get away." I was ready to leap aboard and pull him off with my bare hands, but Edwin came to her rescue, ordering him off the boat. Leslie was shaking. I was furious and my extreme fatigue didn't make me very forgiving. Last night, Leslie had told me a bit about how she had been treated, and I vowed it wouldn't continue—I simply wouldn't allow it. Edwin profusely apologized to both of us, saying, "Douglas not from *hia"* and that he was a stupid man who had no idea of who we were. I let him save face and nodded to Leslie that we should just finish our loading and get away from this drunken free-for-all.

With our precious cans of underwater epoxy now in our possession, we told each other that our escape from this madness would come soon.

One of the items I brought back was a cheap little boom-box shortwave radio, like the ones we had seen the villagers using. I had the Radio Manus broadcast schedule, and with a bit of searching on its very compressed dial band, I figured I should be able to find international stations also. I had made sure that the radio's voltage requirements were only six volts, so that we could run it directly off of our old, spare six-volt Trojan battery. My idea worked. The Voice of America, BBC, Radio Australia, PNG English news, and music entered our home again—we had the world back.

Later, in the afternoon of my first day back, I took a box-load of promised items and gifts for Lynnah and a few others. As I approached her house, the men at the *haus boi* were loudly carrying on, no doubt about our terrible trip. John, *Supamanus'* driver, approached me and soon I was surrounded by the entire *buai*-chewing crowd. It was an uncomfortable, intimidating feeling. All I wanted to do was get through them and over to Lynnah's. John accosted me first.

"You got *moa* of that *gudpela bia* you bring? We *laikim tumas.*"

"No, John. I'm sure you guys got enough last night, and the rest is for us." I tried to keep moving, hoping that this would end their comments and they would just let me pass by. Their laughter and comments increased the more I tried to ignore them. John stepped in front of me aggressively.

"Look, you *lapun meri* (old woman). Why don't you ground that stupid *bot* right there and go home—get out of *hia.* Your *bot*—*em i bagarap.* Two *meri* cannot fix bot. So why you no leave this place?"

The man's attitude was truly hostile, a surprise after what we had just gone through together. Standing there, I knew I had no allies in this bunch. In addition to my incredible tiredness, sore muscles and bruised body, I felt afraid—the same fear that Les had alluded to last night. *Things* have *changed here.* I pushed through them and found safety with Lynnah next door.

Her delight with my "gifts" was apparent. Flour, rice, baking powder, yeast, cooking oil—all were ways to her heart. She promised baking treats from her *bus aven* (bush-oven), but cautioned about people's attitudes, particularly after watching my latest skirmish with the "boys." "*Tumas toktok long beksait hia* now. You, Leslie, *lukautim.*"

She explained that the long-dreaded time for her family to vacate their living quarters had arrived. The new government schoolteacher was arriving soon, and the village council had told them to move out as soon as their new house they were building was habitable.

My attention was diverted from our conversation when I saw a speedie being poled over to *Banshee.* It was Collen's, the smallest boat in the village, with Bill and Collen aboard. They came up to *Banshee's* stern and grabbed the pulpit next to our 8 hp outboard. I couldn't hear the conversation, but could see Les wave her hand in my direction. The men then proceeded to remove our outboard, mount it on the speedie and drive off, circling back and forth in front of the *haus boi* and Lynnah's beach. *What the hell? Les never would have allowed that.* "Gotta go, Lynnah." Hastily paddling out from shore, I motioned for them to return my outboard. They ignored me and threw up a wake as they zoomed past.

Collen and Bill had to sit way aft to keep the little outboard's intake and prop underwater. *Dammit, they could ruin it if they don't keep it down. What's this all about—some crazy "show-face" village male thing again?* After my reaffirming stint back in civilization, and with two confrontations already with the "boys" this morning, I had little patience for their macho games. Les said she was so tired of fighting with them she had just given up. They had told her that they wanted to "test" the engine, and she had tried to get them to "wait till Joy comes back," but emotionally couldn't fight them any more. I assured her that it was probably a male version of the "communal ownership" thing. The outboard had sat on "his family's" veranda for so long, Bill now assumed he could claim it as his. We already knew that Collen was angry that I hadn't purchased the expensive, *"pebek"* diving fins he had demanded when I left Hermit. I had offered him a pair of inexpensive snorkeling fins. *"Em i no gud inap*—me no *laik,"* he said contemptuously. Repairing his badly broken speedie should have been payment enough. "Whatever it's about, it'll stop as soon as I see Paul."

We agreed that a long walk down the isolated beach past Paul's would help our spirits. Time away from immediate concerns, in natural surroundings, always healed. And we had much to discuss. With the new epoxy and capabilities we knew we had, we had to work out our salvage plan, and a lonely beach is always good for that. Stopping by Paul's compound, he welcomed me back "home" and appeared very interested in our plans for repairing *Banshee* for the voyage to Madang. I could tell he was feeling pressured by our continuing presence in his village. He groaned when we told him about Collen and Bill's latest escapade and that our outboard was now beached at Namo's on the back of Collen's boat. They had simply appropriated it. He made it clear that he would personally return it by sundown. We both felt sorry for him—he tried so hard. The remainder of the day gave us rest, togetherness, and an opportunity for planning. *We will be ready to begin our repair work tomorrow.*

Leslie

It was now Wednesday. Joy had been back one day, but she still needed rest. She'd gone over Paul Oman's instructions for the epoxy repair with me, and I knew what to do.

I figured it would take a day to clean up the outside hull, and two days to patch it, inside and out. I'd already degreased, cleaned, and sanded the inside while Joy was away. That is, as far as my short arms could reach. I couldn't get at the forward area of the crack under the shower pan. *Going to have to cut away something up there. Now that Joy's back, she can give me some advice.*

Then there was the matter of cutting away the old transducer still attached to its fiberglass flap, so that I could patch underneath it and over the wood piece fitted into the hole in the hull. That was the tricky part. The flap would have to be sawed off from the inside. One wrong cut and water would come pouring in again. I had to be very sure that the new outside epoxy and fiberglass sheathing I was about to make was thick and strong enough to secure the wood before I attempted this procedure. Menacing seawater still seeped into the hull around the edges of the wood patch and through parts of the crack. Daily bilge pumping kept up with the leak, but it definitely wasn't seaworthy.

We wanted to be out of Hermit by the end of next week. The atmosphere was becoming increasingly hostile ashore and we were afraid to leave the boat unattended—Paul had warned us. Even Lynnah was worried and insisted that if we both came ashore, she would have Ben or her kids watch *Banshee* from the beach. "People come *klostu* (near), me *salim* (send) Ben *long bot. Sapos* trouble, me *singaut long* Paul. Go do your *wok* now, you no *ken* worry."

The hull had accumulated quite a bit of growth, particularly over the old bumpy Z-Spar patch. I scraped away the coral and barnacles with a putty knife. In order for the new epoxy to adhere well, the area then had to be sanded clean and free of all old anti-fouling paint. I had to get down to bare fiberglass before any application of the new products, using the heavy grit sandpaper Joy had brought back. *Glad the compressor still works. Going to need quite a few tanks for this job before it's over.* At the end of the day, I was exhausted, but the prep job was finished. *And they've left us completely alone; maybe Joy's presence aboard keeps them away.*

Thursday was patching day. We lined up two of our new products on plastic drop cloths in the cockpit. The third, "911" (now called Quick-Fix 2300), was a very quick-setting paste used to stop incoming leaks. Paul Oman had told Joy that we probably wouldn't need this in our patching operation, but it was good insurance for the trip. An unnerving thought, but we knew what he meant.

Joy had remembered everything—disposable gloves, respirators, plastic sheeting, plastic spoons, stirrers, squeegees, mixing cups, baggies, and a roll of fiberglass tape. *No convenient Home Depot for forgotten items here.* A final review of mixing and application procedures, and then I geared up in my very old "work" BC and dived over the side. The stuff had a strong toxic odor, and I was glad to be breathing from my tank. Joy peered at me through respirator and goggles. We started out with the Wet/Dry 700 Epoxy Kevlar Paste, a thick orange-colored material I used to fair out the area and build a smooth base for the epoxy-impregnated fiberglass tape to come. Booby's plastic cat toilet boxes provided an excellent mixing tray as Joy carefully measured out and mixed spoonfuls from each of the 2-part cans. Then she plopped a blob of the resultant goo on a plastic bag and floated it to me on a small wood plank. Joy kept her hands clean with plastic gloves. I tried to use them at first, got frustrated with keeping them on in the water, and finally went at it with bare hands. *Yeah, toxic as hell, but I'm savin' the boat.*

That part done, we took a short break and then began the taping part. Neither of us had ever used fiberglass tape underwater before, so we just followed Paul's instructions. Joy mixed up the thinner grey Corro Coat FC 2100 (the brushable version of Wet/Dry 700), soaked pieces of the tape with it, and dropped them one by one over the side to me. I'd grab a piece as it sank, flatten it out, and plaster it over the filled-in crack and around the edges of the wood-covered hole, overlapping each piece as I went along. Each time I needed more, I'd pop up like a trained seal begging for more treats.

During our work, we'd notice Collen in his boat repeatedly speeding out at full throttle from Namo's beach and then back in again. It made me nervous and the resulting wakes tended to lift corners of the tapes, so I had to keep pushing them back down until they set up. It was frustrating and he wouldn't quit. Every time I went in the water, he'd shoot out again. We tried to ignore him and figured that as long as he kept his distance, we could endure it.

When I had completed an overlapping patchwork along the entire length of the crack and had covered the large wood plug in fiberglass pieces, I was ready to quit and let my artwork harden. Clean-up was a mess, and even though we worked hard to keep the epoxy off my diving gear, the deck, and hardware, it defied us, leaving hardening residue in too many places.

Joy

With the Sabbath approaching again, we knew we had only one more day that we could get in the water and do visible work. Early that Friday, Les gave the outside hull its final coat, extending the overlapping patchwork out to about a foot-wide swath along the damaged area.

Collen's antics continued and became dangerous and impossible to ignore. Emboldened by yesterday's runs past us, he came closer—too close for safety. He'd aim directly at *Banshee's* port side where Les was working and come at us at top speed, yell about the swim fins, and then turn away within inches of certain collision. After a few insane runs like this, Les had to quit and get out of the water. The underwater wake lifted her tapes right off the hull, and they would sink before she could grab them. It was impossible to continue, to say nothing about the scary feeling of almost getting smashed between the two boats each time he hurtled by. His last pass was breath-stopping, it was so close. *A crazed nut case.*

"Enough!," I yelled, as I stripped off my gloves and gear. Advising Leslie to stay out of sight, I jumped into the dinghy and paddled off to see "the boss." Luckily, I found Paul at home. He was amazed and angered at Collen's reckless behavior, telling me that his excuse for running the speedie was to test Namo's outboards that he had been working on. "Yeah, right, Paul, I don't believe it for a moment and neither do you." We shook our heads at such stupidity and parted, Paul striding off to Namo's with a vengeance as I quietly paddled back to the boat.

The *banzai* dive bombing stopped.

In my absence Les worked on patching the crack on the inside of the hull, safely out of sight of Collen and the boys. I got back to work mixing and dipping for her, and soon we had the framework of a substantial patch covering all but the transducer area and the unreachable part under the shower pan in the head. That would need a cutout in the heavy fiberglass pan, which required power tools and a generator. A job for another day. After lunch, it was still peaceful, so Les jumped in the water again and finished up her work while the inside patch set up. Then returning inside, we worked together in an assembly line to complete the patch. My concentration was interrupted when I heard the rumbling of a boat's engine and anchor chain rattling down. Peering out through our small windows, I stared in astonishment. Next to us was a very large yacht flying an American flag.

"My god, Les. Look, it's a sailboat—an American one! There's a white guy up on the bow. Oh Les, after all this time."

234ESCAPE234 FROM HERMIT234 ISLAND

All I wanted to do at that moment was to get over there and talk to the newcomer.
Les, sensing my urgency and still bent to her task in the bilge, reassured me that she
could finish up by herself while I went over for a brief visit. She didn't have to say any
more; I was paddling.

What a huge boat. The freeboard is almost as high as I am.

"Hi, I'm Indy," the booming American voice said as I got close. "Tie your painter
up there and climb aboard. Been lookin' for you—missed you in Lorengau. They said
you'd left."

"You were? They did... Who?" I was so amazed I was almost speechless.

"Yeah, I heard about you two stuck here on your boat and wanted to give you a ride
back up. Heard you had kind of a rough trip in that little speedboat."

*Seems to know everything. Who is this guy? Whatever... I'm sure glad to see anybody on a
sailboat. Maybe he'll help us get to Madang.* So many thoughts whirled through my head as
I climbed up and gave him a thankful hug. His boat, *Pegasus,* was a huge motorsailer..
Sort of matches him, all ego and "man in charge" stuff.

"I'm 'Indiana Jones,'" he laughed. "An old girlfriend gave me the name—just call
me Indy, everyone does." My instincts said caution, and I kept that in mind as we
talked, keeping my agenda under wraps. I let him ramble on before he turned the
conversation to us. He was amazed that we had been on Hermit so long, and questioned our reasons at every turn. "I woulda' got a barge and crane up here long ago—
just lifted her up and taken her outta here." When I told him about the harassment,
pilfering, and payback demands, he retorted, "Just threaten to torch their bush shacks,
if they don't stop it and give back your stuff."

Our interchange was interrupted when the local "officials" motored up in a speedie.
Paul, Stanley, and Bento caught his attention—time for check-in, and time for me to
leave. The Sabbath was closing in.

Later that evening, we sat at anchor next to another boat from our world, feeling
sure that the open harassment would cease as long as "big brother" was here. "Les,
you know, he could put a long line on us and tow us right into Madang—three days is
all it would take. We could go right through the strait—the shortcut between those big
offshore islands and the mainland. Where they told me not to go without an engine,
'cause the wind dies at night and the currents are so strong. He could get a crew from
here easily if he wanted some help, and we wouldn't have to steer all the time—we'd be
able to sleep in shifts. Oh Les... Am I dreaming? Would he do it?"

ESCAPE FROM HERMIT

Joy

Morning. Same island, same village, same people, but different now—one of our own sat next to us, quietly anchored in the morning calm. Just to reassure myself, I glanced through the porthole. *Yeah,* wan bikpela bot *right there. Damn, I've been here so long I'm even thinking in Pidgin.*

And no Sabbath duties either. Paul allowed us to visit our *wantok* (as he termed Indy) as much as we wished during the Sabbath, although we were admonished to keep things quiet and *insait long bot* during the sacred hours. No problem with us. We were over-joyed to have someone to talk with, and his boat was huge inside. An invitation to dinner was in the offing for the evening, and we could hardly wait.

Leslie's job for the day was to finally remove the offending transducer, now that the outside hull surrounding it was thoroughly encased in cement-like epoxy. The "menace" was still attached to its flap of hull and hung there innocently in the under-seat locker. She had been planning for this day, gathering all the necessary tools be-forehand. Knowing that Leslie works best alone at projects like this, I gratefully took off for *Pegasus* and Indy, my agenda yet to be sprung.

Leslie

Only two things stood between me and finishing my inside patch job. One—cutting an access hole in the head shower pan—required negotiating the loan of power tools and a generator from Paul. The other—slicing off the transducer—I could do alone. I needed a large, sharp knife with a partially serrated blade, like a hunting knife. An earlier visit to Lynnah had provided the solution—the loan of August's large knife that he always wore at his belt, although I was cautioned to be very secretive about borrowing it. Head down in the restricted locker, I was able to puncture the tough fiberglass and pry open holes along the flap. Then using my little square cut saw, I laboriously sawed and ripped through the tenacious material, all taking a couple of hours of backbreaking work. My wrists and hands emerged bleeding again with scrapes and imbedded fiberglass shards, but the transducer finally lay at my feet, still attached to its share of hull.

Done. I wanted to sink the damn thing in waters as deep as possible, but at the same time wanted to parade my victory to Joy. *This is the godamn thing that sank us.*

Joy

Indy greeted me and welcomed me aboard. I followed along as he toured me through his "palace," a motorsailer capable of comfortable worldwide travel. Pilothouse, inside steering, generator, a separate chart table with wide drawers for charts, full-size galley, lounge, three bathrooms, private aft cabin, and a high seas radio setup complete with integral computer with access to email and weather information, were only a few of the conveniences aboard. After months of living village-style and on poor dilapidated *Banshee,* the luxury was overwhelming. I attempted to explain to Indy our difficulties—the hull, the villagers, our physical deterioration, our mental stress, and our concern about the open sea voyage to Madang without an engine, nav lights or autopilot. However, it became apparent that his focus was more on his situation and not on assistance to us.

He continually returned to his favorite subject—women, and finding a suitable "wife" for his travels and lifestyle. He related that he was an American of Russian ancestry and had decided that only a Russian woman would suit his needs.

When he began to show me Internet photos of prospective applicants from a website of Russian "ladies" looking for mates, I balked, especially after viewing the first few. *Better state my case and be direct before he goes somewhere I don't want to go. Strange, he doesn't seem to catch on that we are in an extreme situation here and could certainly use some assistance.*

"Indy, with your boat on a direct course through the straits to Madang, it'll only take three days to the city wharf. We need some help here; could you put a towline on us and take us into Madang? I've been towed before. *Banshee's* light and tracks well, and you could probably pick up a crew here for the watches. I'll pay, Indy, to the best of my ability. Please, we've come so far—we need help and Madang's so damn close with an autopilot and an engine."

The big man looked like he'd been shot, stopping his monologue to stare at me, dumfounded. *Shit, it's never even occurred to him—what's with this guy?* Recovering his speech he loudly sputtered on about his very important mission: Russian women, or to be more exact, finding "the right Russian woman." *Wow, what have we got here?*

"Impossible, I'm in a terrible rush. Got to get to Vladivostok by my deadline. I'm interviewing them, y'know. Very important. And I'm behind schedule—ha, ha, women won't wait, y'know." *Yeah right—got it.* I said some placating words that seemed to derail him, and he eventually offered a copied chart that was a duplicate and access to his sailing directions for Madang. As a consolation he offered to make me some small C-Map charts of the coast and harbor entrance. Then, he went back to his own situation.

Leslie's triumphant yells broke the awkward exchange. Indy peered out and told me Les was waving something over her head at us. I smiled, "Yeah, the transducer—she's finally got it out. Must have been successful, the boat's not sinking and she's smiling." The dinner invitation was still on, and he made it even more tempting by inquiring as to our taste in wine. *Indeed, wine with dinner—where am I?*

Returning to *Banshee,* I found Les immersed in epoxying the now-cleared area formerly occupied by the transducer and its flap of pushed-in hull. "One more to go," she reminded me, motioning to the shower pan, "and we're outta here."

My emotions showed through when I told her that Indy wouldn't give us a tow—he had a "schedule" to keep. "Never mind," I told Les. "We'll do it ourselves," putting on my brave front to mask my anxieties.

Dinner was delightful. Indy certainly knew how to cook and entertain. Table settings, cloth napkins, wine glasses, and dinner music—the conversation flowed. The red wine was wonderful, and for a brief time we were transported to another dimension. We told stories, laughed until the late hours, then toddled home to our musty, dank, little enclave.

Another Sunday came, and we still enjoyed the "protection" of another yacht in the anchorage. Collen resumed his close-in dive-bomb circling of our boat and now Indy's. Yelling and gesturing as he zoomed out of Namo's beach, he was a man possessed. Indy was alarmed and ventured ashore; something must have been said, because the assault ceased, and we gratefully enjoyed the calm respite. Soon though, came more strangeness...

We were both aboard *Pegasus,* copying from Indy's sailing directions, when a wind gust came through the isthmus and the big vessel began to drift out of the bay. Leslie let Indy know that his anchor was dragging. The ensuing drama and uproar was not pleasant, and bordered on frightening. Les and I exchanged looks that said, "don't move or speak," and as soon as his anchor was down again we beat a hasty retreat to little *Banshee. Not my kinda captain, not my kinda guy. Maybe sailing to Madang by ourselves isn't such a bad idea.*

Monday began the "Hermit shuffle" to borrow a generator and power tools to cut out the shower pan and the interliner where the transducer had been. This would give Leslie access to patch the remainder of the crack from the inside.

First, there was the request to Paul, who had to come out to determine if such a request was really required. Then, there had to be approvals from the Council and the equipment's owner, Steven. We knew the bureaucratic drill. In a day or so, a speedie with Stuart (Leslie's boat repair assistant), the generator, and tools were parked alongside *Banshee*. Paul, of course, came to supervise. Leslie got to work, and soon access holes to the rest of the damaged hull showed in the thick fiberglass shower pan and interliner. The rest, Les told me, although a killer to her back and arms, "was easy."

We were informed that when Les had her hull job completed, Paul would visit again and inspect the soundness of the hull, as it was his duty to approve all voyages leaving Hermit. Not wanting any further difficulties, we played our role and solemnly went along with him. At our request, he appeared the next day and performed his leader's duty, officially thumping the hull and peering into all the compartments.

"Em i gudpela! Strong! You *ken* leave Hermit now."

He asked us not to tell anyone of the date of our departure, not even Lynnah. Control was becoming an issue. Rumblings of potential problems and even potential piracy from the *bekslaiders* on our way out were beginning to surface. The village needed us to be gone and needed to return to normal routines without the tempting presence of "the outside world" dangling in easy reach. Paul suggested Friday afternoon, right before the Sabbath. Stanley and August could lock down the gasoline supply early and village rules prohibited engine use and non-religious gatherings or movement from sundown to sundown. Paul and his trusted few would tow us out beyond the reef.

The stage was set—we had a window. We had to go for it.

Pegasus and Indy left on the passage to Palau. On her own, Leslie had made another futile plea for towing assistance, as I wouldn't touch the subject. However, Indy did promise to do one thing:

"When I arrive in Palau I will contact the search and rescue authorities in PNG, and if you haven't shown up in Madang in two weeks from today, I will ask them to consider you overdue, or a victim of foul play, and request that they begin an investigation and a search."

Ominous as it sounded, we appreciated his efforts and thanked him.

For the rest of the week, at Paul's request, I began daily progress conferences with him. He was a man under pressure trying to keep the lid on. He asked that we speak to no one but him or Stanley and promised that he would always be available. He did allow us to visit with Lynnah and Ben, but "keep *toktok long* family, *tasol.*"

Each day I would watch from *Banshee* as Paul returned along the beachfront from church—my signal to go in for our conference at his compound. We both came to enjoy our "leader to leader" exchanges, sitting at his beachfront table under the shade trees. We trusted each other, and neither would betray that trust—anarchy would be the alternative. I told him we were contemplating writing a book about our "story," as he termed it. He became very solemn and thoughtful, and nodded his head. I asked him what I should say about some of the more unpleasant things that had happened here. He looked me straight in the eye and said, "You tell truth, Joy. The good, the bad, *tasol.* But you *mas* tell truth. They will live with it—both ways."

"I agree, Paul—the honest truth."

The change in the village ambiance was palpable. Tension was in the air. Most of the time Leslie remained on the boat, and only occasionally did she visit Lynnah in her new house on the other side of the isthmus. We had to watch which path we took to our destinations, avoiding the loungers at the *haus boi,* not too close to Collen's, and tracking clear of Namo's and Okip's. *Meries* who once had been friends only covertly smiled at us now, and we avoided eye contact with most of the men. Temptation, greed, envy, and the payback cultural norm had taken their toll—a sad ending.

Last minute requests for us to fiberglass this and fix that were numerous, fielded to us through Bento, Ben or Lynnah. They knew we were going, but we weren't telling when.

A new disaster loomed: the large socket for the wrench that we used to rotate the engine split apart. We had seen growing stress cracks in it from the months of daily turning and had hoped it would hold up a few more weeks. We had had a spare, but it never returned. Paul and Stanley were concerned, but any thought of the spare being "found" now was out of the question. Our engine sat there motionless, the grip of corrosion seizing it more firmly each day.

After living in PNG now for four months, I knew how real the concept of compensation was. The Hermit clan had *wantoks* in every walk of life all over PNG, and I didn't want claims to follow us to Madang. Paul understood and acknowledged my fears. At my urging, he agreed to sign a statement that cleared us of any claim.

"You *raitim* (write), I sign, no problem. But first, you *mas raitim* story *long* 'Hermit Yacht Book,' then I give you *pepa long* time you leave. You write "true" story so there are no questions *sampela* time (sometime). You give to Stanley so he *ken* read."

As he extended his hand to shake, his eyes said it all. I knew what he was asking. *Nothing comes for free.*

The week was rapidly rolling to a close. We packed up, checked our rigging and sails, and made ready for sea—as ready as our poor dilapidated *Banshee* could be. *Never have I put to sea more unprepared than this. We're taking a big chance, but it is our only way out.*

We weren't sure that our inflatable life raft would open, if we had to ditch in an emergency. It had been underwater in the sinking and since refloating had steadily leaked a stream of rust out of its canister—we thought from the CO_2 inflation bottle. Our plan was to carry our inflated Avon hard floor boat upside down on top of our hard dinghy on the foredeck. Should the hull not hold, and the life raft fail to inflate, we could go to the Avon. We put together a last resort "ditch bag" that included the EPIRB. Its battery checked out, so we were hopeful that it could still put out a signal if we needed it.

More concerns: a compass light, pencils, and paper. We had pens, but there wasn't a pencil on the boat. Navigating on a chart can get awfully messy if ink is used; that's why it's not done. A piece of blank paper for navigating would be helpful too. I took my needs to Paul. In more affluent times I had given Joen and the school stacks of clean white paper along with numerous pencils and pens. Vanished—all gone. Paul thought that perhaps Natalee would be able to come up with a pencil. As for the compass light, he would try. He knew its importance, as he had made many ocean night crossings himself.

I worked on the "Yacht Book" reluctantly, putting it off at first. Paul and I had our tacit agreement and I would follow it. I got into my task and filled two large pages with glossed-over details and a lot of thank-you words. We meant the thanks, but the errors were those of omission. A worried Stanley was visibly pleased when we presented it to him and he read through it. *We were keeping our bargain.*

Natalee found a pencil—one only, and we found an eraser. She was proud of her find and laughed when she said, "Hermit's not exactly a 'writing' society." *Natalee, our friend with the expensive private school education.* Paul "found" a little red compass light. His son had picked it up on the beach, he said. Leslie identified it as coming from her former boat. Our little supply of electricity from the solar panels and the salvaged batteries would keep it running in the dark night.

Tomorrow would be Friday. Our secret plan would be hatched. Paul and a few trusted others would be out very early to assist us. With his speedie, he would move us over to the village mooring off the reef in the center of the bay. He'd post a watch from shore to see that we were left alone while we cleaned up the anchor line mess and readied for sea. Then after mid-day, Stanley and August would lock down the gasoline supply, and Paul would return to take us out through the pass.

We were almost there.

A WEEK'S PERILOUS VOYAGE

Joy

We saw them coming. We were ready—exhausted after the morning's anchor retrieval drill, but ready. Earlier, when Paul motored us over to the mooring and tied us up, he had acted like a man in a hurry; all of them kept glancing nervously shoreward, scanning the beach. Zooming off, he said he would be back after mid-day to take us out the pass.

"*Stap long hia tasol*. Please, you no go *long* village. You no *mekim toktok*. Time you leave Hermit, now."

We had heard the rumors of a take-over. This made it all too real. The strain showed on his face—*he had to get us out of there*.

They leaped aboard, tying the speedie astern. They barely spoke. It was obvious they had a plan. Paul's demeanor had changed—an authoritarian air surrounded him. I spoke; he didn't answer, but strode directly back to the steering wheel, grabbed it and sat down. He gave commands in Pidgin and Bento scurried up the mast to the lookout position. There were only two others with them—teen-aged boys, Paul's son and Namo's, and they looked deadly serious.

"I am pilot now. I sail you out *long* lagoon. You tell boys what to do *long* ropes. *Em save* English."

"Paul, you said you will tow us out while I steer. You agreed. This is my boat and I am the captain. I don't want to sail in here, it's dangerous—the reefs are everywhere. I agreed to pay you for the gasoline for the tow. I …"

He cut me off. "You *harim* me. I am pilot, *mipela* sail. You *pulimap* sail now!"

I was dumfounded—speechless and afraid. I had never seen Paul like this. I motioned to Les not to speak. Our boat had been literally taken over. *Good god, what is this all about?*

Okay, got to think fast. "Paul, the wind is straight behind us and it's strong now. We can only use one sail; the main will cut off the wind from the jib." *They can handle jibing with the headsail alone, but with the main up too, the potential for disaster's just too much. Got to keep things simple and slow by only using one sail. Surely they'll use the outboard if things get in a pinch.* "We'll need to jibe (making a zigzag with my hand) through the reefs. You *save*? The little staysail jib will let us do this, and we can see around it. If we have to, we can even come pretty close to the wind this way." He nodded and translated to the others, shouting up to Bento on the mast.

I knew there was no dissuading him. He acted like a man possessed—determined to do this his way. *Some macho face-saving gesture maybe, showing the Ninigo crowd that he could also command and sail a boat?* Right then I didn't care; all I knew was that we had to comply or maybe lose *Banshee* altogether. Les watched in horror as we silently communicated to run the lines and get the sail out. The two boys were agile and followed our directions. Paul kept up a continual Pidgin dialog with his cohorts as *Banshee* swung downwind to the unfurled staysail. Bento conned from the mast and we were off.

As we maneuvered through the menacing reefs it became obvious that we were superfluous to their plan. Our opinions or directions didn't matter; they didn't speak to us or allow us to help. We retreated to the bow and held hands as we huddled fearfully under the inflatable. *Was this still our boat? Banshee* jibed through the reefs to the tune of Bento's calls from his perch on the spreaders. It *seemed* to be working. As we got further away from the sheltering mountains the northwest wind came around on our beam. Paul finally yelled for help when the sail began to luff.

"Pull it in, Paul. The winch, winch it in."

A boy cranked on the winch and got the idea as the sail filled. The worried kid stayed crouched in place once he realized his important position. *This is dumb and plain crazy. He's got a 40 hp outboard right there. Damn, why can't we just be towed out in a safe, civilized manner?* There was a lot of current as we approached the pass, and the reefs to leeward got closer and closer. To point higher, Les re-sheeted the jib to the inside track and led it inside the shrouds. We had to change-over the jib fast and smartly so not to lose any forward momentum. Surrounded by reefs there had been no room to luff up and set the main. Without it we couldn't point as high and were crabbing off to leeward toward the coral.

"Please, Paul, get someone in the speedie now to keep us off. They can push us on the side."

Silence. He stared through me. *Damn his stupid ego*—I was boiling inside. I could see the pass coming up and the dark blue open sea outside.

"Come up, Paul. Now!"

Fear crept over his steely-faced countenance. I knew what he was thinking—we all did. Les ran back to the cockpit, sat beside him and calmly but firmly told him what to do.

"Come up slowly, a little at a time. Watch the wind arrow up there, it points to the wind. Turn left, closer, closer. Easy now...Ease her up, Paul."

I watched in horror to leeward as the water turned from blue to green and tinges of brown reef appeared. I remember seeing fish. I held my breath, praying that our sharp angle of heel would provide a shallower draft and keep the keel from scraping the coral. Miraculously, the reef slid past under our keel and in a split second we were spit through the pass into safety in the ocean's cobalt blue.

We were out.

"Papa God. We ask you *long* protect *dupela meries, pren long Hermit*," their prayers began. I was respectfully offered the *stia* and we bowed our heads and joined hands as *Banshee* bobbed slowly along under her solo sail.

Paul rose and looked at us.

"I am sorry *long* your *propeties*. For the way *sampela* treat you. It is not our way. Papa God *blesim* you and keep you safe."

On an unspoken command they pulled in their speedie, jumped in and followed along as I luffed up and Les raised the main. A cheer rose as *Banshee* laid to her sails. I felt at home—our life was ours again.

The afternoon wind and sea was kind. Fluffy tradewind clouds chased us. Sunlight danced on the waves. *Banshee* settled into her familiar "slot" on a comfortable broad reach. I set a course of 165° magnetic to allow for the set and drift of current, particularly around Manus and the smaller islands. We took turns with the steering duties until way past nightfall. The supreme exhilaration of sailing free again belied our exhausted state.

The inside of the cabin was still in a sorry state, and we tried to pick our way around, ignoring the peeling paint and imbedded salty crud. Our big concern was the hull's soundness. Purposely we hadn't reinstalled the big water tank under the sole so we could have access and monitor the repair area in the bilge. We might have to do additional patching at sea. The concern about leaks and stress cracking weighed heavily on us, and checking the hull became a frequent task.

Without our electric autopilot, we had to steer by hand. Our Aries wind vane had once worked well, but long ago its performance had ceased being so wonderful and we had installed a much-preferred Raymarine electric autopilot. That modern convenience had fallen victim to the sinking. While hand steering can be pleasant for a while in favorable seas and winds, it becomes a backbreaking, mind-numbing chore in double-handed sailing, especially in heavy weather. A burden that robs the crew of sleep, energy, and the will to function efficiently. While one person is steering, the other must do everything else, and sleep and rest become shortchanged.

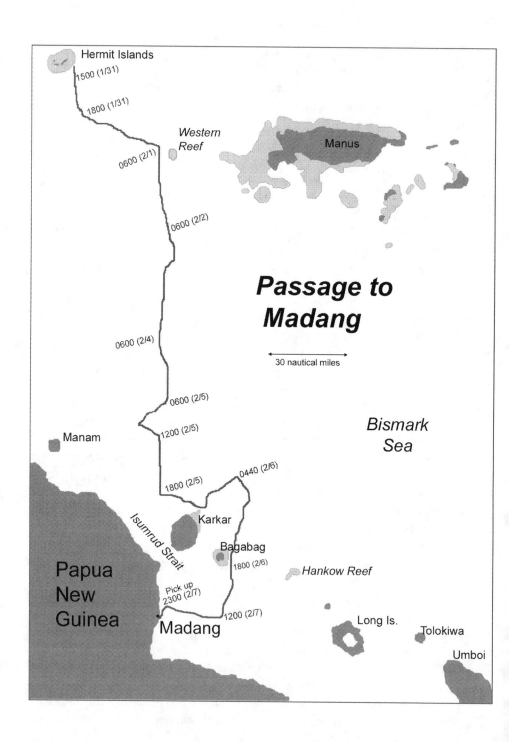

We had two alternatives to constant hand steering. One was playing and fussing with the Aries while adjusting and balancing sails—sometimes successfully, but mostly not. The other was sailing the boat close-hauled, balancing the sails, and tying off the helm. Most well-balanced sailboats will then sail to weather, gradually working their way up until the jib luffs and then fall off until the jib fills again, repeating the process without a lot of attention from the helm.

As night crept upon us, the exhaustion of the day's labors, coupled with the stress, fatigue, and debilitation that we had lived with for so long, overcame our logic and senses. Judgment was clouded, attention to detail was fuzzy, and we were just plain tired. Both of us kept falling asleep where we sat. Les made a hot meal, but it was an effort just to keep the new little cast iron stove from careening off the gimbaled hulk of our former stove. One hand for the stove and one for the pot allowed only the simplicity of one-pot meals. I told her to get a few hours of sleep, and soon I was catching myself falling over the wheel in a stupor.

I looked at the chart and decided we could chance heaving-to and both get some sleep. Not the best practice, but at this point we were in the classic "Catch 22" of singlehanders. Both of us were simply unable to stay awake any longer. I awoke Les long enough to help furl the jib and put *Banshee* in a hove-to position and then collapsed on a bunk. I remember both of us getting up periodically to look out, but we were mostly dead gone until way past daylight.

"Leslie, get up. We've got to get sailing again. Shit, look at our drift. We're only 10 miles from Western Reef, at least according to this damn small-scale chart. The current must be tremendous!"

Refreshed by sleep and pumping adrenaline, we made short work of putting *Banshee* on a course to windward. The most immediate benefit was that she was self-steering when I tied off the wheel. *Fine with me. We're going dead south and that's where Madang and the mainland are.* Les made coffee and food and the helm only needed to be watched and occasionally adjusted when it luffed up too far. A position plot showed that we were now moving safely south and past the lurking menace of Western Reef.

Our euphoria was short-lived though, as clouds steadily accumulated overhead and the rising wind and sea made our steering arrangement more and more tenuous. We partially furled the jib and tucked another reef in the main. It had to be blowing a steady 25-30 knots with higher gusts. As the wind rose, the seas did too and then dark squalls started building on the weather horizon. *Banshee's* heeled-over attitude became even more uncomfortable as we plowed into the seas.

As the squalls passed over us, the waves got nasty as *Banshee* was forced to bite into them. They were like walls of water, sometimes stopping her forward momentum altogether with jarring crash. Our speed slowed. We weren't sailing anymore; it was more like clawing, clawing our way slowly into the wind and toward the long expanse of PNG's mountainous northern coast.

The wind shrieked and howled at us. The sea was white with foam streaks and breaking waves. When we hit a big one, green water cascaded over on the cockpit overheads and waves sped into the cockpit. Who could tell if it was pelting, stinging rain or spray? It was all cold and wet and our foul weather jackets had long since lost their waterproofing. The only one that worked was an old PVC jacket that I had bought in a gas station in Australia years ago. With towels around our necks and flannels under it, some semblance of dryness and warmth was possible. Our stints at the wheels shortened to about two hours each. Then we'd strip down and bundle up, the other sharing our one waterproof jacket. Somehow we ate, more out of necessity than anything else. At times we'd just open a can of anything and dig in. Sleeping was more like falling unconscious. We'd flop on the low side bunk and crash into oblivion until called to the helm.

Nights were the worst. Without any functioning navigational lights it would be easy for us to be run down by a ship. While on the helm we constantly strained our eyes into the darkness. At four feet above the horizon in heavy seas visibility is extremely limited. Fortunately commercial ships are high in the water and carry lights. Those lights we had to see or risk being run down. A call of "Ship, ship" brought both of us on deck with the VHF and the GPS at the ready. Les would steer so we would be sure of a steady course, and I would turn on the GPS, tune up the VHF on the hailing frequency Ch. 16, and call out to the approaching ship in the blackness with our position, course, and speed.

The responses we got to that call were varied and in many accents, but every ship I called answered, and all were kind and concerned. We watched as the big vessels changed course and gave us a wide berth. It was reassuring and I was so glad I had bought that little Uniden Atlantis radio. Sometimes in heavy blinding rain, I would call out an hourly message into the void even if we didn't see any ships.

"Hello all ships in my area," I began, giving the same identifying information, position, course and speed, but adding, "This is a position warning only. We have no visibility in bad weather. If you hear this message, please come back."

The answers to that message were even more varied. Once a Japanese captain I contacted on a very stormy night offered to phone Leslie's mother and send an email to Mitch in Madang giving our position, but he became so concerned that we were disabled without an engine that it occupied most of the conversation. Eventually he accepted our sailboat status and that a lack of an engine for us at the moment was really extraneous. His kind offer made us feel that at least now our family and contacts in Madang would know where we were.

Exhaustion permeated every part of our beings but we kept on—what were our choices? Les was enduring it better than me. I felt every year of my seniority over hers. Food had become unpalatable to me and Les forced me to eat. A new area of concern arose: our strapped-on Avon inflatable boat was losing air and getting quite flat. It was our only alternative if we had to ditch and the life raft failed to open. In the heavy seas the life raft canister dripped a steady stream of rust. *Maybe the CO_2 cartridge was rusting* *through? Then it would never blow open.* All that could be done was for Les to bravely maneuver up on the pitching foredeck and pump it up with our foot pump. This entailed holding on with one hand, holding the tube in the valve with the other and pumping with one of her feet. It got to be a daily horror for her. I remembered that awful trip in *Supamanus* and was grateful for *Banshee's* cabin and our sails. This storm was much worse, but at least we were weathering it in what was proving to be a very sound boat. I began to have a lot of faith in the cement-like compound that was holding our hull together.

The storm lasted four days, until Wednesday, the morning of the 6th. We had covered only 144 miles, but we had maintained our longitude despite the fierce current. Karkar Island, towering 6,000 feet, was only 45 miles ahead of us. At dawn, the wind dropped and the seas eased. A weak sun shone through the thinning clouds. The northwesterly backed to the north, and we could ride it once again. We shook out a reef from the main, pulled out more jib, and footed off. By midmorning we tacked to a more favorable course and by noon we were able to sail a direct course to Karkar. Compared to our progress of the previous four days we were positively flying. As dusk approached we saw the heavy cloud bank over PNG's mountains and the outline of Karkar under clouds and rain.

Land!

All along the horizon dark banks of clouds hugged the sharp slopes of the mountainous coast. Until darkness obliterated our view, we watched bands of heavy rain and flashes of lightning under the bases of the ominous towering clouds. *Warm, moist tropical air from the equator colliding with the coolness of the high altitude slopes. No doubt a nightly occurrence, clearing with the sun's warmth in the morning. It'll probably hit us tonight. Don't want to be too close to land.* By 10 p.m. the clouds covered us, the winds picked up and rain and lightning were upon us in a big way. We tacked out and away from land, and away from the current-laden channel between Karkar and its smaller neighbor, Bagabag Island.

We tried to steer to weather to hold our position against the current. The gusts were insane as they dropped and accelerated off the heights of Karkar. I estimated 50 knots plus. The wheel shook in my hands as the squalls hit with painful stinging belts of cold rain from the mountain top. *Banshee's* whole hull trembled while the rigging took up a terrible cadence. I held on as long as I could, determined to hold her to weather. Then Les took a stint as long as she could hold on. Fatigue was killing us. After midnight, we surrendered to the onslaught, hove-to and stood short watches to allow at least one of us to sleep. We were sitting ducks, right in the outflow of the heavily trafficked Vitiaz Strait, the shipping channel from Australia. Watch keeping for ships was crucial. A steady parade of big lighted monsters kept us vigilant for the remainder of the night. By dawn the fierce wind abated, and a position check confirmed an unwanted northeast drift. A northwest wind pushed along the leftover storm swells as the sun rose. Although totally spent, we fell off the wind a bit and enjoyed a brief sleigh ride south to Bagabag. For some reason even the Aries wind vane worked.

Peering at the horizon, we tried to make out Bagabag. While smaller than Karkar, it still was over 2,000 ft. high. It was there under its personal mantle of clouds and rain. The closer we got, the more the wind shifted to the west and even a bit to the southwest. Beating again, Leslie took the helm from the wandering Aries to steer the straightest course possible to the island. We needed to get past before nightfall. The current pushed us east and we worried about the underwater danger of Hankow Reef to leeward. With our limited small-scale chart and lack of government sailing directions, we had no idea that 30 feet of water covered it at all times and we could have floated over it. Had we known this, we would have given Bagabag a wider berth. With concentrated hand steering and a full jib, Les was able to work the gusts, catching lifts and heading up to our goal. By late afternoon, we could see the verdant green of the island, the brown of bush houses and the sloping, patchwork hillside gardens.

"Beautiful," we both exclaimed as we sailed past the encircling reef. Fragrant smells of vanilla, flowers, wood smoke, and earth tantalized our senses. We were close enough to see people. Little did they know of our harrowing past. *Just some happy yacht tourists on their way to Madang, they must think. They'd probably seen many.* We floated on our euphoria as the warm colors of the sunset enveloped us.

Then the wind stopped…

We were dead in the water and drifting onto the reef.

"My god… Not now. No!"

Quickly the tropical night descended. I grabbed the GPS and checked our drift. I stared at our tiny chart and plotted. *Shit, right onto the island, as close as I can figure.* I scrambled into the cockpit, my heart pounding. Les was already pulling out the reef and unfurling the big genoa. Lines were everywhere.

It was flat dead calm—the water was a mirror.

I grabbed the wheel and started sculling our large spade rudder, a technique I'd learned years ago with smaller boats. I put the island on our stern and Leslie literally flapped the sails like wings. We moved forward. Adrenaline kept us going. We shouted at each other. I yelled in terror.

"No, I won't lose *Banshee*. No…."

Kerosene lamps appeared on the shore. A bonfire blazed up. "They're trying to show us the shore," I yelled to Les. "Good. I can keep the lights on my stern, it'll give me direction. Keep flapping; it's working." My back ached from the heavy sculling. I stared at the tiny GPS screen, willing it to show movement—movement anywhere but northwest. *Please, east or south but no more west please,* I prayed to any force that was listening. *Just get us out of here.* A miniscule puff of a breeze wafted slowly off the shore. The genny seemed to fill a little. I had steerage way.

We were moving, ever so slowly… Away.

The puffs came and went for what seemed hours. The lights on shore grew smaller. We seemed to be making enough headway south down the coastline to put distance between us and the reef. The steering took constant concentration—we took turns while the other collapsed for an hour. Dark hours passed. Our fatigue was all-encompassing. I remember hallucinating and blacking out. I would fall over the wheel and jerk awake in fear, not knowing where I was for a while. It was frightening.

We kept going.

At some point I awoke in my bunk to sunlight and the smell of coffee. I didn't remember lying down. I had no memory of the rest of that fearful night, but when I looked out Les had *Banshee* hove-to past the southeast side of the island, drifting away innocently in the light morning breeze off the shore.

"You were gone, Joy. It was just like when I was single-handing in Hawaii. I had to steer, had to keep going until I figured it was safe. Like some coffee? Bagabag's beautiful out here."

And it was.

The wind came up as we drifted into the Karkar channel, and soon we had 25 knots on the nose. We reefed and took off, but couldn't lay Madang—that would take another tack. The seas were smaller under the lee of the islands and we fairly flew under very little sail.

Early afternoon and the wind suddenly went dead. The seas were strange—the wind shadow of giant Karkar. It was over in an hour. Then, *bang*—we popped through and right back on the freight train. *But wait,* "We can lay Madang. It's right in front of us—22 miles. Never make it by dark, though." We were scurrying. I saw the same dark rain clouds drop from the mountains. *Damn, not another night out here.*

"I'm going to try the radio. Glenn told me something about a repeater (booster antenna) on Ch. 82. Probably too far out to hear anything—I'll just try."

I sat on the cabin top and turned it on.

Voices.

"My god, Les, I'm going to call."

"Breaker, breaker. This is an emergency. This is U.S. Yacht *Banshee*. Do you copy me?"

Someone answered...

WE MADE IT!

"Stand-by, we'll get Mitch on the radio for you—might take a moment. Wait one." I tried to keep emotion out of my voice so I could be heard clearly, but the strong, clear Aussie accent with its connection to civilization was choking me with pent-up feelings.

"Roger that. Standing by."

Tears welled up in my eyes. "They hear us, Les. They're getting Mitch." It was almost over. The wait, though only minutes, was interminable.

"That you, Joy? We thought you'd be getting close by now. Where are you?"

"We're about 20 miles off. I can give you a position. Mitch, we are so very, very tired. It's been so long."

"Yeah, Joy, but you guys have done it. We'll get you in—no worries now."

I grabbed the GPS and slowly read out our position. It was hard to pinpoint us on our small-scale tattered chart.

"Can you see any landmarks out there—anything?"

"No, Mitch, I can't make out anything. It's nasty out here—squalls, rain, thunder and lightning and we're still banging into this heavy chop. We've got no lights, Mitch, just a weak flashlight that we can turn on when we see yours."

"Look, it'll take us a while to get the boat ready and fueled up. Y'got batteries to keep that VHF going?"

"Yeah, Mitch. I got it wired in to what's left of our ship's banks. I'll keep the radio on."

"Right, hang in there."

Daylight was going fast as we approached the coast. We figured we'd better bathe, even if all we had was salt water. "After all, we might be having company," we joked to each other. After an hour, I called Mitch again.

"Right, Joy, we're just comin' out of the harbor now. Man, it's bad out here."

I gave them my GPS info and we waited, still closing on the coast. I couldn't see anything up ahead. The visibility with the rain was poor. Darkness closed in. We heard nothing from the radio.

The wind stopped. *How close were we?*

Les scrambled for the sails. I tried to maintain steerage way. A brilliant flash of lightning illuminated our world.

"Land, Joy. I saw the black of land in the lightning. Get out of here! Turn her around now. Hurry. Scull, like before. C'mon."

With Les holding out sails, *Banshee* slowly answered her helm. *We're turning, thank god.* A gentle offshore breeze pushed at the outstretched sails and I heard water move past us. *We're going back out—it's okay.*

As the chaotic scene returned to normal, I watched the GPS until I figured we were a safe distance off. The wind died again, but the little box said our drift was offshore. I tried the radio again and Mitch answered.

"Joy, we've been waiting to hear from you. You still okay? We had to go back in 'cause we had no visibility and couldn't make any headway out there."

"Mitch, it's flat calm out here now and I can see lights of the city."

"Yeah? Right, we'll give it another try. Y'know, way back here y'haven't got a clue of what's going on out there."

"Okay, Mitch. We'll be waiting." I gave them the reciprocal bearing and distance to our position. "Give us a call when you think you're getting close. We haven't got much battery left in our flashlight."

We waited, silently drifting in the swells. *Lights, civilization. It's almost over.* My mind wandered with exhaustion and stress. Our little VHF sat in the cockpit companionway. We stared at it, willing it to come to life. Time ticked by in the humid darkness.

"Joy, you there?"

We pounced on the radio.

"Roger, Mitch."

"You should be able to see our red and green by now. We're quite a way out."

Les grabbed the radio and went on deck to scan the horizon. I wasn't able to concentrate anymore. I was nodding off, slumped in the cockpit.

Leslie

I still couldn't see any nav lights. Between swells, the city lights would disappear. I was so tired it was hard to concentrate. I'd stare and things would go blurry.

"This is Leslie. I can't see any nav lights. How far out are you?"

"Straight out from the lighthouse—we've gone quite a ways. You said y'were comin' from Bagabag. Can't see you on radar at all."

Then it hit me. *By the lights we have to be north of the city. These are power boaters, used to driving a straight course between two points.* In my mind I could see it. *Hell, they probably don't even use charts. They know the local landmarks. All this position and bearing stuff's no use to them.*

"Mitch, we're north of Madang and close in. Turn left. That'll put your green light toward me as you come back to the coast. I can watch for that. I'm shining a light on my mainsail so you can see us."

"Roger. *Singaut* when you see something."

I kept straining my eyes. I hung on to the rigging as I pointed our last weak diving light at the main and waited. I thought I saw something in the blackness, but no, I couldn't really focus. At least an hour passed.

"We've got you on radar now. It has to be you, there's no one else out here and we're getting a good return. We'll just track in on you. Shouldn't be long now until you see our lights. We're aimin' straight at you. You should see a red and green and a white over them."

"Joy, come up. They're here. I can see their lights now. They're coming close. I'll get some fenders so they can come alongside." Joy came out on deck staring at their lights as I tied off the fenders. *She's really gone—holding on and shaking. Got to help her.*

Joy

Les has got to do this. I just can't. Is it really over? I was succumbing to the pent-up strain of four months of believing we could do this. I steadied myself and came on deck as the big sportfisher pulled alongside. Guys grabbed me as I came aboard. I almost collapsed right there. *C'mon now, got to pull myself together.*

I stumbled into the cabin, Les followed. Three middle-aged Australian men greeted us. Mitch (Greg Mitchell, owner of Bush Developments), Dave Faithfull, and Mark. Mitch I knew from long talks on the phone in Moresby and lots of emails. Dave owned the boat and was the engineering manager of Luship (Lutheran Shipping Co., Madang). *Perfect guy to meet at this point.* And Mark, as he said, had come along for the ride.

Les and I both talked at once. The words spilled out. We hadn't talked to people of our own culture in so long. They offered us snacks and sodas, apologizing that they hadn't brought more. The strain gone, we were famished.

"Salami—real salami," I blurted as they laughed. *An apple, crackers, and cheese? Civilized snacks.* We could have eaten platefuls. We'd been a long way away, on another planet.

Leslie

Time to go. They told us it would be a long ride back to Madang, as the tow had to be slow. I was stunned when they asked if I had a tow line ready. *Towline? In this mess?*

"Our spare anchor line will work, but I've got to pull it out and unshackle the chain."

The guys waited patiently while we pulled out the anchor line and flaked it on deck, ready to pay out to them. The rumble of their powerful diesel gave me confidence. *We'll be out of here soon.* The towline paid out and they took up the slack. Joy took the wheel.

Banshee was underway again—this time on a dead straight course to civilization.

I watched for awhile from the bow to see that the towline set well and then went back to the cockpit. They kept the speed down so all we had to do was to set the wheel brake, and we snaked along peacefully behind our rescuers. We were both nodding off. I was shaking with cold and exhaustion and my teeth were chattering.

"Relax back there, you two, it'll be a coupla' hours. We're quite a ways out and going slow."

"Fine with us, Mitch," Joy replied. "We're about dead on our feet. If it's okay with you, we'd like to go below and sleep. I can put the radio next to my ear. Just give a shout when you want us."

"No worries. Get some rest."

We were dead asleep as soon as we lay down. *Someone else is in charge now.* I was grateful.

Joy

"Hey there. Copy us? We're comin' up on the copra wharf now. You'll need to get some fenders out on both sides. We'll come alongside to get you onto the wharf."

We both sprang to life. Leslie was on deck before I could get back to them.

"Roger, Mitch," I said, and the little VHF was exchanged for eye contact as they came alongside to guide us into the old wood and rusty steel wharf. No matter how menacing it looked, we were grateful as we fended off and tied spring lines to hold us in the surge of passing ships. I talked with them for a while longer as Les worked with the lines. Someone offered her a rain jacket as she shivered in the intermittent rain.

"Glenn'll be by around eight when he comes into work in his speedie. The officials will be here too. They'll want to see you. You've been reported overdue and they've got a search goin' for you, y'know. Called it off when we heard from you this afta'noon."

"Really?" *Must have been Indy, when he got Palau.*

"Yeah, we're all glad to see you, fer sure. Glenn'll take you over to Luship Engineering so they can get your engine out of there and get Blue workin' on it."

All these names, people wanting to help us. My head was spinning.

"How can we thank you? You've done so much."

"Get some sleep, tomorrow's a big day for you. You'll be safe here." He motioned to the big security guard with a billy-club staring at us. Les caught our lines and they pulled out.

"I'm gone, Joy. Gonna fall down right here. Booby's already tried one escape. I had to grab him off the deck, put him below, and put the hatch boards in."

Les retreated below to her bunk. I crawled below, poured myself a strong one, and went outside and climbed onto the wharf. I sat there touching land and watching civilization—lights, buildings, guards, ships, and *Banshee* tied up so peaceably next to me.

"You *olrait misis?*"

I heard the guard, smiled and nodded. *We must certainly look like a disaster. But we made it!*

Glenn arrived on schedule in the morning, telling us that Customs wanted us to move to the commercial wharf to clear. Expertly he maneuvered *Banshee* over. I climbed up and they kindly checked us in. Yes, a search and rescue warning was out for us, courtesy of a yacht in Palau—*yeah, thanks Indy.*

The officials were simply in awe. *Dupela meri* did this? Passers-by stared at us and shyly smiled. Paul, the Customs and Immigration official, kept me in rapt conversation until Glenn motioned that we'd better get on over to Luship. They were waiting for us. *So many people wanting to help—so many light years away from Hermit.*

Underway, with Glenn's speedie alongside, we watched the city pass by. Roads, cars, businesses, people coming and going. *My god, we have been so far away.*

Soon we were tied up next to *Rita*, a huge coastal passenger ship in for repairs, and in the midst of a busy engineering facility where it seemed anything could be built, welded, or repaired. A hose was passed down. Clean water ran into the cockpit. We tried to clean up some of the filth and disorder. They told us a shower was near the office—"kinda' primitive, but it's a room with a door."

"Primitive?" They've got no idea; this is high class from where we've been. People came by—we were introduced to so many. The workers passed by to stare in amazement at *"Dupela Meri,"* as we came to be known.

It was Saturday and the place would shut down at noon. We had to make our arrangements with the office now before closing. They wanted to haul the engine out first thing Monday. "Blue" would be by in the afternoon, we were told.

Schedules, appointments—my head was spinning and my legs were weak as I stumbled into Dave's office and sat down in front of my rescuer of the night before. Tall, gaunt Dave Faithfull greeted me and set forth what Luship could do for us.

"Just go through me, and she'll be right. Afta' we git yer engine out, we'll find a place fer ya somewhere, no worries."

He took us to lunch at the Madang Club, and he was amazed when two plates of food vanished in minutes. Then we went to an ATM for some *kina*, and by some miracle it all worked and I walked out with a full wallet. Walking back to his truck, I dodged traffic on my unsteady legs. *Certainly not up to civilization's speed by a long shot.* We were like time travelers coming out of a long ago warp.

The much-respected, white-haired Australian mechanic, "Blue" Dean, arrived in the afternoon.

"Fix it? No worries. It's a toy engine. Just a rebuild, mate. The guys 'll bring it over t'me shop on Monday. She'll be right."

We found dinner, and many meals thereafter, at the Madang Inn, down the road from Luship. Well fed, clean, and tired, we slowly ambled back to our bunks aboard, assured of a peaceful and safe sleep. It was over.

Stap isi. Mipela kamap pinis.

Banshee is a Bristol 34, Hull #1
designed by Halsey Herreschoff
and built by Bristol/Peterson
in Bristol, Rhode Island in 1971

REPAIRING *BANSHEE*

Our rebuilding of *Banshee* in Madang took two years—from February 2003 to February 2005, when we set sail for Palau. We had a compromised hull, scraped and pock-marked decks and topsides, a gutted, filthy interior encased in layers of peeling paint, a seized engine, and electrical, refrigeration, and instrumentation systems that were reduced to salt-encrusted rubble. Only the sailing rig had survived unscathed, completely intact and functional as it had been when we sailed into Hermit.

The restoration had to be fitted within the weather restrictions of the North Pacific typhoon season (June through November), as we were headed towards waters affected by those dreadful storms. Most of the equipment and supplies had to be ordered from Australia or the U.S. via the Internet. That and local shopping in the town became my responsibility while Leslie did most of the hands-on repairs.

Our budget only allowed for two regular local workers. Kunanga Pangul, a PNG bushman, became our six-day-a-week companion. As Leslie said, "He started out as an extension of my arms, hands, and back, and became an excellent fiberglasser, finisher, and artistic painter." Later, his cousin-sister, Hamang Sibo, joined our team, beginning with the customary PNG *wok bilong meri* and graduating to sanding and finishing.

During the entire rebuilding of *Banshee,* we lived aboard. The daily tasks of preparing our meals and those of our workers, shopping, and doing laundry had to coexist with endless projects and the mess of grinding dust, fiberglassing, and painting.

Banshee was on the hard at the government marine railway in Madang for six weeks while Leslie and untrained helpers restored the integrity of the hull. Living aboard became a balancing act as the railway was built on an incline, and we commuted to our home by way of very tall ladder. Large areas of the damaged hull had to be removed, dished out with a grinder, and re-fiberglassed with epoxy resin, woven roving, mat, and finishing cloth.

"Splash-down Day," when *Banshee* returned to her water home, was only the beginning. We focused on refinishing the ghastly mess of the interior and then did a complete re-wiring project. Over a year later, with Kunanga's help, we were still at it, installing the rebuilt engine and restoring the decks and topsides. More projects ensued: plumbing, and pressure water systems; sailing instrumentation and radar repair; restoring the autopilot and windlass; rebuilding the winches; renewing the foam seat cushions and covers; and installing a computer navigation system.

When we left Madang, we had a beautiful boat once again. The interior, now rebuilt with PNG tropical hardwoods, sparkled with varnish, and Awlgrip LP-painted bulkheads, lockers, and ceiling provided an attractive and comfortable living space for our ocean voyaging. The decks and topsides also gleamed with Awlgrip and were topped off with new graphics for *Banshee's* name and hailing port.

As our long-time sailing friend, the late Dan Millar, commented when he visited *Banshee* on our return to Palau: "Joy, this boat did not sink."

Joy Smith
Palau
2005

AUTHOR'S NOTE

This is a work of non-fiction. It is an actual experience that we lived. We have attempted to portray it as it happened to us in the most truthful manner possible. The people mentioned in the book are living people; the places actually exist. The events are actual occurrences as we saw them. Any errors are the responsibilities of the author and collaborator. The book is written in two voices, Joy's and Leslie's, because specific experiences happened to each of us. Our words "in thought" are italicized to indicate such to the reader.

The people of Hermit do not speak English among themselves. Their vernacular is extinct and so they use Pidgin. Some knew English, a bit of broken English, or a mixture of English and Pidgin. Many spoke only Pidgin, having no knowledge of English at all. I have written the dialogue parts exactly as they were spoken. When we arrived on Hermit, we did not speak Pidgin, although from my previous travels in PNG, the Solomons and Vanuatu, I had a feel for it. Out of necessity we learned and used it during our two-and-a-half year stay in PNG.

The Pidgin language of Papua New Guinea, *Tok Pisin* or Neo-Melanesian, is an official language of the country. It is a recognized language in world universities. The Bible has been translated into Pidgin, and it is used in text books, magazines, music, newspapers, radio and television. Varieties are also used similarly in the Solomon Islands and Vanuatu. Pidgin is Melanesian in both grammar and orthography.

In PNG Pidgin orthography there is no tense, no plurals, and no gender. These are understood through contextual meaning and modifiers. In general terms, the adjective *"ol"* pluralizes. There are no hyphenations in PNG Pidgin. Double words, i.e. *"toktok,"* are written as one word. Pidgin words are italicized in the text.

For the ease of the English language reader, certain liberties have been taken with the writing of Pidgin words. Where there are Anglicisms (borrowed words meaning and sounding the same as in English), the English spelling is used instead of the Pidgin spelling. No italics are used for these English words, i.e. *"haus,"* is written as house and not italicized. If they are used in combination with another Pidgin word, i.e. *"haus kuk,"* and the result is a Pidgin term, then the Pidgin spelling is used and the term italicized.

In a country with over 800 vernacular languages, called *tok ples,* Pidgin is the communication and trade language of the people. It is a colorful and descriptive language of many derivations. Its existence allows people of a vast country to communicate with those beyond their sometime isolated homeland village areas.

For further interest to the reader we now have a website, www.bansheeboat.com, showing photos taken on Hermit by visiting cruising sailors after we departed. The actual characters in the story are showcased in the village of Hermit. The website will change as our sailing continues.

Joy Smith
Puerto Galera, Mindoro, Philippines
2006

PIDGIN NOTES

The following are Pidgin words and idioms that are used in the text. Many have their basis in English or German. Some words came from the early plantation times and those used by traders and whalers in the days of sailing ships. However, they may have undergone changes in meaning, pronunciation, or spelling as they became incorporated into Pidgin. Some are two-word terms, always used together, that mean a single concept. Anglicized Pidgin words—from English, spoken as English, but having Pidgin spelling—have been written in English for the ease of the English reader.

bagarap *v.* broken, not good, impaired, messed-up. From the English idiom "buggered-up."

bai *v.* shows the future tense and is pronounced "by." It means will, then, after that. From the idiom "by and by" something happens.

baket *n.* bucket but it is pronounced differently than bucket, so it is spelled in Pidgin.

bek *a.* back; *n.* bag.

bikman *n.* a "bigman," or high ranking man in the culture. The "k" replaces "g" in the sound shift.

bikpela heve *idiom* for "big problem." The accompanying word *heve* is written in Pidgin as together they are a Pidgin term.

bilong *prep.* for, of.

cassowary *n.* a large flightless bird common in PNG. The English term is used.

em nau affirmative *idiom* in Pidgin discourse meaning, "it is so." It is used as an expression of agreement or understanding. Literally it translates as "it is now."

gudpela *a.* good.

haus boi *n* the men's house or men's gathering place that is off-limits to women.

haus kuk *n* cook-house. The singular word *kuk* is an Anglicism and is written as in English, i.e. cook.

haus meri *n.* a female housekeeper or nanny.

haus toilet *n.* a latrine (for bush villages); a little house extending over the water (for coastal villages); a public toilet building.

heve *a.* by itself is an Anglicism and is spelled as in English – heavy.

isi *a.* slowly, gently, smoothly. *Stap isi* is an idiom meaning relax.

kina *n* unit of currency. It relates back to the days when shell money was used as currency.

laikim *v.* means to like or to want. *Wanem* (interrogative) means "what?" or "when?"

laplap *n.* wrap-around skirt worn by both men and women; a rag or cloth.

liklik *n.* something or someone who is little.

long *prep.* Pidgin word that has a different meaning from English. In Pidgin it covers in, by, on, with, from, to, at.

lusim *v.* "let it go," quit, stop doing something, or to forget or lose.

maski *adv.* derivation unknown by author. A commonly used term meaning never mind, forget it, or don't bother.

mekim, wokim *v.* "to do" and "to make," but the Pidgin meaning has changed from English. *Mekim* is intransitive and means to make or to do. *Wokim* is transitive and means to make something or to do work, i.e. it takes an object.

meri *n.* woman; *bilong meri* is possessive; and *ol meri* is plural. However, *meri's* for the possessive and *meries* for the plural is substituted in this book because it is currently used as an Anglicism in vernacular Pidgin as is *man's* (possessive) and *mans* (plural).

pe *v.* pay. Used singularly, is an Anglicism and is spelled as in English – pay.

pebek *n.* compensation.

pebekim: *v.* to compensate.

pela *suffix* of many words, is often shortened to "pla" in pronunciation. It comes from the old trader's vernacular of appending the term "fella" (meaning "fellow" or a person) to many descriptive adjectives when talking to the local population. The "f" became a sound shift to "p." So *bikpela* comes from "big fella," *wanpela* from "one fella," and *gudpela* from "good fella."

pen *n.* pain; paint.

pukpuk *n.* crocodile.

raus *n.* leave or get out (from the German command).

rausim *v.* to leave or remove.

stap *v.* be present; remain; be in progress; be. It does not mean to stop, cease, or quit. That word is *lusim*.

siubim *v.* to shove, push. There is no "sh" spelling in Pidgin. After an "s" the diphthong "iu" takes on the function of an "h" and provides the "sh" sound.

soim *v.* to show, point out.

solwara *n.* ocean water (salt water).

Toksave *n* message or instructions.

toktok *v.* is one word.

tok ples *n.* is two words.

wait *a.* (pronounced as, and meaning the color white). It is an Anglicism and is given its English spelling, white, when it is used as one word. *Waitskin, waitmeri, waitman* are one word Pidgin terms. For this text *waitmeries* spelled as in Pidgin is used. It is current day Pidgin vernacular.

waswas *a.* and *n.* bath or shower.

EPILOGUE

It has been almost four years since those terrible minutes that changed the course of our lives. *Banshee* now sits comfortably and safely on a mooring at the Puerto Galera Yacht Club in the Philippines. The log on our PNG-installed GPS stands at 4,751 nautical miles; a lot of water has passed under our keel in one-and-a-half years.

A push through the southern hemisphere's stormy northwesterlies gave us a sleigh ride on the end of the northern trades and brought us into our old home of Palau. Sailing was good again. The beautiful Philippine archipelago lay before us where we happily wandered for over a month, harbor hopping from one island to the next.

The memory lingers; the disaster changed much in our life. Our sailing continues: new countries, new challenges and so many new anchorages ahead of us.

Puerto Galera
Mindoro Island
Philippines
August 2006

ACKNOWLEDGEMENTS

We have so many to thank in six countries. The generous kindness, caring, and hospitality we have received has been overwhelming and continuous. Over the last four years, these people, companies, and governmental agencies have made our progress, *Banshee's* re-building, and this book possible. We are indebted to all. Thank you so much.

Editor: Anne Carlson
Graphic artist and contributing editor: John Lanier
Sketch artist: Debra K.Thomas
Photography: Edward Vaughan, Lois Bayyom Nai, Carolina Pilhelgas, and
        Bernadette Willes

United States:
David Rothenberg, New Jersey
Jeannine Talley, writer and artist, Pinellas Park, Florida
Larry and Barbara Brown, Wilton and Westport, Connecticut
Max-Air Diving Compressors, Kerrville, Texas
Nobeltec Marine Software
Paul Oman, Progressive Epoxy Polymers, Pittsfield, New Hampshire
Rob Pace, Town Executive Center, Boca Raton, Florida
Stephen Tenney, formerly of Raymarine, Nashua, New Hampshire
Sue Brown, Sue Brown Travel, staff and travel consultants, Boca Raton, Florida
Susan Stepan, Andrew Corp., Chicago, Illinois

Steve Shores, West Marine sales representative, Hollister, California
Tammi Lauder, Chappaqua, New York
Tom Spangler, ACCO Chain Products, York, Pennsylvania
Tracy Coulter, Bob Hansen, and John Payne, Hansen Marine, Marblehead,
    Massachusetts
Wendy Johnson, U.S. Bureau of Consular Affairs, American Citizen's Bureau

Papua New Guinea:
Air Niugini staff, Lorengau Air Niugini Office, Lorengau
Andrew Barter, Madang Resort, Madang
Blue Dean, Mobile Machinery, Madang
Clint Rooke and Rooke's Marine, Madang
Colin, Carol and family at Tony's Boatyard, Madang
Daniel Tarie, Manager, Binnen Slipways, Madang
Dave Faithfull, Manager, Luship Engineering, Madang
Dr. John Mackerell, Madang
Ela Joinery and Hardwoods, Madang
Glenn Richie, Fibertech, Madang
Greg "Mitch" Mitchell, Bush Developments, Madang
Internet Café, Madang
Kunanga Pangul and Hamang Sibo, Madang
Lindsay Swanson, Aisi Bishman Electrical Supplies, Madang
Lois Akau, Akau Guesthouse, Lorengau
Luship Engineering, Madang
Lynnah and Ben and children, our family on Luf
Michael Lensim, Luship RFD Liferaft Services and Repair Shop, Madang
Mikah and Mack, Papua New Guinea, *Sip Keptans*
Neil Keenan, Taubman's Paints, Madang
Paul Burke, Manager, Gateway Hotel, Port Moresby
Paul Male, Papua New Guinea Immigration Officer, Madang
Paul Silas and Stanley, Luf village, Hermit
Pioneer Bible Translators, Madang
        With special thanks to: Martha Wade, Kyle and Kathy Harris, Lois Witham,
        Jan and Eunice Messersmith, William and Robin Butler, Steve, Rhonda
        and Jason Hayward, Dave and Christine Robinson, Chris, Lori and Ryne
            Urton, Ellen Rohrer, Jesse Pryor, Lois Bayyom Nai, and Laurua Ronnie
Sir Peter Barter, Minister for Inter Government and Health, Papua New Guinea
Sir Rabbie Namaliu, Minister for Foreign Affairs and Immigration, Papua New
Guinea
Susan Jacobs, U.S. Ambassador to Papua New Guinea, and Heather Guimond, U.S.
Embassy staff

The People of Luf Village, Hermit
Thomas Polume, Papua New Guinea Diplomat and Consul, Lorengau
Tony and Lorraine Collins, Madang
Tony Beirne, Tony's Boatyard, Madang
Tracey Taraika, Supervisor, DHL Madang Office, Madang
Valerie Knight, V. and R. Knight Shipping, Lorengau
Wep Kanawi, Provincial Administrator, Lorengau, Manus Province

Sailboat Cruisers:
Carolina Pilhelgas and Bent, Yacht *Disalagraptus*
Edward Vaughan, Yacht *Mas Alegre*
Frank Schliewinsky
Josh Buchan and the late Dan Millar, Yacht *Lazy Days*

Palau:
Blue Marlin/Palau Sport, Malakal, Koror
Café Palau Internet Café, Koror
Crew and Captain of the *President Remeliik*, Palau Navy Frigate, Malakal, Koror
Cruise Control, Malakal, Koror
Ignacia Oilouch, formerly First Lady of Airai, teacher at Palau High School, and
        dear friend, Koror and Airai
Mandy Etpison, Koror
Neco Marine Center, Malakal, Koror
Palau Community College instructors and staff, Koror
        With special thanks to Dean Alvina Timarong, Marianne Tamaungil, Natalia
        Rekemesiik, Epimachus Moses, Soledad Garcia, and Wilma Sukrad
        Richard and Rita Brungard, friends and supporters, Koror
Tom Watson, Surangel and Sons, Koror
Tova and Navot Bornowski, Fish 'n' Fins Dive Center, Koror

Australia and New Zealand:
Australian Search and Rescue Office (SAR), Canberra
Jeff Dodd, Freight Consolidation Services, Brisbane
John Byrne, Maxwell Windlass, New Zealand

Philippines:
Martyn Willes, DeBe Enterprise and Service, yachtsman, water sports photograher, &
        Bernadette Willes, water sports photographer, dear friends, Manila
Puerto Galera Yacht Club, Mindoro
Rodney Hegerty, Broadwater Marine, yachtsman, yacht chandler and dear friend,
Manila and Subic Bay

CORPORATE CONTRIBUTORS

We wish to thank the companies that so generously made contributions toward the rebuilding of *Banshee* in Madang.

ACCO Chain Products, York, Pennsylvania – replacement of 300 ft. main anchor
    chain
ACR Electronics – replacement of EPIRB battery
Andrew Corp., Chicago, Illinois – GPS antenna for Magellan GSC 100
Balmar, Arlington, Washington – alternator regulator Max Charge MC612
Blue Sea Systems – 12v electrical components and gauges for re-wiring project
Garmin International Corp. – Garmin 128 GPS and external antenna
Mike's Marine Exchange, Hawaii – diving mask and booties
PADI, Santa Ana, California – new scuba diving instructional teaching materials
Raymarine, Nashua, New Hampshire – extensive refurbished instrumentation, parts
and repair
Shakespeare Electronics Products Group – antenna for Magellan GSC
Speedy Kiwi Signs, Lae, PNG – new hull graphics
Underwater Kinetics, UK International – underwater UK lights, rechargeable
batteries and chargers
Xaxero Marine Software, New Zealand – computer weather forecast products

A SPECIAL THANKS

I wish to express a special gratitude and thanks to my partner of eleven years, Leslie Brown. The credit for saving and rebuilding *Banshee* goes to her. Without her drive, desire, and mechanical skills our boating home would not be here today. I will always be grateful.

Anne Carlson, my editor, taught me to write. For three years she persisted and stayed with us through internet and satellite email as we created this book. When we finally met it was as though we were old friends. We knew so much about one another. Thank you, Anne. I could not have done it without you.

ABOUT THE AUTHOR
AND COLLABORATOR

Joy Smith has been sailing her entire adult life. She is a native of Los Angeles, where getting hooked on sailing is easy. She had owned and raced four sailboats before buying *Banshee* in 1971. *Banshee* and Joy have crossed the Pacific three times with various crews. After the third Pacific crossing, Joy, a science teacher, became an assistant principal of a high school on Guam, and Leslie Brown joined her there in 1996.

Leslie Brown is from New York, where she worked as a N.Y.C. bike messenger. She became a sailing enthusiast after moving to Hawaii. She restored an old 24-foot plywood sailboat and sailed on her own around the Hawaiian Islands for ten years, working as a scuba diving instructor.